# Rediscovering the New Testament Church

# Rediscovering the New Testament Church

Anthony Jacomb-Hood

# Rediscovering the New Testament Church

by Anthony Jacomb-Hood



Library of Congress Control Number: **2014956423**

---

**Publisher's Cataloging-in-Publication data**

Jacomb-Hood, Anthony.

Rediscovering the New Testament church / by A. Jacomb-Hood.

p. cm.

ISBN-13: 978-1978377585 / ISBN-10: 1978377584

1. Bible. New Testament. 2. Church --Biblical teaching. 3. Bible. New Testament--Criticism, interpretation, etc. I. Title.

BS2545.C5 .J33 2014

262/.7 --dc23

---



The following abbreviations are used to refer to other Bible translations: GNB for the Good News Bible; and NASV for the New American Standard Version.

# Table of Contents

# Foreword

Anthony Jacomb-Hood is a detail person. No wonder, for he is an engineer by trade. In *Rediscovering the New Testament Church*, Anthony has carefully compiled, organized and given commentary on the many aspects of how the life of Christ continued and was expressed in the 1st Century *ekklesia*.

I think it is safe to say that Anthony has left no stone unturned when it comes to *ekklesia*-life! I have read this book twice, and he has indeed done a masterful job of giving the flavor and ethos of the exciting New Testament story. Here is one of his statements that caught my interest:

> One of the surprising things about the New Testament is how rarely shepherding/pastoring is mentioned as an activity of Christian leaders.

In our culture of small bytes, *Rediscovering the New Testament Church* will challenge readers with huge chunks! For those who are daring, curious and seeking, this book will spread out a feast of the supernatural narrative revealed in early church life.

Although Anthony has unearthed and organized untold details, his heart is for our generation to discover and enter into *ekklesia*-life, where Jesus is leading, directing and expressing Himself through each and every brother and sister.

Welcome aboard and enjoy the ride!

**Jon Zens**

Author of *The Pastor Has No Clothes*, and

*58 to 0: How Christ Leads Through the One Anothers*

# Acknowledgements

I thank the many people who have stimulated my thinking about the nature of the New Testament church. I particularly thank Fred Kluempen, Nick Coates, Rad Zdero, Rochelle Vollmerding and my wife Elizabeth for reviewing drafts of this book. Their comments and recommendations have resulted in many improvements. I also thank Jon Zens for editing this book and writing the foreword. And of course my deepest debt of gratitude is to our wonderful Trinitarian God, who is bringing forth the bride of Christ.

# Preface

No single passage of Scripture provides a comprehensive description of a New Testament church and the roles and responsibilities of the participants. This is not surprising, given that the New Testament authors wrote in response to specific situations. They were not attempting to provide a "church manual." For years I assumed that there was no coherent picture of New Testament church life within the Bible, just some scattered glimpses provided in passages responding to particular topics. Only recently did it occur to me that it might be worth gathering these glimpses together to see if, like pieces of a jigsaw puzzle, they do form a coherent picture. This book is the result of this study. I had a two-part surprise when I brought all of these pieces together. Firstly, I discovered that they did form a coherent picture. Secondly, I discovered that this picture or pattern of church life appears to be very different from the various patterns of church life, which have been most widely embraced by the Christian community over the last 17 centuries.

In discussing this topic I have discovered that when I use the phrase "pattern of church life" some individuals assume that I am only considering typical church organizational structures (*e.g.*, pastors, priests and bishops, boards of elders, church councils or whatever). In this book I use the phrase "pattern of church life" very broadly. A pattern of church life can mean an organizational pattern with a clearly defined authority structure, but it can also mean something much more flexible and relational. The New Testament often refers to all believers as "brothers" so we should consider the possibility that the pattern or style of church life might be like the pattern of life in a family. Healthy family patterns are all about living relationships. They are not about organizational structures. Similarly, the New Testament describes the church as being like a body, so we should also keep open the possibility that the pattern or style of relating to one another within a church may be like the relationships between the organs within a live body. Part of the point of this book is to discover, which sort of pattern of church life existed in the New Testament church. We can only discover this if we keep an open mind.

Similarly, when I use the term "church" most people assume I am discussing an organization, which holds weekly services led by a pastor or priest. This individual provides teaching and organizes the weekly services. The congregation participates in worship and prayer and listens to the teaching and Bible readings. In many churches it is also assumed that church leaders have the authority to make most decisions about the life of the church. In this book I will often refer to this style of church as a "leader-centric" church, as so much of the life of the church is centered around the human leader of the church. A goal of this book is to discover if church during the period of the New Testament was like this. In this book I often use the phrase "the New Testament church," and by this phrase I mean church as described in the New Testament.[1] Please keep your mind open to the possibility the New Testament church was radically different from most churches today.

My goal in undertaking this study is to base it on Scripture, especially the New Testament. The New Testament authors wrote their books to be read by the New Testament church. They wrote assuming a certain level of background knowledge and understanding on the part of their readers. In particular, much of the content in several of the epistles is highly specific to the circumstances of the church receiving the epistle. We need to be aware that our experience of church life may be very different from the experience of believers during the period of the New Testament. So we need to be very careful to avoid reading our interpretations into passages. These interpretations may fit our experience of church life, but may be totally different to the experiences of the authors and original recipients of these documents. It is easy to pick out a handful of verses, which seem to support our opinions about the nature of church life. When we do this, there is a risk that we will reach a wrong conclusion, because some detail obvious to the original authors and readers is not obvious to us. Before we assume that our interpretations of particular passages are correct we need to open our minds to the

---

1. Sometimes I use the word "assembly" instead of the word "church." "Assembly" is the primary meaning of the Greek word *ekklesia*, which is commonly translated "church." *Ekklesia* always refers to a group of people who have gathered together. It does not refer to a building or an organization. In the New Testament the word *ekklesia* is used in three ways: the universal church, the overall church in a city or region, and the Christian assembly which meets in a particular home. In this book I also use the term house church to describe assemblies associated with a particular home, which follow the pattern of church life described in the New Testament.

possibility that New Testament church life was totally different from our experience of church life. We then need to review the passages in the context of all of the information provided for us in the Bible. We need to be like the Bereans who checked what Paul and Silas were saying from the Scriptures.[2]

2. Acts 17:11. The Scriptures referred to in this verse are what we now call the Old Testament.

# Introduction

This introduction first addresses a couple of key questions we need to consider prior to investigating Biblical teaching concerning the nature of the New Testament church. It then introduces the specific questions, which this book seeks to answer.

### *Does the New Testament teach that there was a pattern of Church practices that applied to all New Testament churches?*

In 1 Corinthians 11:16, Paul closes a discussion on the appropriate role of women in the church by saying "If anyone is inclined to be contentious, we have no such practice, nor do the churches of God." This verse shows that there were established practices within New Testament churches and that individual churches were expected to follow these practices. As noted previously, the existence of an expected pattern or style of church life during the New Testament period does not necessarily mean that the pattern was the description of an organization. The pattern may be about relationships, similar to the pattern of life in a healthy family.

Other key scriptures that may reveal the existence of an expected pattern or style of church life include:

> I urge you, then, be imitators of me. That is why I sent you Timothy, my beloved and faithful child in the Lord, to remind you of my ways in Christ, as I teach them everywhere in every church. [1]

> Be imitators of me, as I am of Christ. Now I commend you because you remember me in everything and maintain the traditions even as I delivered them to you. [2]

---

1. 1 Cor. 4:16-17
2. 1 Cor. 11:1-2. The context of these verses includes teaching on church practices.

> What you have learned and received and heard and seen in me—practice these things, and the God of peace will be with you.[3]

> So then, brothers, stand firm and hold to the traditions that you were taught by us, either by our spoken word or by our letter.[4]

At first glance, to many readers these verses may seem to have no relevance to patterns of church practices. Many of us assume that Paul is talking in these verses only about his teaching of doctrine and of what constitutes righteous behavior. Clearly, these two topics were important to Paul and are part of what he is talking about in these verses. However, it is clear from his epistles that Paul's "ways in Christ," which he teaches "everywhere in every church"[5] include teaching on how things should be done within a local church. So this passage is telling us that Paul sent Timothy to Corinth to remind them not only of Paul's doctrinal and ethical teaching but also of his teaching concerning appropriate church practices. This verse shows that just as Paul teaches the same doctrine to every church, he also teaches and demonstrates the same pattern of church life and practices to every church. As we shall see it is a pattern that allows substantial freedom.

For many of the original readers of Paul's letters, their primary opportunity to meet Paul and to observe his behavior would have been at Christian assembly meetings. So commanding people to imitate him implicitly includes commanding them to participate in church life and meetings in a similar manner to the way Paul participated. One way new believers would have learned the pattern of New Testament church life was by watching and participating in assembly meetings and other aspects of church life.

1 Corinthians 11:1-2 is Paul's polite introduction to a multi-chapter section of the epistle, which addresses various aspects of Corinthian church meetings. Given this context it is reasonable to assume that the word "traditions" in 1 Corinthians 11:2 primarily refers to church practices. This verse is commending the Corinthians for following and maintaining the pattern of church life, which Paul had taught them. Paul then goes on to give them a series of reminders and a few corrections concerning church practices. Towards the end of this multi-chapter section, in 1 Corinthians 14:37 Paul says that the things he is writing are a command of the Lord. The context of

3. Phil. 4:9
4. 2 Thess. 2:15
5. 1 Cor. 4:17

this verse indicates that this verse applies to the pattern of church life described in these chapters.

In 1 Corinthians 11:2 and 2 Thessalonians 2:15, 3:6 Paul uses the Greek word *paradosis*, which is typically translated tradition or teaching. Nowadays we view traditions as fun things we like to continue to do, but we are free to ignore them if we wish. This word has a much stronger meaning in the New Testament. It describes a required pattern of behavior. The majority of the uses of this word in the New Testament[6] are negative references to Jewish traditions, which had become more important to the Jews than the commands of God recorded in the Old Testament. It is likely that the letter mentioned in 2 Thessalonians 2:15 is the letter we call 1 Thessalonians. So it is likely that this is an example of New Testament traditions becoming Scriptural truth. It is reasonable to assume that God has caused the traditions of New Testament church life, which He wants us to know about, to be included somewhere in the New Testament.

The teachings in Paul's epistles concerning patterns of church life are focused on specific topics relevant to the church(s) or individual(s) receiving the letter. When Paul planted new churches some of the new believers came from Judaism and others from the variety of other religions, which existed in the Roman Empire. Paul would have introduced all of these new believers not only to Jesus but also to the New Testament pattern of church life, which was very different to their previous religious experiences.

### *What risks are associated with searching for patterns of church life in the New Testament?*

Today, many churches claim that their practices closely follow the patterns of church life mentioned in the New Testament. However, it turns out that the practices of these churches are highly varied. They cannot all be correct. Searching for patterns of church practices in the New Testament is a tricky undertaking.

Perhaps the greatest risk is that we will read back into Scripture things that we take for granted today about church life. For example, many churches today are led by a pastor or priest who organizes the Sunday services and does most of the teaching in these services. In some churches the pastor also has final decision-making authority on most other matters related to the church. If one has spent all of one's Christian life in this kind of church, it is natural to

6. *E.g.*, Matt. 15:2-6, Mark 7:3-13

interpret certain verses as supporting this pattern and to inadvertently overlook other verses, which do not support this pattern. It is just like wearing tinted glasses. If the glasses have a blue tint, everything seems blue and it is hard to see things that are not blue.

In my experience many believers unconsciously assume that the pattern of church life in the New Testament is "organizational." They assume that church life, like most work places is based on an organizational pattern. The essence of an organizational pattern is that everyone has a place in the organization. Many tasks, especially decision-making, may only be undertaken by the individual holding the appropriate leadership position. For example, in many churches only a pastor or priest may preach or lead a communion service or baptize. Commonly, only these individuals have the authority to plan services and decide who may minister in particular areas.

For those of us who have grown up in organizational churches, it is easy to impose our organizational presuppositions on Scripture. An example of this is to assume that New Testament churches were governed by a board of elders. The logic flow may go as follows: all organizations need leaders to make decisions; the only local leaders mentioned in the New Testament are elders; it seems that most local churches had several elders; so these elders must have worked together to govern the church. This is impeccable logic. But the logic is only valid if the presupposition that the church is an organization is correct.

As we undertake this study it is critical to keep open the possibility that the New Testament pattern or style of church life might not be organizational. Is it possible that the pattern could be more like a family or a living organism? If we intentionally keep ourselves open to all of these possibilities, it will become much easier to see and consider all relevant Scriptures. Then we will be better placed to find the pattern of church life and practices, which emerges from the available evidence.

Another risk of searching for patterns of New Testament church practices is that we will stop too soon and end up with an incomplete and in some cases inaccurate picture. Also, it is possible to interpret God's blessing on a church or group of churches, which embrace a particular pattern of church life, as evidence that the pattern they follow is God's preferred pattern and the same as the pattern of the New Testament church. This is not necessarily the case.

Once we have identified a pattern of church life in the New Testament, a new group of risks become relevant as we seek to put this pattern into practice. Patterns of church life are like "wineskins." [7] The wineskin is important only because it provides a container for the wine. What really matters is the wine. Similarly, what really matters about church life is that it is full of God's life-giving vitality and truth. If we focus too much on the pattern of church life and not enough on our life-giving God, the pattern can rapidly become an old wineskin, which is unable to contain all of God's life. The pattern can become a dry and empty shell, which lacks the flexibility to accommodate all that God wants to do. If we do not focus on maintaining a fresh relationship with Jesus, our pattern of church life can become like an old wineskin. This can happen even if we have a correct understanding of the New Testament pattern of church life and practices.

Is it possible that our God has given us a "wineskin," which is like the clothing of the people of Israel during their forty years in the desert? Deuteronomy 8:4 tells us that the Israelites' clothing did not wear out during this time. This verse is placed between verses, which talk of close relationship with God. For the wineskin of church practices to remain fresh and flexible over a long period of time we definitely need to maintain a close relationship with Jesus. Is it possible that the New Testament pattern or style of church life and practices is particularly well suited to helping individuals maintain a close relationship with Jesus? Is it possible that the New Testament pattern of church life and practices is less vulnerable to become like an old wineskin than other possible patterns of church life? Is it possible that the New Testament pattern of church life and practices is particularly well suited to hosting the full vitality of God and maintaining the full flexibility and freedom that Jesus wants in His bride?

### *What were the practices of the New Testament church?*

In the first chapter of this book I consider 27 practices related to the day-to-day activities and decision-making of New Testament churches. [8] Many of these practices relate to different types of ministry (*e.g.*, teaching, praying, baptizing) that occur in the life of the church. For each of these ministry activities I seek to discover from Scripture who could be involved. For instance, were ordinary

---

7. *Cf.*, Matt. 9:17

8. For 21 of these practices, further discussion of the relevant Biblical material is provided in Appendix 1. A detailed outline of the contents of this book is provided in Appendix 8.

believers in New Testament churches excluded from certain types of ministry, and were ordinary believers required to ask permission from a leader before entering into other types of ministry? If so, what ministry roles were restricted in this manner? Similarly, did leaders have decision-making authority? If so, what decisions were made by leaders?

### *What leaders existed in local New Testament churches?*

The majority of references to leaders in the New Testament are to leaders like Peter, Paul, Barnabas, Timothy and Titus who traveled around planting new churches and helping existing churches. In this book I refer to these leaders as "traveling leaders." In the New Testament there appears to be a clear distinction between these "traveling leaders" and local leaders who were continuing members of a particular local church. These local leaders were typically called elders (Greek, *presbuteros*) or overseers (Greek, *episkopos*). In Chapter 2 I examine the role of local leaders and in Chapter 3 I examine the role of traveling leaders.

### *What does the New Testament teach about obeying and submitting to leaders?*

Chapter 4 addresses New Testament teaching on obedience and submission to leaders. Does Hebrews 13:17 command believers to obey their leaders? If this is the correct translation of this verse, in what areas is obedience expected? What does submission to a leader look like? What boundaries may believers draw to protect themselves from unhealthy leaders? How do these teachings fit with the pattern of New Testament church life and practices, which emerged in the first three chapters?

### *Who had power in New Testament churches?*

It can be uncomfortable discussing who has the power to make decisions for a church. It seems so unspiritual. The reality is that the distribution of decision-making power within a church is a key aspect of the pattern of church life and practices. There are a few unhealthy church leaders who grab power for bad reasons. But in most cases the intent of Christian leaders, when they create a church structure, is to distribute power in the manner, which will best keep the church in a healthy place.

Chapter 5 looks at the distribution of power within local New Testament assemblies and the balance of power between local assemblies and traveling leaders. This chapter addresses how this distribution of decision-making power contributed to keeping each church in a healthy place and how it contributed to minimizing problems associated with the abuse of power.

### *Is the essence of the pattern of church life organizational or organic?*

A unifying thread running through all of the questions addressed in the first five chapters is whether the pattern or style of New Testament church life was at heart organizational or "organic." The word "organic" is chosen to describe a pattern or style of church, which is first and foremost a living being (or organism) not an organization. In the organic model of church life the emphasis is on the community being held together by relationships of mutual respect and submission. Everyone has an equal place in the body and every member is expected to contribute to the life of the church. All believers are free to choose, based on the leadership of the Holy Spirit, what they contribute. They do not need to ask permission from a human leader before making a contribution.

### *Other New Testament Church Practices*

In Chapter 6 I discuss a series of important topics concerning New Testament church practices, which do not relate to the question of whether New Testament church life was organizational or organic. In particular this chapter addresses such topics as teaching methods, preaching, the gift of prophecy, the role of women, the time and place of church meetings, interactions between churches, and church finances.

### *What is the relevance of New Testament church practices to today?*

The final chapter examines the impact of church practices on the spiritual development of the members of the local church. Does the organizational model or the organic model provide a better context for individuals to mature spiritually and minister fruitfully? Which model best fits with the priesthood of all believers? Is a participatory style or a leader-centric style of church meetings more likely to result in mature believers? What is the best way to keep the wineskin of church life fresh, flexible and healthy? How can we best accommodate the Holy Spirit who wishes to blow wherever He wills through those who have received Him?[9] I encourage you to keep these questions in mind as you read this book and study related passages in the Bible.

---

9. John 3:8

# Chapter 1
# New Testament Assemblies

In order to gain as comprehensive a picture of New Testament church life as possible, the first section of this chapter addresses 27 roles and activities that took place in New Testament Christian assemblies. For each topic, I seek to find out from Scripture who was expected to (or free to) undertake or participate in these roles and activities. One goal of this study is to understand who was involved in different aspects of church life. In particular, I investigate which roles and activities were open to all members of the community, which roles could only be undertaken by recognized leaders (elders, overseers), and which activities required the involvement of the whole church assembly. A picture of the life of New Testament Christian communities emerges from this study. The following sections of this chapter discuss how this picture fits with other Biblical material concerning the nature of the church and Christian leadership.

## 1.1 Roles and Responsibilities in New Testament Christian Assemblies

Table 1[1] summarizes 27 roles and activities mentioned in the New Testament concerning local Christian assemblies. For each role or activity, the table notes who could participate in or who was responsible for the role or activity. This table is a high level summary of many topics. For some of these topics, the relevant New Testament material is absolutely clear and straightforward. In other cases there are significant nuances, and in a few cases there is some uncertainty. However, before discussing these important details underlying the summary shown in Table 1, I will discuss the patterns evident in this table. Table 1 only addresses the roles and activities of believers and leaders within local Christian assemblies. The roles and activities of traveling leaders and their interactions with local leaders and other believers will be discussed in Chapters 3 and 5.

1. Pages 22 and 23

| Role or activity | Responsible individual or group | Relevant Scriptures and Comments |
|---|---|---|
| Serving as a priest | Any/Everyone as led by Spirit | 1 Peter 2:5, 9 |
| Ministering in the main weekly meeting and other settings | Any/Everyone as led by Spirit | 1 Cor. 14:26-33<br>Heb. 10:24-25, Col. 3:16, 1 Peter 4:10-11 |
| Deciding who does what ministry | God | Eph. 2:10, 1 Peter 4:10, Col. 4:17 |
| Making church discipline decisions | Whole church assembly | Matt. 18:15-17, 1 Cor. 5:1-13 |
| Testing revelatory words | Whole church assembly | 1 Cor. 14:29, 1 Thess. 5:19-22, 1 John 4:1 |
| Loving and caring for one another | Any/Everyone as led by Spirit | Matt. 22:39, Gal. 6:9-10 (about 60 verses total) |
| Teaching | Any/Everyone as led by Spirit | All: Col. 3:16<br>Rom. 15:14, Heb. 5:12, James 3:1<br>Elders: 1 Tim. 3:2, 5:17, Titus 1:9 |
| Admonishing | Any/Everyone as led by Spirit | Col. 3:16, 1 Thess. 5:14, 2 Thess. 3:15, Heb. 10:24 |
| Challenging an individual about his sin | Any/everyone as led by Spirit | James 5:19-20, Gal. 6:1 |
| Rebuking an individual about his sin | Any/Everyone as led by Spirit | All: Luke 17:3-4<br>Elders: Titus 1:9<br>Also: Gal. 6:1, Eph. 4:29 |
| Hearing a confession of sin | Any/Everyone as led by Spirit | James 5:16 |
| Assisting with conflict resolution and lawsuits among believers | Any/Everyone as led by Spirit | Matt. 18:15-17<br>1 Cor. 4:3, 6:1-6 |
| Protecting church unity | Any/Everyone as led by Spirit | Eph. 4:3, Rom. 14, 1 Cor. 10:15 - 11:1 |
| Reaching out with the Gospel | Any/Everyone as led by Spirit | Jude 1:23, 1 Peter 3:15, Matt. 5:14-16, Matt. 22:39, Acts 8:4 |
| Preaching | Any/Everyone as led by Spirit | Acts 8:1-4, 11:19-21, 15:35, Mark 1:45, 5:20, 7:36, Luke 8:39. New Testament preaching is evangelistic. |
| Baptizing | Any/Everyone as led by Spirit | Acts 8:12, 9:18, 10:48, Matt. 28:19, 1 Cor. 1:10-17 |
| Serving the Lord's supper | Any/Everyone as led by Spirit | 1 Cor. 11:17-34 |

Table 1. List of roles and responsibilities in local assemblies

Table 1 cont'd. List of roles and responsibilities in local assemblies

| Role or activity | Responsible individual or group | Relevant Scriptures and Comments |
|---|---|---|
| Praying publicly | Any/Everyone as led by Spirit | All: 1 Cor. 11:1-16, 14:6-20, Jam. 5:16 Elders: James 5:14, 1 Tim. 4:14 |
| Praying for healing | Any/Everyone as led by Spirit | Mark 16:18, 1 Cor. 12: 9, 28, James 5:14-16 |
| Praying for deliverance | Any/Everyone as led by Spirit | Mark 16:17, 1 Cor. 12:10 |
| Prophesying, Tongues | Any/Everyone as led by Spirit | Acts 19:6, 1 Cor. 12:10, 28-30, 14:1-5, 39 |
| Living as an example | Any/Everyone as led by Spirit | All: Hebrews 6:12 Elders: 1 Peter 5:3 |
| Overseeing | Any/Everyone as led by Spirit | All: Hebrews 12:15 Elders: 1 Peter 5:2 |
| Building the church | Jesus | Matt. 16:16, Eph. 5:23-32, Psalm 127:1 |
| Deciding who is a local or travelling leader | Holy Spirit working through existing leaders and whole church | Luke 6:12-13, Acts 6:1-6, 9:15, 13:1-4, 14:23, 16:2, 20:28, 1 Tim. 4:14, Titus 1:5 |
| Shepherding/Pastoring | New Testament only mentions elders | Acts 20:28, 1 Peter 5:2, Heb. 13:17. Unlikely that non-elders were excluded |
| Protecting sound doctrine | New Testament only mentions elders | Titus 1:9. Unlikely that non-elders were excluded |

It can be seen from Table 1 that 20 of the 27 roles are open to all believers as led by the Holy Spirit. Three of the roles are reserved to God and two are reserved to the whole assembly. The remaining two roles (shepherding and protecting sound doctrine) are listed as being only mentioned in the context of elders. This is because I have found no Scripture explicitly linking these roles to believers in general. However, it is very hard to argue that believers who were not elders were excluded from providing pastoral care and from helping to protect sound doctrine. As can be seen from the table, the New Testament links many aspects of pastoring to all believers.

It can be seen from Table 1 that the New Testament expects all believers to be active and responsible in almost all areas of local church life. As will be discussed later, New Testament assembly meetings were characterized by every member contributing to each meeting as he or she was prompted by the Holy Spirit. Contributions might include leading the meeting into worship through a hymn or psalm or song, reading a passage of Scripture, teaching, praying, speaking in tongues, providing an interpretation to a message in tongues, sharing a vision or sharing a prophetic word. Meetings were planned and led by God moving through every member of the community. [2] The main weekly meeting of New Testament assemblies was not planned, organized and led by a small group of leaders.

New Testament believers were expected to contribute both to the main weekly meetings and to ministry outside of these meetings. [3] Jesus prompts each believer (or group of believers) to do the ministry He wants done. In some cases this will be a prompting to perform a specific ministry act. In other cases the prompting may be a call to an ongoing ministry. Acts 13:1–4 is an example of this. God, not a group of human leaders, decided to send out Paul and Barnabas.

Believers in the New Testament church were free to minister in ways that have commonly become reserved to ordained clergy. Examples of this include serving the Lord's Supper (communion), baptizing and hearing confessions of sin. The role of New Testament elders was not defined by tasks that only elders were permitted to perform. [4]

### *Decision-making in local assemblies*

Church discipline and the testing of revelatory words relevant to the local church represent two of the hardest and most significant decisions that a local assembly needs to make. Scripture is clear that these two decisions were made by the whole church. [5] In Acts 6:1–6 the whole church selected seven men to distribute food to those in need. Another example of a decision relevant to a complete assembly being made by the complete assembly is given in Acts 11:29. This verse mentions the decision of the church in Antioch to send famine relief to the believers in Judea. Similarly, 1 Corinthians 14:39 presumes that any decision to limit speaking in tongues would be made by the whole church. In the next verse Paul assumes that

---

2. Subsections 1.1.2, 1.1.3
3. Eph. 4:12
4. See Table 1 and Appendix 1.20, 1.21
5. Subsections 1.1.4, 1.1.5

the full gathering was jointly responsible to ensure that "all things... be done decently and in order."[6] It seems reasonable to conclude that most decisions, which impact the whole church were made by the whole church. This conclusion is consistent with Paul writing letters to whole churches and not just to the elders. In many cases these letters expect the whole church to address issues relevant to the whole church.

Acts 15 records elders and apostles making a decision concerning a doctrinal issue: did Gentile believers need to be circumcised and did they need to abstain from food offered to idols? Based on verses 2, 6 and 23 it appears that the whole assembly was not involved in this decision. However, verse 22 records that the decision to send representatives with a letter describing this doctrinal decision was made by the apostles and elders with the whole church. It is possible that decisions concerning matters of doctrine are the only decisions, which elders and apostles may make in isolation from the full assembly. This is consistent with there being no mention in the Bible of individuals who are not leaders having a role in protecting sound doctrine.[7]

In general, New Testament elders do not have a decision-making role in the life of the church that is any different from any other believer.[8] Obviously elders, like all other believers, are meant to decide (based on God's leading) how they will individually contribute to the life of the church. Elders do not get to decide how others will contribute to the life of the church.

---

6. Some individuals interpret this verse as requiring meetings to be planned and led by human leaders. This interpretation takes this verse out of the context of the rest of the chapter (and the rest of the New Testament). The context of this verse shows that the order under discussion is God's order, not human order. The rest of the chapter discusses meetings where every member contributes based on the gifting (and prompting) of the Holy Spirit. Verse 39 makes clear that it is the brothers (*i.e.* the whole community as a group) who have authority over the content of the meeting. Obviously in many cases, if an individual is concerned about a specific contribution to a meeting, he may be able to resolve this concern by speaking to the relevant individual without needing to involve the whole assembly.
7. Section 6.6, Appendix 1.21
8. Sections 4.1 and 4.2 discuss obedience to and submission to local church leaders. These sections conclude that elders do not have authority to direct other believers. They do have substantial authority to influence other believers.

The general principle that the whole church has authority to make decisions on matters relevant to the whole church, does not give the whole church authority to intrude into decisions, which individuals should be making for themselves. Acts 11:29 and 1 Corinthians 16:2–3 are examples of each individual within the community making and implementing their own decisions. In this case, each individual decides how much to give.

Very few passages describe the full process used by the church to make decisions. For example, Acts 6:1-6 records that the apostles proposed to all of the believers that they select seven men to distribute food to those in need. We are told that this idea pleased the believers and that they chose seven men. We are not told how they chose these men.

Acts 14:23 and 2 Corinthians 8:19 both use the Greek word *cheirotoneo* to describe the appointment of leaders. The literal meaning of this word is to "stretch forth the hand." In Greek city state democracies, this word was used for voting because Greeks voted by stretching out their hand to drop a stone into an urn. Sometimes this voting was part of the decision-making process used by a city assembly (*ekklesia*). It is possible that New Testament Christian assemblies (also called *ekklesia* in Greek) made some decisions, including the appointment of elders, by voting. However this same word may also be used for stretching forth one's hand to lay hands on someone in prayer. So it is possible that these verses are not referring to a vote but are referring to prayer with laying on of hands after a leader had been selected by some other method. Acts 1:23-26 mentions the casting of lots to select a new apostle. The Israelites made many decisions by casting lots,[9] but this decision-making process does not seem appropriate after the coming of the Holy Spirit. Consensus decision-making is implicit in many Scriptures. [10] It is probable that New Testament assemblies made many, possibly all, of their joint decisions by consensus.

Making decisions by consensus can be difficult. It sometimes requires deep humility and a commitment to sacrificial love for other members of the assembly. Needing to make tough decisions by consensus can be a wonderful opportunity for growth. Elders

9. Lev. 16:8-10, Num. 26:55-56, 33:54, 34:13, 36:2-3, Josh. 7:14, 14:2, 18:11, 19:1-51, Judg. 20:9, 1 Sam. 10:20-21, 14:42, 1 Chron. 24:5-9

10. John 17:23, Acts 15:22, Rom. 15:5, 1 Cor. 1:10, 2 Cor. 13:11, Eph. 4:3, 5:21, Phil. 2:2, 1 Pet. 3:8

will often have a significant role in helping a local church assembly reach consensus on a tough topic in a godly manner. I believe that consensus decision-making is the best way to make decisions within a local church assembly. This does not guarantee that the resulting decisions will always be correct. [11]

In summary, New Testament churches were characterized by the priesthood of all believers. All believers were empowered to minister as led by God and decisions impacting the whole community were made by the whole community. Unlike many modern churches, the community was not divided in two tiers: a priestly class that organizes ministry and leads the main weekly meeting; and ordinary believers who have limited opportunity to contribute to the main weekly meeting and may only minister in certain other settings with the permission of a priest or pastor. The main weekly meeting of New Testament churches was not organized and led by a small group of leaders, with the rest of the community following their lead. Every member was expected to contribute to the meeting as led by the Holy Spirit. Similarly all of the members of the community were expected to be active in ministry outside of the main weekly meeting as led by the Holy Spirit.

### *Leadership within local assemblies*

The leadership provided by elders to New Testament churches was not defined by specific roles and decision-making authority that were reserved to elders. Elders did not have the authority to govern a local church. It appears that most decisions in the life of New Testament churches were made by the whole church mostly by consensus. Elders were influencers, encouragers and facilitators, not organizers and decision-makers. Teaching was a shared responsibility of the community, not a role reserved to elders. [12]

Given that several of the New Testament churches had major problems, I consider it very significant that the New Testament authors

---

11. A possible example of this occurs in Acts 15:39-40, which implies that the church assembly in Antioch supported Paul in his dispute with Barnabas over Mark. The implication of Philem. 1:24, 2 Tim. 4:11, Col. 4:10 and 1 Pet. 5:13 is that Barnabas was correct to continue to invest in Mark. So it is possible that both Paul and the local church were wrong about Mark's potential and destiny. Barnabas' decision to continue to invest in Mark was an individual decision and the local church had no authority to stop him doing this. However the local church may have missed the opportunity of blessing Barnabas and Mark before they departed for Cyprus.
12. See Appendix 1.1. Some elders were active teachers (1 Tim. 5:17).

taught this narrow role for elders. Paul and the other apostles did not try to solve church problems by reserving decision-making authority and organizational leadership to elders. As previously discussed, Paul's teaching that all things should be done decently and in order is referring to Spirit-led meetings with all of the brothers and sisters discerning the Spirit. Paul is not referring to meetings planned and led by elders. [13] In 1 Corinthians 14:37 Paul says that the things he is writing are a command of the Lord. The context of this verse indicates that this verse refers to the whole passage, including the teaching on Spirit-led meetings and on the whole church jointly testing revelatory words.

The New Testament is clear that good leadership is critical to the health of the local church. [14] It is commonly assumed that it is necessary for a local church leader to have organizational authority over key areas of the life of a church in order to be able to provide this leadership and maintain the health of the congregation. In an assembly the size of a house church, it is possible for the elders to provide high value leadership without needing to give them organizational authority or an exclusive role in the life of the church.

So in what ways did elders provide leadership within local churches? Elders led by influence, not by decision-making. As they did the things that all believers are free to do (*e.g.*, teach, read scripture, admonish), they had a highly influential role in the life of the church. In particular, one of the most important leadership roles is to watch over the souls of other members of the community. [15] As leaders do this, they are positioned to pray for and influence others, perhaps with a word of encouragement, an admonishment, a teaching or by giving advice. In some cases elders may make a recommendation concerning ministry. A key goal is to encourage the whole community to abide in Jesus. [16] As we all abide in Jesus we receive leadership directly from Jesus, and God brings forth much good fruit.

A second important dimension of leadership by influence, which is sometimes needed in churches, is facilitating meetings. This may include:

---

13. 1 Cor. 14:40
14. *E.g.,* 1 Tim. 3:11
15. Heb. 13:17. In Heb. 12:15 all believers are commanded to watch over the complete community (Appendix 1.17, 3.2.3).
16. John 15:1-17. Paul uses the phrase "in Christ" about 80 times. In many cases he may be using the phrase to communicate the same meaning as Jesus communicated by using the phrase "abide in me."

- Encouraging quieter members to contribute
- Encouraging individuals who contribute a great deal to contribute slightly less
- Stepping in when an inappropriate contribution may result in someone feeling disrespected or hurt
- And facilitating consensus-based decision-making

Elders may also lead by protecting sound doctrine and by pastoring. [17] The leadership provided by elders is in many ways similar to good parenting especially of older children. [18] It is also similar to older children helping their younger siblings. Non-elders may also lead by influence in a manner similar to elders. Non-elders who do this consistently are likely to be recognized as elders in due course. [19]

The following six subsections discuss in greater detail the roles shown in the first six lines of Table 1. The remaining 21 roles are discussed in Appendix 1.

### 1.1.1 Serving as a priest

1 Peter 2:5, 9 teach that all believers are a royal priesthood, and Revelation 1:6 and 5:10 say that all believers are priests. This represents a staggering break from Judaism (and most other religions) where the role of priesthood is restricted to a small group. This teaching is fully consistent with the roles of believers summarized in Table 1. As can be seen from this table, roles that many Christian denominations (and other religions) restrict to priests (or pastors) were open to all believers in the New Testament church. This includes leading portions of the main weekly meeting, teaching at the main weekly meeting, hearing confession of sins, baptizing, serving the Lord's Supper, admonishing, assisting in conflict resolution and challenging an individual about his sin. In New Testament churches, matters of church discipline and the testing of revelatory words relevant to the complete church were addressed by the complete

---

17. In cases where an individual continues to teach false doctrine after being refuted by an elder, it may be appropriate to initiate the church discipline process. Similarly it may be appropriate to engage the whole congregation if an individual continues to dominate meetings after being repeatedly asked to contribute less so that others may contribute more.
18. 1 Tim. 3:4-5. Unlike parents, elders do not have authority to discipline. This is reserved to the full assembly.
19. A fuller discussion of the responsibilities and authority of elders is provided in Section 2.5.

congregation. All of these roles are commonly considered to be priestly roles.

The Greek word translated priesthood in 1 Peter 2:5, 9 is *ierateuma*. The emphasis of this word is on a body (or group) of priests. Two other Greek words are translated priesthood in other New Testament passages where the emphasis is on the priestly office.[20] Peter was careful to select a word that emphasized a group of believers serving in a priestly manner rather than a word that emphasized a particular office within the religious community. The New Testament teaches that Jesus is our only high priest, so believers as priests should follow His leadership. [21]

### 1.1.2 Ministering in the main weekly meeting and other settings

1 Corinthians 14:26 says, "What then, brothers? When you come together, each one has a hymn, a lesson, a revelation, a tongue, or an interpretation. Let all things be done for building up." This verse makes it clear that every member is expected to contribute to the main weekly meeting. Potential contributions to meetings listed by Paul in this verse include: hymns, lessons, revelations, tongues and interpretations (of tongues). So the contribution of each member to the meetings is much more than joining in worship and prayers selected by someone else. Each member is expected to contribute to the meeting content that he (or she) has selected as prompted by the Holy Spirit. In this sense every member is expected to contribute to the leadership of the meeting. Paul also says in verse 26 that the purpose of these contributions is to build each other up. In verse 31 he goes on to say that contributions from each member may also result in people learning and being encouraged. This type of meeting is fully consistent with every participant being a priest.

Similarly Colossians 3:16 says, "Let the word of Christ dwell in you richly, teaching and admonishing one another in all wisdom, singing psalms and hymns and spiritual songs, with thankfulness in your hearts to God." And 1 Peter 4:10-11 says, "Each one should use whatever gift he has received to serve others, faithfully administering God's grace in its various forms. If anyone speaks, he should do it as one speaking the very words of God. If anyone serves, he should do

---

20. *Ierateia* is used in Luke 1:9 and Heb. 7:5, and *ierosune* is used in Heb. 7:11, 12, 14, 24. These words are not used to describe believers.
21. Heb. 2:17, 3:1, 4:14-15, 5:5, 10, 6:20, 7:26, 8:1, 9:11, 10:21

it with the strength God provides, so that in all things God may be praised through Jesus Christ. To him be the glory and the power forever and ever. Amen" (NIV). Both of these passages apply broadly to our lives. In the New Testament church, believers had the freedom to obey these commands in their weekly assembly meetings.

1 Corinthians 14:26-33 teaches that every member of the community was expected to contribute content to each meeting as led by the Holy Spirit. Clearly there was an expectation of order and harmony between contributions. This can be achieved with an appropriate attitude of mutual submission and humility, without needing to have a human leader or group of leaders control the meeting. One of the great joys of following the pattern described in this passage is discovering that the Holy Spirit is fully competent to lead meetings! In fact on occasion one might have to admit His omniscience gives Him a distinct edge over the best human leader.

There is no mention in this passage, or elsewhere in the New Testament, of a human leader deciding the flow of a house church meeting. In verse 32 Paul does not say that the spirits of the prophets are subject to the elders. If New Testament church assembly meetings were organized and led by one or more elders, one would have expected Paul to say that contributions by prophets are subject to review by the elders. The New Testament does, however, expect individuals to exercise self-control for the good of the group.

In the middle of a multi-chapter section providing direction concerning Christian meetings, Paul teaches that the church is like a body and is the body of Christ.[22] This context indicates that that a primary application of this teaching is to the main weekly meeting of the Christian community. For the body to be healthy, it is necessary for every member to play his part. Structuring the main weekly meeting to allow each member of the body to minister to everyone else is a natural fit with the truth that everyone is a valuable and unique part of the body. Restricting the main weekly meeting so that only a few key leaders can minister distorts the body. Some members are overworked and others are underworked. Some needed types of ministry will either not happen or will be done less well if the person with the optimal gift is not free to minister.

---

22. 1 Cor. 11 to 14 addresses meetings and 1 Cor. 12:12-27 teaches about the church as body. Immediately before and after this passage Paul is teaching about spiritual gifts. The healthy use of spiritual gifts flows from an understanding that the church is the body of Christ.

Hebrews 10:19-25 provides another insight into New Testament church meetings. Verses 24 and 25 make it clear that the purpose of regularly meeting together includes "stir(ring) up one another to love and good works" and "encouraging one another." Obviously it is common in traditional church services for the leader to do these things. This is good, but is not what is commanded in these verses. These verses teach that these are activities to which every believer should contribute. It is difficult for believers to be obedient to this command in the context of a traditional church service. The whole leader-centric model of traditional church services can easily send the message that only the ordained clergy are good enough to provide such spiritual leadership.

This passage also contains the command to "not neglect meeting together." This command relates to participating in meetings where every member can contribute to "stir(ring) up one another to love and good works" and "encouraging one another." This is fully consistent with type of meeting described in 1 Corinthians 14:26-33.

All of the discussion in this subsection so far has related to the main weekly meetings of Christian assemblies. The Biblical evidence shows that these meetings were based on every member contributing as led by the Holy Spirit. According to Acts 2:46 the Jerusalem church met both in homes and at the temple. It is reasonable to assume that these home meetings followed the pattern described in this subsection. Owing to the larger number of people present at the temple meetings it would not have been possible for every member to contribute. This does not necessarily mean that these meetings in the temple were similar to typical modern day leader-centric church services. It is possible to have large meetings where there is freedom for any participant to contribute as led by the Holy Spirit. Acts 15:35 notes that "many others" taught and preached alongside Paul and Barnabas in Antioch. This shows that even when two apostles were in town they did not do all the teaching and preaching. It is likely that this principle applies to larger meetings such as the meeting in the temple as well as in other settings.

Meetings in a public hall are mentioned in Acts 19:9. From the context of this passage it seems likely that the focus of these meetings in Ephesus was evangelistic, but it is possible that they were similar to the temple meetings mentioned in Acts 2:46. There is no mention in Scripture that such large meetings were widespread. It is likely that in several cities the opposition was so strong that it was not possible to hold large meetings. It seems that believers were expected to participate in small meetings where they could contribute and form strong relationships with one another. Participating in larger meetings may have been an occasional additional opportunity.

### 1.1.3 Deciding who does what ministry

In John 10 Jesus says:

> But he who enters by the door is the shepherd of the sheep. To him the gatekeeper opens. The sheep hear his voice, and he calls his own sheep by name and leads them out. When he has brought out all his own, he goes before them, and the sheep follow him, for they know his voice. A stranger they will not follow, but they will flee from him, for they do not know the voice of strangers.
>
> I am the good shepherd. I know my own and my own know me, just as the Father knows me and I know the Father.

These passages teach that each believer is expected to know and recognize Jesus' voice. Each believer is to be led both by watching where Jesus is going and what He is doing and by listening for His commands. This passage emphasizes the direct communication between Jesus and each believer. This communication, which includes Jesus communicating to believers through the Bible, provides believers with the information they need to follow Jesus.

John 10:14-15 make the staggering statement that each believer is expected to come to the place of knowing Jesus in the same way that Jesus knows the Father. This is not only "knowing about" as in believing correct doctrine, but also the deep personal intimate knowing that makes the Father and the Son (and the Holy Spirit) truly One, within the mystery of the Holy Trinity. [23] Taking John 10:14-15 together with John 5:19-20 [24] and John 16:13-15 [25] it is reasonable to

---

23. The Greek word for "know" in John 10:14-15 is also used in Matt. 1:25 and Luke 1:34 to describe sexual intimacy in marriage.
24. John 5:19-20 So Jesus said to them, "Truly, truly, I say to you, the Son can do nothing of his own accord, but only what he sees the Father doing. For whatever the Father does, that the Son does likewise. For the Father loves the Son and shows him all that he himself is doing. And greater works than these will he show him, so that you may marvel."
25. John 16:13-15 When the Spirit of truth comes, he will guide you into all the truth, for he will not speak on his own authority, but whatever he hears he will speak, and he will declare to you the things that are to come. He will glorify me, for he will take what is mine and declare it to you. All that the Father has is mine; therefore I said that he will take what is mine and declare it to you.

conclude that believers should do what they see or hear Jesus and the Father doing or saying just as Jesus only did what He saw the Father doing. The Holy Spirit provides the necessary communication. There is no hint that God wants an elder in the communication path telling us what ministry the elder thinks God wants us to do. Similarly Matthew 23:10 teaches that we have only one guide, leader, teacher, instructor—Jesus.[26] In John 15 Jesus teaches that the branches (individual believers) should abide in the vine (Jesus). Jesus does not teach that twigs (individual believers) should abide in branches (elders) that abide in the vine (Jesus).[27] Elders can have an important role, especially with less mature believers, helping them to discern the leading of the Holy Spirit and helping them to follow this leading in a wise manner.

The weekly meetings of New Testament church assemblies provided a wonderful opportunity for believers to minister in response to what they saw and heard Jesus and the Father doing. The weekly meeting was a great opportunity for the gathered community to minister to one another and was also a safe place for individuals to learn how to minister in this manner. A healthy body needs to receive from all of its parts, not just from leaders.

Luke 22:25-26 teaches that the role of the leader is like a servant (rather than a lord) and Ephesians 5:21 teaches that all believers including leaders, should be moving in mutual submission to other believers. This style of leadership is inconsistent with leaders assuming the authority to be ministry permission givers/withholders. For example, there is no hint in the New Testament that individuals can only pray for other believers if they have taken the prayer team training class and been approved by the elders. In fairness to leaders who restrict ministry in this manner, it is often true that they have excellent motives for their behavior. A common motive is to protect individuals from being hurt. In a house church setting (due to its small size) it is possible to achieve this important goal without introducing a culture of needing to ask a leader's permission to minister. Of

---

26. Appendix 4.5.7 discusses the Greek word (*kathegetes*) for leader used in this verse. Section 1.4 provides further discussion of Matt. 23:8-10.

27. See also 1 Cor. 14:26, Eph. 2:10, 1 Pet. 4:10 and Col. 4:17 which imply that believers are accountable to God to do what He has created them to do. 1 Pet. 4:10 and Col. 4:17 command believers to do the ministry they were created to do. Col. 4:17 shows that a church may command a believer to do the ministry God has given him to do. This is very different to commanding a believer to do the ministry selected by the elders.

course, leaders can contribute to teaching individuals how to minister effectively.

A New Testament example of a leader assuming the authority to direct individuals to refrain from ministry is mentioned in 3 John 1:10. Diotrephes was stopping believers from welcoming visiting brothers, the ministry of hospitality, and punishing those who did so by putting them out of the church. John makes clear that this permission withholding and punishing is wrong. The exception to this is if an individual is teaching error. In this case an elder is expected to refute the error. [28]

Another way to address the question of who decides who does what ministry is to consider the question: Does the Holy Spirit have a preference in how He leads? Does He prefer to lead through a single pastor (or a small leadership group) or does He prefer to lead through a wide range of people giving each one a small piece of the action? It seems to me that the teaching on spiritual gifts in the New Testament shows that He prefers to lead through all believers. [29] When He leads through a diversity of individuals it is much clearer who deserves the glory.

Another dimension to this question is whether the Holy Spirit has a preferred leadership model based on its impact on the believers. Is one leadership model more conducive to spiritual growth among the believers? As will be discussed in Section 7.3, I believe that leading through all of the believers rather than through a leadership group can be more helpful to the spiritual development of the believers. If human leaders provide most leadership, we can slip into passivity and into looking to human leaders when we should be looking to God.

Given the major problems in some New Testament churches (*e.g.*, Corinth) it is amazing that Paul (and other New Testament leaders) did not seek to fix the problems by empowering elders to have more control over the life of the church, and over who could serve in particular ways. In fact it seems that he saw this as a danger to be

---

28. Titus 1:9. Some may cite verses where Paul says he sent a ministry partner to a particular city as evidence that Paul could direct the ministry activities of his teammates. When all verses related to this topic are considered, it becomes clear that Paul did not have this authority (Section 3.6, Appendix 2.2).

29. *E.g.*, in Rom. 12:4-8 Paul encourages his readers to use the gift(s) they have received. Much, but not all, of our ministry will flow out of our giftedness. The Holy Spirit chooses which gifts He gives to each believer so He is the one who decides how we will serve, not human leaders.

avoided. In Acts 20:29-30 Paul warns of savage wolves attacking the Ephesian church. It seems that Paul expected some of the elders listening to him on that day to become wolves who would "entice the disciples to follow them." It seems that Paul is warning against leaders who want disciples to have their primary allegiance to them rather than to Jesus. Jesus said "if the Son sets you free, you will be free indeed." [30] Part of this freedom is to obey and follow Him without needing permission from a religious leader.

The earliest record we have of a Christian leader moving towards giving elders the authority to make ministry decisions is in a letter written in the last decade of the 1st Century. In this letter, written by Clement to the church in Corinth, he suggests the application of the Levitical priesthood to the church. This is taken a step further in the letters written by Ignatius in the first decade of the 2nd Century. Ignatius wanted elders to have more control and decision-making authority than is taught in the New Testament. It seems that by the early 4th Century (reign of Constantine) most churches had moved to the leader-centric pattern which has been the predominant style of church ever since. [31]

### 1.1.4 Making church discipline decisions

The use of the plural form of the word "you" in 1 Corinthians 5:2, 4, 13 shows that the whole house church assembly was to be involved in disciplining an immoral believer. [32] Similarly 2 Corinthians 2:6 refers to a discipline decision made by the "majority" of the congregation. Evidence from two or more witnesses was required before a church considered charges against someone. [33] In some cases traveling leaders may have a role in the church discipline process. [34] Also, as discussed in Section 5.2, God may directly intervene in a church

---

30. John 8:36
31. Much more detail on this transition in leadership is provided in Chapter 16 of *Nexus, The World House Church Movement Reader* edited by Rad Zdero and published by William Carey Library.
32. This is consistent with the final step in the conflict resolution process. Matt 18:17, Appendix 1.6
33. Deut. 19:15, Matt. 18:16, 2 Cor. 13:1, 1 Tim. 5:19
34. See: 1 Cor. 5 and 1 Tim. 5:19 and Sections 2.8 and 5.2. In 1 Cor. 5:3 Paul says that he has already pronounced judgment over the immoral brother. Whatever this means, it is still the responsibility of the complete church assembly to make the church discipline decision. I suspect that when Paul says he has already judged the immoral brother he is saying that he has already made up his mind that this brother should be disciplined. This does not mean that Paul is claiming that he can make this decision unilaterally.

discipline process. It seems from Scripture that only the whole local church assembly may authorize any discipline. There is no hint that elders or traveling leaders may discipline someone without getting the agreement of the full congregation.

Exclusion is the only form of discipline that I have found in the New Testament. [35] Individuals who were disciplined were excluded from house church meetings and from contact with members of the house church in other settings. [36] In order to have every member support the exclusion, they would need to be convinced that the discipline was appropriate. This was achieved by having them involved in the decision process. Making church discipline decisions by consensus provides a further opportunity for every member to be fully engaged in the decision-making process. The severity and redemptive purpose of this discipline is taught by 1 Corinthians 5:5, which contains the powerful phrase "hand this man over to Satan" (NIV). I do not consider rebuking to be a form of discipline, because if you reject the rebuke it need have no power over you. [37]

2 Corinthians 10:6 may imply that it is only appropriate to undertake church discipline when the bulk of the congregation is walking in obedience to Jesus. If the bulk of the congregation is not walking in obedience to Jesus, the first priority is to help as many as possible to return to a close walk with Him.

Involving the whole house church in church discipline provides a measure of protection against abusive leaders. It does not provide protection from an abusive leader who has inappropriately strong influence over most of the church community. It is possible that this circumstance underlies 3 John 1:10.

### 1.1.5 Testing revelatory words

1 John 4:1, 1 Thessalonians 5:19-21 and 1 Corinthians 14:29 are commands to the whole church assembly to jointly weigh potential prophetic words. [38] Such words were not to be evaluated by the elders

---

In several places in this chapter he makes clear that the whole assembly needs to make this decision jointly.

35. Matt. 18:15-17, 1 Cor. 5:1-5, 9-13
36. Rom. 16:17, 2 Thess. 3:14-15, 2 Tim. 3:5, Titus 3:10
37. Section 4.3, Appendix 6
38. 1 Cor. 14:29 says "Let two or three prophets speak, and let the others weigh what is said." Some interpret the phrase "the others" to mean "the other prophets," which implies that only prophets are engaged in evaluating potential prophetic words. It could also mean "the others present," which

only, nor were they to be evaluated only by a group of prophets. Prophetic words had a key role in the life of the New Testament church. Prophecy "speaks to people for their upbuilding and encouragement and consolation" and were part of assembly meetings "so that all may learn and all be encouraged." [39] Prophecy was also used by God to guide ministry decisions, bring individuals to faith and to identify future traveling leaders. [40] The teaching that decisions concerning revelatory words were to be made by the complete community (as opposed to leaders only) is another indicator that important decisions impacting the full community were made by the complete community.

### 1.1.6 Loving and caring for one another

"One Anothering" was a very important dimension of the life of the New Testament church. In about 50 verses we are commanded to do some positive aspect of one anothering, and in another ten verses we are commanded to refrain from some negative aspect of one anothering. These specific commands all flow from the broad command to "love your neighbor as yourself" [41] and Jesus' new commandment: "love one another: just as I have loved you, you also are to love one another. By this all people will know that you are my disciples, if you have love for one another." [42] Galatians 6:9-10 restates these commands placing particular emphasis on the importance of loving other believers. [43] This focus of particularly loving other members of the community of faith is apparent in many of the one-anothering commands. For example, ten of the one-

---

implies the whole church is involved. Verse 31 mentions the potential for everyone to prophesy, so in this context "the other prophets" is equivalent to "the others present." I believe that these verses apply to words relevant to the full church, and that words relevant to individuals should be submitted to the individual for evaluation. See Section 6.3 for further discussion of the role of the prophetic in New Testament churches. I use the term "potential prophetic words" to describe words which may be prophetic but have not yet been tested. Factors to consider in testing revelatory words include: the consistency of the word with Biblical truth especially concerning Jesus and the importance of loving and obeying God; and the prophet's track record of accuracy (1 John 4:1-3, Deut. 13:2-6, 18:20-22, 1 Sam. 3:19-20).

39. 1 Cor. 14:3, 31
40. Acts 11:27-30, 1 Cor. 14:24-25, Section 3.2
41. Matt. 22:39
42. John 13:34-35
43. And let us not grow weary of doing good, for in due season we will reap, if we do not give up. So then, as we have opportunity, let us do good to everyone, and especially to those who are of the household of faith.

anothering verses mention brothers or brotherly love.[44] We are to love one another like family. However, some of these one-anothering commands apply equally to everyone with whom we interact.

Far and away the most common command associated with one anothering is to "love one another." This command is contained in 15 passages.[45] Other closely related commands include:

- Serve one another in love using one's gifting (Galatians 5:13, 1 Peter 4:10)
- Wash one another's feet (John 13:14)
- Bear one another's burdens in love (Galatians 6:2)
- Be kind to one another (Ephesians 4:32)
- Do good to one another, do not repay evil with evil (1 Thessalonians 5:15)
- Care for one another (1 Corinthians 12:25)
- Comfort one another (2 Corinthians 13:11)
- Live in harmony, peace, agreement with one another (Romans 12:16, 15:5, Mark 9:50, 2 Corinthians 13:11)
- Bear with one another in love (Ephesians 4:2, Colossians 3:13)

Other things we are commanded to do concerning one anothering include:

- Instruct, teach, admonish, exhort and stir one another up to love and good works (Romans 15:14, Colossians 3:16, Hebrews 3:13, 10:24)
- Encourage one another (1 Thessalonians 4:18, 5:11, Hebrews 10:25)
- Build one another up (1 Thessalonians 5:11)
- Greet one another with a holy kiss (Romans 16:16, 1 Corinthians 16:20, 2 Corinthians 13:12, 1 Peter 5:14)
- Welcome one another (Romans 15:7)
- Show hospitality to one another (1 Peter 4:9)
- When you come together to eat, wait for one another (1 Corinthians 11:33)
- Forgive one another (Ephesians 4:32, Colossians 3:13)
- Show honor to one another (Romans 12:10)
- Clothe yourselves in humility towards one another (1 Peter 5:5)

---

44. Rom. 12:10, 15:14, 1 Cor. 4:6, 11:33, Gal. 5:13, 1 Thess. 4:9, 2 Thess. 1:3, James 4:11, 5:9, 1 Pet. 1:22
45. John 13:34-35, 15:12, 17, Rom. 12:10, 13:8, 1 Thess. 3:12, 4:9, 2 Thess. 1:3, 1 Pet. 1:22, 4:8, 1 John 3:11, 23, 4:7, 11-12, 2 John 1:5

- Submit to one another (Ephesians 5:21)
- Pray for one another (James 5:16)
- Speak to one another with psalms, hymns and spiritual songs (Ephesians 5:19)
- Confess your sins to one another (James 5:16)

Things we are commanded not to do concerning one anothering include:

- Do not speak evil against one another (James 4:11)
- Do not bite, devour or consume one another (Galatians 5:15)
- Do not grumble against one another (James 5:9)
- Do not judge one another (Romans 14:13)
- Do not lie to one another (Colossians 3:9)
- Do not provoke one another out of conceit (Galatians 5:26)
- Do not envy one another out of conceit (Galatians 5:26)
- Do not take pride in one over against another (1 Corinthians 4:6)
- Do not compare yourself to one another (2 Corinthians 10:12)
- Do not hate one another (Titus 3:3)
- Do not have lawsuits against one another (1 Corinthians 6:7)

Peter says that through God's "very great and precious promises... [we] may participate in the divine nature." [46] A primary element of our participation in the divine nature is being a community characterized by love for one another just as the members of the Holy Trinity are a community who love one another. This love between the members of the Holy Trinity is so profound that the three persons of the Holy Trinity are one God. Jesus says that the Father is in Him and He is in the Father. In this context Jesus prays that the believing community will have the same unity as He has with the Father. [47] He goes on to pray that the united believing community will also enter into this unity both with Him and with the Father. Jesus and His Bride, the church, shall become one when we are married. [48] We are to passionately love God and love one another because this is the nature of our God and it is our heavenly destiny. It was also humanity's privilege and joy to fully love God and to fully love one another prior to the fall.

---

46. 2 Pet. 1:4 NIV. See also Eph. 4:24, Col. 3:10, 1 John 4:8
47. John 17:20-21
48. Eph. 5:31-32, Rev. 21:2

## 1.2 The church is the body of Christ

In many passages,[49] Paul says that the church is the body of Christ. Jesus is the head of His body, which means that He is the source of all of our life and energy.[50] Romans 12:3-10 and 1 Corinthians 12:11-31 also say that the church is like a body with diverse organs and members, which form a single whole. Just like the organs and members of a human body, each member of Christ's body is intended to perform a unique and needed function. In several cases these varied functions are associated with spiritual gifts. These gifts and functions should be humbly exercised according the measure of our faith within a context of mutual love. Christ's body is united as its members experience both good and bad times, rejoicing with those who rejoice and weeping with those who weep.

In Ephesians 4:11-16 Paul again touches on this picture emphasizing the importance of varied gifts for our ongoing equipping, building up, and growth into Christ our head and into knowledge of Him as well as into unity and maturity. The latter part of verse 16 beautifully summarizes God's intent: "when each part is working properly, [Christ] makes the body grow so that it builds itself up in love." God wants to move through every member to mature and grow His body. This is totally consistent with the pattern of New Testament assembly meetings where everyone contributed to each meeting as prompted and enabled by the Holy Spirit. This style of meeting is conducive to building the friendships and love bonds that makes the assembly a single body rather than a collection of disconnected individuals.

In 1 Corinthians 10:16-17 Paul says that the bread we share in the Lord's supper is a participation in the body of Christ. As we partake in the one bread we become one body. In 1 Corinthians 11:23-30 he emphasizes the importance of being in healthy relationship with our brothers and sisters in Christ before participating in the Lord's supper.

---

49. *E.g.*, Eph. 1:22-23, Col. 1:18, 24, 2:19, see also Heb. 13:3.
50. The Hebrew and Greek words translated "headship" in the Bible do not, in general, mean authority to direct the activities of those who are under the headship. In general, these words indicate the source of life. So when the Bible says that Jesus is the head of the church it means that He is the source of life for the church. However, as discussed in Section 1.1.3, other passages teach that God desires to lead His church by guiding and directing each believer.

In Ephesians 5:21-33 Paul links the truth that the church is the body of Christ with the truth that the church is the bride of Christ. Jesus is committed to presenting to Himself a splendid bride. Part of the splendor of God's creation of our human bodies is the wonderful way in which all of the members and organs work together to form a beautifully functioning whole. As King David said, "our bodies are fearfully and wonderfully made." [51] Part of the beauty and splendor that Jesus wishes to see in His bride and body is every member harmoniously participating, in a manner that expresses the uniqueness of their individuality and gifting, and yet also forms a single wonderful whole.

### 1.3 Freedom and authority of believers

Jesus said, "if the Son sets you free, you will be free indeed" and "you will know the truth, and the truth will set you free." [52] There are many dimensions to this freedom; perhaps the most important is that "the law of the Spirit of life has set you free in Christ Jesus from the law of sin and death." [53]

In the context of the meetings and ministry of New Testament Christian assemblies, a very important freedom of believers was to minister as they were led by God. [54] Christian assembly meetings were based on every member's participation with everyone contributing as prompted by the Spirit. We are to use this freedom to do good and we must ensure that the way we use our freedom does not become a stumbling block to the weak. [55]

The foundational authority given to all who receive Jesus is the right to become children of God, indwelt by the Holy Spirit and a member of a royal priesthood. [56] This authority is the foundation for the freedom believers have to minister and to participate in joint decision-making within the church assembly. The protection of sound doctrine is the only activity mentioned in the New Testament where local leaders may have had authority that was not available to

---

51. Psalm 139:14
52. John 8:32, 36. *cf.* Matt. 17:26, Gal 5:1
53. Rom. 8:2. Other dimensions of freedom mentioned in the New Testament relate to: money (Acts 5:4); meat offered to idols, special days (Rom. 14); marriage (1 Cor. 7:35-37); circumcision and the law (Gal. 5:1-6).
54. Subsections 1.1.2, 1.1.3
55. 1 Pet. 2:15-16, 1 Cor. 8:9
56. John 1:12, Acts 2:38, 1 Pet. 2:9

ordinary believers.[57] A more complete discussion of New Testament teaching on authority is provided in Appendix 2.

All believers are priests, and priests have the privilege of access to God. In other religions where only some individuals are priests, the priests lead the religious ceremonies and non-priests need to come to a priest to perform certain key transactions with God. In a spiritual community where all members are priests, all members are free to come into the presence of God and minister as He directs. For example, in 2 Corinthians 1:3-6 Paul says that we comfort others with the comfort we have received from God. All believers are, as priests, free to enter into the presence of God to receive comfort for their afflictions, which then equips them to minister comfort to others.

## 1.4 New Testament teaching on leadership

The most profound teachings about leadership in the New Testament are implicit in the most general commands to all believers as to how we should treat one another. The most important of these is the commandment that Jesus identified as the second greatest commandment "Love your neighbor as yourself" (NIV).[58] Jesus also expressed this command in Matthew 7:12 as "So whatever you wish that others would do to you, do also to them, for this is the Law and the Prophets," and the parallel passage in Luke 6:31 says, "Do to others as you would have them do to you" (NIV). Similarly in Philippians 2:3-4 Paul says, "Do nothing from rivalry or conceit, but in humility count others more significant than yourselves. Let each of you look not only to his own interests, but also to the interests of others." It is wonderful when Christian leaders live out these commands. Almost all spiritual abuse results from disobedience to these commands.

Another closely related group of commands includes Ephesians 5:21 where Paul commands all believers to move in mutual submission. This means that Christian leaders need to submit to all believers.[59] Similarly in Luke 22:25-27 Jesus says that Christian leaders should be like servants and not "lord it over" their followers. The parallel passages in Matthew and Mark[60] not only say that Christian leaders

57. Titus 1:9, Acts 15:2, 6, 23
58. Matt. 22:39, Mark 12:31, Luke 10:27, Rom. 13:9, James 2:8
59. See Section 4.2 for a discussion of submission within the Christian community, and Appendix 5 for a broader discussion of New Testament teaching on submission.
60. Matt. 20:25-28, Mark 10:42-45

should not "lord it over" their followers, but also make the point that the path to greatness and being first in the kingdom of God is to first become a servant or slave. Peter uses the same phrase in 1 Peter 5:1-3 "To the elders among you, I appeal as a fellow-elder,... not lording it over those entrusted to you, but being examples to the flock" (NIV). In 2 Corinthians 1:24 Paul also uses this phrase to describe his relationship with the Corinthians. The essence of mutual submission in the context of Christian ministry is for groups of individuals working together to make jointly decisions relevant to their joint ministry. In my opinion it is only the individuals who are involved in a particular ministry who participate in the consensus decision-making process for that ministry. Others may of course provide advice.

The link Jesus makes in Matthew 20:25-28 between Christian leadership and service/being a servant is a recurring theme throughout the New Testament. Several passages[61] make clear that Christian leaders are expected to serve other believers. Several other passages[62] teach that Christian leaders (like all believers) are servants of Jesus.

The word "ministry" is often used to translate the Greek word *diakonia.*[63] It has become so widely used as a word describing the work of Christian leaders that it is easy to forget that the root meaning of the Greek word is serving. Similarly, the modern term "minister," which is often used to translate the Greek word *diakonos,*[64] is so commonly used as a title for a Christian worker that it is easy to forget that the root meaning of this word is "servant."

The Greek word *doulos* (slave or servant) is also widely used of Christian leaders. In several passages[65] this word is used to describe Christian leaders as the slave or servant of other believers. In many passages[66] this word is used to describe Christian leaders as the slave or servant of God. In other passages[67] this word is used to describe all believers as slaves or servants to God. In Philippians 2:7

---

61. *E.g.*, Matt. 23:11, Mark 9:35, 1 Cor. 16:15, Col. 1:25
62. *E.g.*, 2 Cor. 6:4, Phil. 1:1, Col. 1:7, 1 Tim. 1:12, 4:6
63. *E.g.*, Acts 1:17, 25, 12:25, 20:24, 21:19, Rom. 11:13, 2 Cor. 4:1, 5:18, 6:3, 2 Tim. 4:5
64. *E.g.*, 1 Cor. 3:5, 2 Cor. 3:6, Eph. 3:7, 6:21, Col. 1:23, Col. 4:7
65. *E.g.*, Matt. 20:27, Mark 10:44, 2 Cor. 4:5
66. *E.g.*, Acts 16:17, Rom. 1:1, Gal. 1:10, Phil. 1:1, Col. 4:12, 2 Tim. 2:24, Titus 1:1, James 1:1
67. *E.g.*, 1 Cor. 7:22, Eph. 6:6

we are told that Jesus became a slave and that this is an example for all believers to follow.

It is implicit in the command for leaders to "not lord it over" other believers and in the use of the words servant and slave to describe leaders, that Christian leadership is not about organizing and directing ministry. Servants and slaves do not tell others what to do, nor do they have special rights. Leaders are expected to state clearly what the Bible[68] teaches on moral and doctrinal matters. This teaching may include training for ministry.

Paul commands leaders to be gentle when dealing with those who oppose them. For example, in a personal conflict where Paul had been unjustly criticized he chose to "entreat...by the meekness and gentleness of Christ."[69] However, sometimes it is appropriate for a Christian (either a leader or an individual who is not a leader) to rebuke another believer.[70] Paul also expects leaders to lead in humility. Humility and gentleness are key to Christian unity.[71]

Christian leadership is not defined by certain roles and responsibilities that may only be performed by the leader. Believers who do not serve in a formal leadership role are free to contribute and lead in the same ways as identified leaders (*e.g.*, elders). All believers, including leaders, are expected to contribute to church assembly meetings and to participate in other ministry as Jesus leads them. As individuals do this, they often end up providing leadership to a portion of an assembly meeting (*e.g.*, by teaching or by leading the assembly into worship using a particular song) or they may provide leadership to ministry outside of assembly meetings. Being a Christian leader is about watching out for the spiritual community and encouraging and helping individuals to walk closely with Jesus so that they are available to be used by Him.[72]

---

68. For the first few decades after the birth of the church the only available written scripture was what we now call the Old Testament. The material which now forms the Gospels was in some measure known to some believers.
69. 2 Cor. 10:1-2, see also Philem. 8, 9.
70. Section 4.3
71. 2 Tim. 2:25, Gal. 6:1, Acts 20:19, Eph. 4:1-3
72. Heb. 13:17. Obviously any believer can minister in this manner. See Sections 2.5 and 3.5 for further discussion of the important leadership role provided by local and traveling leaders.

## *Matthew 23:2-12*

Matthew 23 records an extended rebuke by Jesus of the scribes, Pharisees and rabbis. From this chapter we can learn several principles of healthy spiritual leadership. Verses 2 and 3a contain the only positive thing that Jesus says about the scribes and Pharisees: "The scribes and the Pharisees sit on Moses' seat, so practice and observe whatever they tell you." The point of this verse is that we should obey Biblical teaching even if the teacher has substantial sin in his life.

In verses 3b-7 Jesus brings four specific charges against the scribes, Pharisees and rabbis. First, He brings the charge of hypocrisy. They do not practice their own teaching. In six of the seven woes that form the second half of this chapter Jesus repeats this charge. It is very important for Christian leaders and teachers to avoid hypocrisy. We need to allow Jesus to transform our character, before we presume to take an ongoing leadership role.

Second, Jesus charges the scribes and Pharisees with placing heavy burdens on individuals. The burden that Jesus is discussing in this verse is the burden of defining righteousness as being primarily about obeying rules, rather than walking in humble relationship with God, doing justice and loving kindness.[73] Once the scribes and Pharisees started down this path they ended up with the problems Jesus addresses in verses 16-28 of this chapter. What God cares about most is our heart attitude towards Him and towards others.[74] Obviously, the heart attitude God desires will express itself in specific patterns of behavior that can be described in broad terms.[75] Attempting to come up with comprehensive lists of do's and don'ts to cover all circumstances tends to result in an inappropriate focus on observable behaviors, instead of heart attitudes. The scribes and Pharisees ended up going beyond what is taught in Scripture and focusing on relatively minor points (*e.g.*, tithing herbs) that caused them to neglect really important issues (*e.g.*, justice, mercy and faithfulness). They also ended up introducing some ridiculous hair splitting into the mix (*e.g.*, concerning oaths).

The second part of Jesus' concern in verse 4 is that the scribes and the Pharisees did not help people carry the burdens they plac-

---

73. Micah 6:8
74. Matt. 22:36-40
75. *E.g.*, Gal. 5:13-26

ed upon them. The best way to help individuals to live righteously is to connect them to God's power to transform us.[76] Christian leaders and teachers must be careful to keep our part and God's part of sanctification connected. Jesus said that His yoke is easy and His burden is light.[77] Christian teaching and leadership should be encouraging and uplifting. It should not leave people feeling abandoned with a heavy burden.

The third charge (v. 5) that Jesus brings against the scribes and Pharisees is that they do all their deeds to be seen by others. This is closely related to the fourth charge (vv. 6-7) that they love to be given a place and title of honor. Leaders want to be followed and followers typically follow people they respect. So the temptation to show off in order to earn respect from potential followers is ever present for leaders and teachers. Similarly being given a prestigious seat or title is often taken as evidence that an individual is worthy of respect. So it is tempting for leaders to pursue these honors as evidence that they have earned the respect of those around them.

In verses 8-12 Jesus changes his focus to the Christian community. In verse 8 He commands us not to use the title "rabbi" because we only have one teacher (Greek, *didaskalos*) and we are all brothers. Verse 10 is very similar to verse 8. In verse 10 Matthew uses the Greek word *kathegetai*, which has a slightly broader meaning than *didaskalos*. *Kathegetai* may be translated guide, leader, teacher or instructor.[78] In verse 10 Jesus commands us not to use the title "instructor" (ESV, NRSV), "teacher" (NIV) or "leader" (NASV, GNB), because we have only one instructor, teacher or leader—Jesus. In Jeremiah 31:33-34 it is prophesied that as part of the new covenant God will directly teach His people.[79] It is likely that Jesus had this Scripture in mind when He spoke Matthew 23:8-10. In this passage Jesus is implying that the new covenant has come and that He is God.[80] The implications of God directly teaching his children are discussed in Section 6.1.

---

76. *E.g.*, Gal. 5:22-23, Eph. 3:20, 5:26-27, Jude 1:24
77. Matt. 11:28-30
78. Appendix 4.5.7
79. *Cf.*, John 6:45 ("It is written in the Prophets: 'They will all be taught by God'" [NIV]), Heb. 8:8-12, Job 36:22, Psalm 51:6, Isa. 2:3, 54:13, Micah 4:2.
80. *Cf.*, Isaiah 30:20 "And though the Lord give you the bread of adversity and the water of affliction, yet your Teacher will not hide himself anymore, but your eyes shall see your Teacher." KJV and NIV have "teachers" instead of "Teacher" in this verse. RSV, NRSV, NEB and ESV have "Teacher" in the singular.

In verse 9 Jesus commands us, "do not call anyone on earth 'father,' for you have one Father, and he is in heaven" (NIV). J. Duncan and M. Derrett[81] state, based on inscriptions on tombstones, that the term father in this time period was used for major patrons of synagogues. In some cases a patron might pay for the construction of a synagogue.[82]

In verses 11-12 Jesus says, "The greatest among you shall be your servant. Whoever exalts himself will be humbled, and whoever humbles himself will be exalted." This is the exact opposite of how the scribes and the Pharisees led. They were busy exalting themselves and telling other people what to do. In Matthew 11:29 Jesus repeats His offer to teach us directly and again He links teaching to humility saying "learn from me, for I am gentle and humble in heart, and you will find rest for your souls" (NIV).

When verses 8-10 are considered in the context of verses 5-7 and verses 11-12, it is reasonable to assume that Jesus' concern with specific titles is that the individuals who hold the titles will consider that they are entitled to special status and rights within the church. Jesus is concerned about individuals seeking special status and rights based on their teaching or any other form of spiritual leadership. He is also concerned about individuals seeking special status based on their generosity. Jesus is absolutely clear that only God is to have special status. All of the rest of us are brothers and sisters. We are all equal before God and have equal direct access to God. God wants to teach each one directly. He wants to be our personal instructor. The essence of greatness in God's family is to be a servant and to humble oneself. Humble servants do not have fancy titles, which imply special status and rights. In particular humble servants do not have the right to make unilateral decisions impacting the local community of faith. We are all brothers.[83]

This interpretation of Matthew 23:8-10 fits well with the context of Matthew 23 and fits well with the teachings on spiritual leadership found throughout the New Testament. However, there is one aspect of this interpretation that at first glance is inconsistent with other New Testament passages: the New Testament church did use titles to

---

81. "Matt. 23,8-10 a midrash on Is 54,13 and Jer. 31,33-34," *Biblica* 62 no 3 1981, pg. 372-386.
82. *E.g.*, Luke 7:5
83. The protection of sound doctrine is a partial exception to these general principles (Titus 1:9, Acts 15:2, 6, 23).

describe the roles various individuals typically played in community life. In particular the word "teacher," using the same Greek word (*didaskolos*) that the best Greek manuscripts use for teacher in verse 8, is used eight times in Acts and the epistles to refer to Christians.[84] Three of these references can be interpreted as using this word as a title and three other references refer to the spiritual gift of teaching.[85]

The New Testament church understood the title "teacher" to indicate that the individual regularly moved in the spiritual gift of teaching. Similarly they also understood the title "apostle" to be a spiritual gift.[86] Paul teaches in 1 Corinthians 12 that spiritual gifts are given by God to various individuals within the church as He sees fit. For the local assembly to be complete and healthy we need all of the gifts. To the New Testament church the gift of teaching is one valuable gift among many. The believers who receive this gift are ordinary brothers and sisters with no special rights.[87] Given this understanding of the title "teacher" within the New Testament church community, there is no conflict with Matthew 23:8.

If a gifted teacher sets himself up (or allows himself to be set up) with special status and rights within a group of believers rather than as one believer among many, he may have crossed the line that Jesus sets in Matthew 23:8-10. In our day we are more likely to call such an individual pastor, or priest rather than teacher or rabbi, but the point is not the specific title. Some critical questions are: does he see himself or is he seen by the congregation as more than one brother among many? Also, does he see himself, or is he seen by the congregation, as coming between individual believers and God? For example, does he claim an exclusive right to teach, organize and direct the spiritual community and does he expect other believers to be loyal to his leadership? Crossing the line set in Matthew 23:8-10 can be a form of idolatry. The teacher is taking a place of honor that God reserves to Himself.

---

84. Appendix 4.5.1
85. Title: Acts 13:1, 1 Tim. 2:7, 2 Tim. 1:11; Gift:1 Cor. 12:28, 29
86. 1 Cor. 12:28, Eph. 4:11
87. They have the privilege of being judged more strictly (James 3:1). Gal. 6:6 does mention sharing "all good things with the one who teaches." This is a command to generosity and generosity is expected to all of our neighbors (Luke 10:25-37), so it is hard to make a case based on this verse that teachers in the New Testament church had special status and rights. See Subsection 6.7.4 for a discussion 1 Tim. 5:17-18.

### *The Parable of the Tares*

The parable of the tares (or weeds)[88] teaches that there is an enemy who causes problems in God's kingdom. The key point of the parable is the appropriate response by the servants to these problems. This provides insight into the appropriate role of both local and traveling leaders.

Jesus taught in the parable of the tares that there will be "tares" in the kingdom. This parable also teaches that Jesus is responsible for dealing with the tares, and that He will not remove all of the tares from His church until the final judgment. He does this to maximize the growth of the crop, which is a picture in this parable of the fruitfulness of His church.

For some of us, our early attempts at ministry may have looked a lot like tares. We may have made mistakes and we may have unintentionally hurt those we were seeking to help. If we ignore the warning of verse 29 and give power to leaders to pull up tares, individuals who are doing ministry imperfectly may be stopped rather than helped to do it better. This limits the fruitfulness of God's kingdom as described in this parable. The parable of the tares is completely consistent with other New Testament teaching on Christian leadership. Jesus does not delegate control of ministry within His church to His servants. He is personally in charge.

This parable does not mention attempts to deal with tares as seeds before they start to grow. However some churches develop a culture of requiring believers to gain permission from leaders prior to engaging in ministry. In the context of this parable it is fair to interpret such behavior as attempting to deal with tares as seeds by checking all seeds before they have a chance to start to grow. God delights in using individuals who seem, to human wisdom, totally inappropriate.[89] So an unfortunate result of checking for tare seeds before allowing individuals to minister is that human leaders may decline permission to an individual who has been called by God. Also the need to ask permission may deter some individuals from moving forward into ministry areas where God wants them to serve.

A common justification for requiring believers to ask permission before initiating ministry is to protect people and to prevent false

---

88. Matt. 13:24-30
89. 1 Cor. 1:26-29

teaching. Typically the heart attitude of the individuals who set themselves up to oversee other people's ministry initiatives is excellent, just like the heart attitude of the servants in Matthew 13:28. However having excellent intentions does not guarantee a good outcome as shown by verse 29.

In a house church setting where everyone is well known it is possible to maintain a culture of ministry freedom while still protecting people. In particular, in situations where an individual's immaturity in ministry creates a risk of hurting others, a mature believer can use his influence to maximize the good and minimize the bad.

## 1.5 Old Testament foundations for New Testament Christian assemblies

### *Ekklesia*

The primary meaning of the Greek word *ekklesia* is an assembly. In the New Testament this word is commonly translated "church."[90] *Ekklesia* and the related verb *ekkaleo*, which means to summon an assembly, are used about 100 times in the Septuagint Greek translation of the Old Testament.[91] In the Septuagint *ekklesia* is commonly used to refer to the "assembly of the Lord" or the "assembly of Israel."[92] Paul regularly refers to churches as "assemblies of God."[93] It is highly likely that this phrase is intended to communicate that the church is the true continuation of the "assembly of the Lord" mentioned in the Old Testament.

---

90. *Ekklesia* is used in the singular to describe: a church assembly which meets in a particular house (Rom. 16:5, 1 Cor. 11:18, 16:19, Col. 4:15, Phm. 1:2); the whole church in a particular city (Acts 8:1, 11:22, Rev. 1:11) or region (Acts 9:31); and the universal church (Eph. 1:22, 3:10, 3:21, Heb. 12:23). It seems that the singular is used to emphasize the unity of the church within and between cities. *Ekklesia* is also used in the plural to refer to churches in different cities (Rev. 1:4, Acts 15:41, 16:5) or within a region (2 Cor. 8:1, Gal. 1:22). In more than a hundred New Testament verses the word *ekklesia* is translated "church." Only once (James 2:2) is a different Greek word (*sunagoge*) used to refer to a Christian assembly. *Sunagoge* is almost always used to refer to Jewish synagogues.
91. The Septuagint translation was undertaken during the second and third centuries BC. It is a translation of what we now call the Old Testament from its original languages (mostly Hebrew) into Greek.
92. Assembly of the Lord: Deut. 12:1, 2, 3, 8, 1 Chron. 28:8, Micah 2:5; assembly of Israel: Deut. 31:30, Josh. 8:35, 1 Kings 8:14, 22, 55, 1 Chron. 13:2, 2 Chron. 6:3, 12, 13. Old Testament assemblies often included both men and women: Num. 20:8, Deut. 31:12, Josh. 8:35, Ezra 10:1, Joel 2:15-16.
93. Rom. 16:16, 1 Cor. 1:2, 11:16, 22, 2 Cor. 1:1, Gal. 1:13, 1 Thess. 1:1, 2:14, 2 Thess. 1:1, 4, 1 Tim 3:5

The primary purposes for assembling the people of Israel were for teaching/learning,[94] worship/prayer,[95] for the whole community to jointly make decisions,[96] and to form an army for battle.[97] These activities are all a good fit with activities within the life of the New Testament church so this may be another reason why the early church chose to use the word *ekklesia* to describe their meetings and their community.

In the Greek culture that continued to strongly influence the Roman Empire during the New Testament period, the word *ekklesia* was used for both impromptu and planned assemblies. Prior to the rise of the Roman Empire, many Greek cities were democracies and these assemblies of citizens were the highest decision-making authority in the city. Even within the Roman Empire these city assemblies continued to have substantial decision-making authority. Two key principles of these Greek *ekklesia* were "equality" and "freedom." All citizens could participate and they all had the same rights and the same responsibility to contribute.[98]

By choosing to use *ekklesia* as the word for what we now call the church, the New Testament Christian community chose to focus itself not on a building or an organization or a leader, but on a community worshiping, praying, learning and building the Kingdom together. Both the Old Testament (Septuagint) and the broader Greek uses of the word have overtones of a self-governing community with every member involvement in decision-making. This is consistent with other New Testament teaching concerning decision-making and leadership within New Testament Christian assemblies.

---

94. Deut. 4:10, 9:10, 31:12, Josh. 8:35, Neh. 8:2, 13:1
95. 1 Sam. 19:20, 1 Kings 8, 1 Chron. 29:10-22, 2 Chron. 1:1-6, 20:4-19, 29:23-32, Esther 4:16, Psalm 22:22, 25, 26:12, 35:18, 40:9, 68:26, 89:5, 107:32, 149:1
96. Jud. 21, 1 Chron. 13:2-4, 2 Chron. 10:1, 19, 29:22, 30:1-5, 23. In 2 Chron. 10, Rehoboam rejects the request of the assembly, which results in the ten northern tribes rebelling.
97. Jud. 20:2, 1 Sam. 17:45-47, 2 Chron. 11:1
98. See William Barclay, "*New Testament Words*," SCM Press 1964, pages 68, 69. *Ekklesia* is used in Acts 19:29-41 to refer to an impromptu assembly in the city of Ephesus. This is an example of a normal usage of this word within Greek speaking communities at this time. Verse 39 refers to a lawful or regular assembly, which had some decision-making authority to address the concerns of the people.

### *Exodus 19-20 and Numbers 16 Leadership by Holy Priests*

God's intent for the people of Israel was that "you shall be to me a kingdom of priests and a holy nation" and He wanted all of the Israelites to hear Him speak.[99] However, Exodus 20:18 records that "the people were afraid and trembled, and they stood far off" and in v 19 they said to Moses, "You speak to us, and we will listen; but do not let God speak to us, lest we die." So it appears that God's intent at the time of the Exodus was to use Moses and Aaron not only to lead his people out of Egypt but also to bring them to the place where they could all be priests hearing His voice and being directly led by Him. However this was too frightening for the people and they chose to hang back and allow Moses to be an intermediary. This decision delayed God's goal of creating for Himself a kingdom of priests until Pentecost. All believers are forgiven by Jesus and indwelt by the Holy Spirit making us "saints"—literally "Holy Ones"—and all believers are priests.[100]

Numbers 16:1-40 records the rebellion of Korah. He and his associates rejected the leadership of Moses and Aaron and were in effect rejecting God (v. 11). In verse 3 Korah and his associates centered their argument on the holiness of the congregation and the presence of the Lord amongst the assembly of the people. In verse 5 Moses agrees this is a valid basis on which to decide who should lead. In verses 9-10 Moses goes on to say that Korah is wrong to desire to be a priest. He should be content with the ministry opportunities he has as a Levite. God killed some of the rebels by having the ground swallow them up (vv. 31-33) and the rest by sending down fire (v. 35).

Some Christian leaders believe that it is appropriate for them to have the same authority to rule that Moses had. The problem with this perspective is that since Pentecost all believers are indwelt by the Holy Spirit and they are all holy priests. All believers now meet the conditions given in Numbers 16 for their involvement in decision-making. So the question of verse 3 becomes relevant: "Why do you exalt yourself above the assembly of the Lord?"

---

99. Exod. 19:6, 9

100. All believers are saints: Acts 9:13, 32, 41, 26:10, Rom. 1:7, 8:27, 12:13, 15:25-26, 31, 16:2, 15. All believers are priests: 1 Pet. 2:5, 9, Rev. 1:6 and 5:10. The priesthood of all believers is prophesied in Isaiah 61:6, *cf.*, Isa. 66:21. See also Subsection 1.1.1.

## *Numbers 11, Gift of the Holy Spirit*

Exodus 18:13-26 and Numbers 11:16-30 discuss the sharing of the "burden of the people" on Moses. Much of this "burden of the people" involved settling the disputes that arose among the people. Exodus 18:15-16 says that "the people come to me to inquire of God; when they have a dispute, they come to me and I decide between one person and another, and I make them know the statutes of God and his laws." No doubt many simple cases came up that exactly fitted with statutes and laws that had already been given. These cases could be handled by the leaders who were appointed in Exodus 18. These leaders were only expected to handle "small matters;" harder cases were referred to Moses.[101]

In Numbers 11, seventy individuals who were already both elders and officials received the Holy Spirit. This equipped them to "inquire of God" so that they could handle some of the harder cases, which had previously only been handled by Moses. In this way they further reduced the "burden of the people" on Moses.

Numbers 11:29 records Moses' wish that all of the people would receive the Holy Spirit and be prophets. In the context of this passage the implication of this desire is that all the people would be equipped to "inquire of God" and share the burdens of the community. Since Pentecost, Moses' wish has been granted. All believers receive the Holy Spirit and share the role of bearing the burdens of the spiritual community. The presence of the Holy Spirit is essential for this role.[102]

In the New Testament this role, like most other leadership roles, is shared by the whole believing community. It is not restricted to a few leaders.

The predominant teaching in the Old Testament concerning the Holy Spirit is that He equips individuals for various forms of ministry or service.[103] Given this background and given the outpouring of

---

101. It is possible that these leaders were restricted to handling "small matters," because they did not have the Holy Spirit, so they were not equipped to inquire of God. They could only handle small matters which exactly fitted the situations addressed by specific statutes and laws.

102. Gal. 6:1-2

103. 177 verses in the NIV translation of the Old Testament contain the word spirit. About 80 of these verses refer to the spirits of human beings or to demonic spirits. Just under 100 Old Testament verses refer to the Holy Spirit. About 60 of these verses relate to the Holy Spirit equipping individuals for ministry.

the Holy Spirit on all believers since Pentecost, it was completely natural for the New Testament church to be based on every member participation.

In the Old Testament community of faith there were two classes of believers: those with the Holy Spirit and those without the Holy Spirit. Most Godly leadership and ministry in the Old Testament were associated with individuals who were appropriately equipped by the Holy Spirit. Those who did not have the Holy Spirit had a much more limited role. In contrast to this there was only one class of believer in the New Testament community of faith: believers with the Holy Spirit. Every member was equipped for ministry. Every member was expected to contribute to the leadership of weekly assembly meetings and to be active in other ministry outside of these meetings. All believers were priests and decisions were made by consensus of the whole community of faith. There were no clergy organizing meetings and making decisions for the whole community.

## 1.6 Desire for a king

There is a parallel between the desire of the Israelites for a king and the desire of some believers for a conventional pastor/priest. Many people like to have strong human leaders to take responsibility for making decisions and for setting direction. Jeremiah says "An appalling and horrible thing has happened in the land: the prophets prophesy falsely, and the priests rule at their direction; my people love to have it so, but what will you do when the end comes?"[104] The desire to have a priest or king rule over us is widespread in every age, but this is not God's preferred way to interact with His people.

Part of the appeal of having strong leaders who make decisions for us is that we can avoid our responsibility to contribute to leadership. Contributing to leadership is challenging and helps to develop maturity. It is very attractive to leave this to a religious professional. Also if we leave it to a religious professional we can avoid accountability for leadership decisions. It is wonderful to have a leader to blame when things go wrong. Another reason why some individuals like to have a human leader is because they prefer to have an intermediary between them and God. God's holiness is frightening, and just like Peter in Luke 5:8, our reaction is often "depart from me for I am a sinful man, O Lord." Also it is easier to trust a human leader we can see to guide, teach and protect us than to have faith in a God

---

104. Jer. 5:30-31

we cannot see. These are some of the reasons why the Israelites wanted a king and why some believers like to have a pastor who is responsible for leading their church. Another major factor is that most believers are totally unaware that any other leadership model exists.

In 1 Samuel 8:4-20 we are told that the Israelites wanted a king to be "like all the nations." I do not see this as being in conflict with the reasons for desiring a king that I discussed in the previous paragraph. In fact the phrase "go out before us and fight our battles" is fully consistent with the reasons stated in the previous paragraph. The desire to copy the leadership structure of those around us is another parallel between the desire of the Israelites for a king, and the desire of some believers for a pastor. Some believers want a pastor who leads using methods embraced by the secular world.

1 Samuel 8-12 recounts the appointment of Saul as the first human king of Israel. This passage says that God directed Samuel to anoint Saul as king in response to the people's desire for a king.[105] God instructs Samuel to warn the people of the abuse of power that will follow from the appointment of a king.[106] God also used Samuel to define in writing the rights and duties of the king.[107]

A repeated theme in this passage is that God considers this desire of the people for a human king to constitute a rejection of his personal kingship over them.[108] In 1 Samuel 12:17 Samuel says that this is a great wickedness and he prays for a storm to destroy the wheat harvest as a sign that he is correct. In 1 Samuel 12:19-20, after the storm has come, the people agree with Samuel that they sinned.

After Saul is anointed king, God promises the people that things will go well for them if they and the king fear, serve and obey Him.[109] Given that God considers the people's desire for a king to be a rejection of Him, this is a most gracious promise. However, compared to many of the other promises of blessing contained in the Old Testament, it is somewhat limited. Having a human king was not God's best for His people, but He was willing to allow them to have what they wanted and He was prepared to continue to bless them (if they obeyed) even though they were ruled by a king.

---

105. 1 Sam. 8:7, 9, 22, 12:13
106. 1 Sam. 8:9-18
107. 1 Sam. 10:25, *cf.* Deut. 17:16-20
108. 1 Sam. 8:7, 10:19, 12:12, 17-20; *cf.*, Isa. 41:21, 43:15, 44:6
109. 1 Sam. 12:14-15

There are several specific parallels between God's leadership of His people in the Old Testament and His leadership of His church. Firstly, God wants to directly lead His people.[110] He does not wish to lead His people through a human intermediary such as a king or a typical current-day priest or pastor. Jesus is our king; He wants all believers to look to Him for leadership.[111] This includes looking to Him for leadership as to what each one of us should contribute to church assembly meetings and in all other situations. In a conventional pastor-led church, believers sometimes end up looking to the pastor for leadership instead of to Jesus. This is a rejection of God's personal kingship over us, comparable to the Israelites rejection of God's personal kingship.[112]

Secondly, God allows his people to be led by a human king or pastor/priest if this is their wish. God gave Samuel permission to appoint a king for the Israelites.[113] It was not His best for His people but He was willing to allow them to have what they wanted. Similarly in my opinion, conventional leader-centric churches are not God's best for His children, but He is willing to allow us to have what we want. As discussed in Section 7.3, I believe that leader-centric churches are less conducive to healthy spiritual growth than New Testament style house church assemblies where each believer directly relates to God as King.

Thirdly, God graciously continues to bless his children and their leaders, even if they choose to have a human king or pastor or priest, as long as they continue to obey Him in other matters.[114] The history of the Israelite kingdom shows that God was faithful to His promise in 1 Samuel 12:14. Whenever the king and people chose to obey Him He blessed them. There are also a huge number of wonderful examples of this in church history. Some of the Old Testament kings were great spiritual leaders who greatly helped their people to walk in righteousness. Many pastors and priests similarly help other believers walk in righteousness.

Fourthly, God commanded Samuel to give the Israelites a solemn warning concerning the negative consequences of choosing to have

---

110. 1 Sam. 8:7, 10:19, 12:17-20, Isa. 43:15, 44:6 and Subsection 1.1.3

111. Matt. 2:2, 21:5, Rev 17:14

112. 1 Sam. 8:7, 10:19, 12:12, 17-20

113. 1 Sam. 8:7, 9, 22

114. 1 Sam. 12:14-15

a king.[115] Some elements of this warning are relevant to believers in leader-centric churches. In particular, believers in such churches often lose a great deal of their ministry freedom and they often lose the opportunity to participate in the making of decisions concerning their ministry contributions. In some churches believers are commanded to tithe to their local church to pay for the church staff and facilities.[116] In a few churches the leadership is abusive and controlling, treating the members of the congregation a bit like slaves.[117]

As we have seen, 1 Samuel 8-12 describes the appointment of the first king of Israel, and this passage emphasizes God's desire for Israel to have no human king. I believe that this passage is also relevant to church leadership. However, there is some ambiguity in the Old Testament concerning the appropriateness of the Israelites having a king. So in the next two paragraphs I discuss some of the passages that present the Israelite monarchy more positively to show that these passages do not undercut the conclusions I have drawn from 1 Samuel 8-12.

Deuteronomy 17:15 says, "you may indeed set a king over you whom the LORD your God will choose." But it is clear from the preceding verse that the desire for a king came from the Israelites and not from God. Also the next four verses contain a series of commands for the king. This passage anticipates that kings will abuse their position of power to benefit themselves at the expense of their people, which is part of the reason why God preferred for Israel not to have a king.

One of the positive aspects of the Kings of Israel is God's prophetic use of this institution to help individuals understand Jesus' Kingship.[118] Similarly King David is presented as a type of Christ.[119] In several places the Royal Psalms prophetically jump to Jesus from material related to the human kings of Israel.[120] It seems that in these passages God is choosing to use the context of the Israelite monarchy to help us to understand Jesus. This does not prove that

---

115. 1 Sam. 8:9

116. *Cf.*, 1 Sam. 8:15

117. *Cf.*, 1 Sam. 8:17. Obviously, unlike slaves, church members are free to leave. Some abusive leaders seek to prevent this by pressuring individuals to stay.

118. *E.g.*, Isa. 9:1-7, 11:1-6

119. *E.g.*, Ezek. 34:23-24

120. *E.g.*, Psalm 2:6-12, 21:3-4, 45:1-6, 72:8, 110:1-2

having a human king was God's best plan to lead the people of Israel. It is an example of God using the situation His people were living in to teach them about Himself. God did not need the Israelites to have a monarchy to teach us about Jesus' Kingship. He can and does use our knowledge of the kings over other nations to teach us about Jesus' Kingship.[121]

### 1.7 Summary

This chapter has considered four areas of New Testament teaching related to Christian assemblies: roles and responsibilities in New Testament Christian assemblies; the church is the Body of Christ; freedom and authority of all believers; and New Testament teaching on leadership. A common picture has emerged from all four of these areas.

New Testament Christian assembly meetings are planned and organized by the Holy Spirit who prompts each member to contribute. They are not planned, organized and controlled by a group of leaders. All believers are priests and they are free to minister in any way at any time as led by the Holy Spirit. Key decisions impacting the whole community, such as church discipline and the testing of revelatory words, are made by consensus of the whole community. The community is characterized by loving and caring for one another. This "one anothering" flows freely in the main weekly meetings (and outside of these meetings) as every member ministers in response to the promptings of the Holy Spirit.

The church is the body of Christ and each member is a part of that body with a particular role to play. For the body to be healthy every member must play its part. New Testament Christian assembly meetings are intended to be a beautiful expression of body life.[122] The meetings are not dominated by a small group of leaders with everyone else following along. During these meetings (and, of course, outside of these meetings) each believer is able to bless God and the community by living out whatever part of the body God has chosen for him to be. Each person receives from the individual whose gifting is best suited to their need.

The New Testament teaches that Jesus has come to set us free. Part of this freedom is the priestly freedom to minister as led by the

---

121. *E.g.*, Dan. 2:25-45 and possibly Isa. 44:28 - 45:7

122. Obviously, as happened in Corinth, human sin can prevent this potential blessing from being realized.

Holy Spirit. We do not need to get permission to minister from a leader. This freedom applies to ministering in the main weekly meeting and to ministry outside of this meeting. The New Testament also teaches that believers who have no formal leadership title and believers who are local leaders (elders) have the same authority. Leadership is not defined by the authority to make decisions, organize meetings and perform certain ministry acts (*e.g.*, baptisms, teaching, hearing confession of sins). All believers have the freedom and authority to participate in all areas of the life of the community as led and equipped by the Holy Spirit.[123]

The essence of Christian leadership is relational leadership. Christian relational leadership focuses on influencing and encouraging others to walk closely with Jesus and to fully enter into His plans and purposes for their lives. The foundations of Christian leadership are the broad Biblical commands as to how we should treat one another (*e.g.*, "love your neighbor as yourself," "do unto others as you would have them do unto you"). Christian leadership is not about lording it over others. It is about being a servant of God and His people. The command to all believers to walk in mutual submission requires Christian leaders to submit to all believers including those who are not elders or traveling leaders.

Jesus came to bring forth His body and bride. He did not come to create an organization. Christian leadership is not about leading within the context of an organization. Leadership within the context of an organization is defined by certain roles and responsibilities that may only be performed by the leader. This is not how the New Testament describes leadership within local Christian assemblies. Christian leadership is about being part of a living body and watching over the souls of each member of this organic community.

Jesus commands us to treat everyone in the community of faith as equals. We are all brothers and sisters. He alone is our leader and teacher. We are not to give anyone a title or position, which grants him special status, authority or rights.

The New Testament authors chose the Greek word *ekklesia*, which means assembly to describe their local communities. This word is translated "church" in most English translations of the New Testament. Most of us commonly associate the word "church" with weekly services led by clergy and the building where these services

---

123. Protecting sound doctrine is a partial exception to these general principles.

are held. This is not the association that would have been natural in the 1st Century A.D. In the Septuagint translation of the Old Testament this word is used of the assembly of the people of Israel. These assemblies were typically called for teaching, worship and prayer, for the whole community to jointly make decisions or to form an army for battle. This is an excellent fit with the weekly assembly meetings described in the New Testament.

The word *ekklesia* was also used in the Greek speaking community at that time to describe the city assemblies, which used to govern Greek city states when they were democracies. These assemblies continued to have some decision-making authority in the Roman Empire. This also is a good fit with the expectation of every member contributing and consensus-based decision-making of New Testament Christian assemblies.

The Old Testament consistently teaches the linkage between the presence of the Holy Spirit and equipping for ministry. At Pentecost the Holy Spirit was poured out on all believers. So it is not surprising that all believers are now expected to use what they have received and contribute to the main weekly meetings and to ministry outside of those meetings.

Another parallel between Old Testament and New Testament teaching on leadership concerns the desire of many people to have a defined human leader. At the time when the people of Israel asked for a king, God made clear that His preference was to lead them directly. He did not want to lead through a king. He also promised that He would still, in some measure, bless His people if they and the king walked in obedience. Similarly, God wants to directly lead each of His children. He does not want to be restricted to leading through priests and pastors. However if communities choose to give this role to a priest or pastor He is still willing to bless, in some measure, as long as the leaders and people are still obedient in other areas.

Figure 1a, shown on page 62, provides a graphical representation of the relationships in a New Testament church assembly. Every believer is in direct relationship with God and is also in "one another" relationship with all of the other believers within the assembly. There are multiple elders who interact with the other members of the assembly as peers. This may be contrasted with the relationships within a typical leader-centric church as shown in Figure 1b.

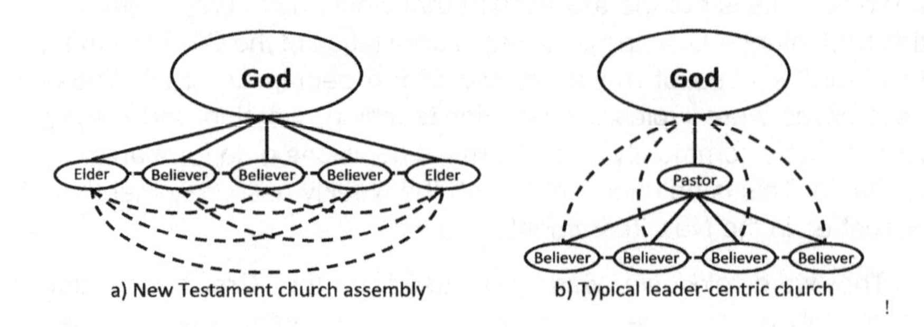


Figure 1. Graphical representation of relationships within churches

# Chapter 2
# Leaders of Christian Assemblies

This chapter looks at the information in the New Testament concerning the leaders of local Christian assemblies. The first section looks at the various words used for these leaders. The following sections look at the appointment, qualifications, training, responsibilities and authority of these leaders. The number of leaders per local assembly and the appropriate response, should one of these leaders fall into sin, are also considered.

## 2.1 New Testament words for local church leaders

This section introduces the words used in the New Testament for the leaders of local Christian assemblies. A more detailed discussion of each of these words is provided in Appendix 3. Subsection 2.1.7 considers whether the choice of words used to describe local leaders tells us anything about how elders provided leadership to local Christian assemblies.

### 2.1.1 *Presbuteros*

Bagster's *Analytical Greek Lexicon* offers the following translations for *presbuteros*: elder, senior, older, ancestor, dignitary. This word is used in four ways in the New Testament: an old man or woman; a category of Jewish leaders; a name for local church leaders; and as a title for 24 individuals in heaven. A detailed analysis of the use of this word is provided in Appendix 3.1.

*Presbuteros* is the most common word in the New Testament for leaders within local Christian assemblies. Even so there are only seventeen definite references to elders as leaders in local Christian assemblies. In the context of local church leadership the emphasis associated with this word appears to be on wisdom, life experience and looking out for the community, rather than on decision-making authority. For example, in Acts 20:28, Paul commands the elders at Ephesus to "pay careful attention to yourselves and to all the flock." This verse shows that elders are people who look out for the community. This is consistent with the conclusions I reached in Chapter 1.

There are numerous references to elders in the Old Testament and in the Jewish community during the New Testament period. It is likely that there were many similarities between the role of elders within New Testament Christian assemblies and the role of elders within the Israelite and Jewish communities.[1] As we shall see the Bible mentions a few differences between the role of Christian elders and the role of Israelite or Jewish elders.

The large number of references to elders in the Old Testament makes it possible to get a fairly clear picture of the role of elders during the time period from Moses to the return from the exile.[2] In the Old Testament elders were important leaders who mainly acted as advisers and representatives, not decision makers. They had a role in certain legal procedures and sometimes had a role in the appointment of kings and leaders. In these last two roles elders had some limited authority. This decision-making authority was partially shared with the assembly of the people. It is not possible to make a compelling case from the Old Testament that part of being an elder was to be a religious leader similar to many modern-day pastors and priests. There is no hint of any hierarchy existing within groups of elders.

The role of elders in the Old Testament is broadly consistent with the role of Christian elders presented in Chapter 1. One area of difference is that elders in the Old Testament sometimes acted as communication intermediaries between the national leader and the people. The New Testament teaches that Jesus wants to communicate directly with all of his people.[3] He also communicates with his people through individuals with relevant spiritual gifts (*e.g.*, teaching, prophecy, wisdom). These gifts are not restricted to elders.

---

1. One possible argument in support of this position is the lack of any introduction within the New Testament to the role of elders within the church. This is an argument from silence, so it should be held lightly. The New Testament does include a brief introduction into the roles of apostles and deacons when they are first mentioned (Matt. 10:1-15, Mark 3:14-15, Acts 6:1-6). Unlike elders, the roles of apostles and deacons are unique to the church.
2. Appendix 3.1.6
3. John 10:3-5, 16

It is slightly harder to get a clear picture of the role of elders within the Jewish community during the New Testament period because there are fewer references to elders in this time period.[4] Most of these references relate to the elders questioning and then opposing first Jesus, and then the apostles. These references show that these elders, like elders within the Christian community, had a role in protecting sound doctrine. It also seems that both Jewish and Christian elders had a role in teaching and that this role was shared with others. There is some uncertainty associated with the exact role of Jewish elders within the legal system during the New Testament period. It is probable that the judicial role of Jewish elders in the New Testament period was greater than in the Old Testament period. This is an area of difference with Christian elders. The full congregation had the final say in matters of church discipline. With this exception it seems that there is continuity between the role of Jewish elders mentioned in the New Testament and the role of Christian elders.

### 2.1.2 *Episkopos*

Bagster's *Analytical Greek Lexicon* offers the following translations for *episkopos*: an inspector, overseer; a watcher, guardian. Strong's lexicon gives: a man charged with the duty of seeing that things to be done by others are done rightly, any curator, guardian or superintendent. This first translation provided by Strong, "a man charged with the duty of seeing that things to be done by others are done rightly," seems to catch the essence of the meaning of this word in the New Testament. This noun is derived from the verb *skopeo*, which may be translated to look at, observe or contemplate.

This word is used in four ways in the New Testament: to describe local church leaders; to describe a visitation of God as a precursor to potential judgment; to describe Jesus' oversight of our souls; and it is once used interchangeably with apostle. More detail is provided in Appendix 3.2.

In the context of local church leadership the emphasis associated with this word appears to be on observing and protecting the dynamics of the church assembly. Part of this is keeping a caring eye on each believer to see if he/she is walking closely with Jesus. This includes observing how believers interact with one another within meetings especially when it is necessary to make a joint decision. This is

---

4. Appendix 3.1.7

consistent with Hebrews 13:17, which links leading to watching over the souls of believers. Even though the Greek verb in Hebrews 13:17 for "keeping watch" is *agrupneo*, not *skopeo*, this verse illustrates why the Christian community selected the term *episkopos* for local leaders. A key part of the role of these local leaders is to watch over the community. If the leader observes that a believer is drifting away from a healthy focus on Jesus or is interacting unhealthily with other believers, the *episkopos* can help the believer get back on track.

All believers are commanded in Hebrews 12:15 to *episkopeo*, which is the verb associated with the noun *episkopos.*[5] In particular this verse commands believers to watch out for one another so that everyone receives the grace of God and so that bitterness does not defile the community. This is the kind of watching out for one another was particularly expected of elders.

The use of the word *episkopeo* in a command to all believers shows that the meaning of this family of words has to be something that everyone can do: watching out for all other believers. This family of words cannot be describing unilateral decision-making and direction-setting leadership because it would be totally chaotic if each believer had the authority to make by himself (or with a few others) decisions impacting the complete local assembly. So the style of leadership implied by the *episkopos* family of words is looking out for the community, not unilateral decision-making and direction-setting leadership. This is compatible with the complete community making decisions that impact the complete community by consensus.

In summary the New Testament use of the term *episkopos* in the context of local church leadership is about seeing that things are done the right way rather than having the authority to decide what should be being done. If something is not being done in the right way, the leader works by influence to deal with the issue. This is consistent with broader New Testament teaching on the limited role local church leaders had in decision-making and direction setting.

Some Bibles translate *episkopos* as "overseer," which is a good single word translation to capture the idea of watching over. Sometimes however, in international corporations the word "overseer" is used to describe a junior manager or team leader with some decision-making authority. This meaning of the word "overseer" does not represent the meaning of the word *episkopos* in the New Testament.

---

5. Appendix 1.17

The New Testament use of the word *episkopos* (overseer) can be illustrated by considering a business that is organized in the following manner. The business has several employees, who all report to the owner. A group of these employees also act as overseers. The owner decides what work should be done and which individual will perform each task. The owner directly tells each employee what task he wants him to do and how it should be done. The overseers assist and encourage the other employees in the performance their work. The overseers do not decide what work should be done or how it should be done or who should do each piece of the work that is being done. All of the employees are free to help and encourage one another in their work. The business owner did not appoint the overseers to prevent the other employees from keeping an eye out for their friends and helping them as necessary. He appointed some individuals as overseers to ensure that at least a few appropriate employees were thinking about the bigger picture all of the time.

The use of the *episkopos* family of words in the *Septuagint* translation of the Old Testament shows that this word family had a wide range of meanings.[6] These words can be used to describe decision-making leaders and they can be used to describe leaders who did not have decision-making authority. In more than 70 percent of the verses where these words are used, the meaning does not relate to decision-making leaders. In these verses, which represent the primary meaning of this word family, the words are used to emphasize visiting and relationship, which result in well informed caring. This emphasis fits very well with the New Testament description of the role of local Christian leaders.

### 2.1.3 *Poimaino*

Bagster's *Analytical Greek Lexicon* offers the following translations for *poimaino*: To feed, pasture, tend a flock, pamper, tend, direct, superintend, rule.

Given the prominence of pastors in many churches, one of the surprising things about the New Testament is how rarely shepherding/pastoring is mentioned as an activity of Christian leaders.[7] When this verb and the related noun are used of spiritual relationships they primarily refer to Jesus. The shepherding, or pastoral role, of

---

6. Appendix 3.2.4
7. Appendix 3.3

humans in the church is secondary and subsidiary to Jesus. The noun "shepherd" is only used once to refer to a human leader: this reference is to leaders with the gift of pastoring who are given as a gift to the church.[8] In three verses the verb "to shepherd" is used to describe an activity of church leaders.[9]

This family of words is used to describe four dimensions of each believer's interaction with Jesus as the chief shepherd/pastor:[10] protection, leadership/direction setting, care and teaching. The first three of these dimensions of pastoral care are brought out in Psalm 23. The role of the shepherd/pastor in protecting the flock is also brought out in 1 Samuel 17:34-35. Some aspects of this protection can only be performed by Jesus. Christian leaders have some role in protecting the flock, for instance in protecting sound doctrine. Psalm 23:2-3 describes Jesus' leading of each believer. Psalm 23 also wonderfully describes Jesus' individual loving care for each believer. Most of this caring can only be done by Jesus. However, He also works through loving believers to provide some aspects of this care.

Local leaders co-shepherd with Jesus by having a role in protecting, leading, caring for and teaching the church. In order to serve in this manner local leaders need to be individuals who are looking out for the flock. Most of the leadership provided by elders is by influence and it includes providing advice and encouraging other believers to stay close to Jesus. All believers have great freedom to contribute in all four of these areas of pastoring. When the New Testament says that local leaders pastor it is not creating an exclusive leadership role for them.

Of the ten uses of the closely related words *poimne* and *poimnion* (flock), seven are specific to the believing community and all of these seven references emphasize Jesus' ownership of the flock. The other three references are generic. Implicit in the emphasis on Jesus owning the flock is his unique authority to lead and direct each believer. He wants to be in direct connection with each believer personally leading them. He does not delegate this to His under-shepherds.

---

8. Eph. 4:11
9. Acts 20:28, 1 Pet. 5:2 refer to local church leaders. John 21:16 applies to Peter who was a traveling leader.
10. 1 Pet. 5:4

### 2.1.4 Interchangeability of *Episkopos, Presbuteros & Poimen*

In the New Testament the words *episkopos* (overseer) and *presbuteros* (elder) do not always refer to local church leaders. However, in cases where *episkopos* (overseer) and *presbuteros* (elder) refer to local church leaders they are interchangeable. [11] For example, in Acts 20:28 Paul commands the elders at Ephesus to "pay careful attention to yourselves and to all the flock, in which the Holy Spirit has made you overseers." Not only does this verse show the interchangeability of the words elder and overseer, it shows that elders are first and foremost people who look out for others, which is also the key role of overseers. [12] Titus 1:5-7 is another example of the interchangeable use of the terms elder and overseer. [13]

Acts 20:28 goes on to say that elders/overseers are expected to pastor. Similarly 1 Peter 5:1-2 says that elders are expected to pastor. There is no explicit link in the New Testament between the noun *poimen* (shepherd) and elders or overseers. The noun is almost exclusively reserved as a title for Jesus (or used to generically describe the shepherds at His nativity).

### 2.1.5 *Hegeomai*

Bagster's *Analytical Greek Lexicon* gives the following translations for *hegeomai*: to lead the way, to take the lead, to be chief, to preside, to govern, to rule. In some circumstances it can also be translated: to think, consider, count, esteem or regard.

A detailed discussion of the use of this verb in the New Testament is presented in Appendix 3.4. It is only used five times in the New Testament to refer to church leadership and in all of these cases the verb is used as a participle to indicate an individual or group of

---

11. Both words are used by a range of New Testament authors. All three authors (Luke, Paul, Peter) who use the word *episkopos* also use the word *presbuteros*. *Presbuteros* is used in the context of Christian assemblies where most of the believers were of a Jewish background and of assemblies where most of the believers were of Greek background. *Episkopos* is used in the context of Christian assemblies where most of the believers were of a Greek background. However, the related verb (*episkopeo*) is used in the context of Christian assemblies where most of the believers were of a Jewish background. So the use of these words does not correlate with the ethnic composition of the community.
12. *Cf.*, Subsection 2.1.2, Heb. 13:17
13. In most manuscripts *presbuteros* and *episkopos* are also linked in 1 Pet. 5:2.

people who are leading. As with pastoring the emphasis is not on an office of leader but on the people who are doing the leading. Given that in the New Testament church all believers are expected to hold themselves open to being used by the Lord to lead a portion of a meeting, or to lead in some other ministry opportunity, it is likely that this word includes a broader range of people than just the elders of a local church and traveling leaders.

*Hegeomai* is used both in Luke 22:26 and in Hebrews 13:17. It is possible that these verses represent the two poles of potential Biblical teaching on the authority of New Testament leaders. Luke 22:26 unambiguously teaches that leaders should not lord it over other believers and that they should act as servants. Hebrews 13:17 is interpreted by some as a mandate for Christian leaders to expect obedience from other believers. This verse is discussed in Section 4.1, where I conclude that at most this command applies to matters of doctrine and moral behavior, not ministry. It is likely that the use of the word "obey" in English translations of Hebrews 13:17 is a mistranslation. The contexts of the other three references to *hegeomai* give limited insight into what part of the spectrum of meanings of this word the author had in mind.

### 2.1.6 *Proistemi*

Bagster's *Analytical Greek Lexicon* gives the following translations for *proistemi*: to set before, (metaphorically) to set over, to appoint with authority, to preside, govern, superintend, to undertake resolutely, to practice diligently, to maintain the practice of.

Appendix 3.5 provides a detailed discussion of the New Testament use of this verb and of the related noun *prostatis*, which is used for Phoebe. In 1 Timothy 3:4, 5, 12 this verb is used of leading a household and it is twice used of all believers. [14] Only three uses of this verb in the New Testament may relate to church leaders.

In Romans 12:8 this verb is used to describe a spiritual gift. As always with spiritual gifts the focus is on God as the giver equipping us to do what we would not otherwise be able to do. This fits particularly well with the first three potential translations listed above, which imply that someone else (in this case the Holy Spirit) is doing the setting before/setting over/appointing with authority. As with all spiritual gifts, the gift of leadership may be given once to a particular individual

14. Titus 3: 8, 14

to address a particular circumstance or repeatedly to address many situations. So this passage is almost certainly addressing a broader gift of leadership than being an elder or a traveling leader. For example this gifting could describe an appointing with authority to do deliverance ministry. Many individuals who are not elders or traveling leaders are given authority to do deliverance ministry.

1 Thessalonians 5:12 is a command to know or respect three groups of people defined by participles. This form of the verb places the emphasis on what they are doing not on any office or title. The first and third participles define activities expected of all believers (hard work and admonishing).[15] The second participle uses the verb *proistemi*, which may be translated in three ways: those who are appointed by God with authority; or those who are leading; or those who are diligent. The third of these activities is expected of all believers,[16] and some measure of leadership is also expected of all believers.[17] It is plausible that *proistemi* is being used in this verse to broadly address those who exercise any kind of leadership; even if they only do so briefly during a meeting or some other ministry. Given that two of the three activities listed in this verse are expected of all believers and that possible translations of the third activity are expected of all believers, it is likely that this verse is addressing all believers who minister in the ways that Paul mentions, which includes many believers who are not elders. This interpretation is consistent with the broader context of the passage, which is addressed to all believers. So this verse provides no information about the type of leadership elders are expected to provide. Translations of this verse that imply that elders govern are at best questionable.

Only in 1 Timothy 5:17 is *proistemi* used explicitly in the context of elders. The context of this verse can equally support several of the meanings of this verb. A literal translation of this verse is "The well set before you elders double honor..." The emphasis in Paul's choice of words in this verse is on God as the one who does a good job of setting individuals in front of the community to lead. 1 Timothy 5:17 may be translated: "Let the elders, who were well appointed by God, be considered worthy of double honor." This translation

---

15. 1 Thess. 5:14
16. Titus 3:8, 14
17. 1 Cor. 14.26

does not imply any particular style of leadership so it maintains the breadth of possible meanings of the Greek. It also links the adverb *kalos* (well) to the adjacent verb *proistemi* (appointed) placing the emphasis on the quality of God's raising up of the elders rather than on the quality of the service provided by the elders. Translations of this verse that refer to elders who "rule well" (ESV) or who "direct the affairs of the church well" (NIV) are not demanded by the Greek and they are inconsistent with other New Testament teaching concerning the role of elders.

### 2.1.7 Discussion

Why did the early church (and the New Testament authors) pick these words for local leaders? What is the leadership message implicit in the choice of words for local leaders? Is there any significance in their relative frequency of use?

The predominant noun for a local church leader is *presbuteros* (elder). This word is used roughly three times more frequently than *episkopos* (overseer), which is used six times to refer to local church leaders. In a handful of verses the New Testament uses two verbs (*hegeomai* and *proistemi*) as participles to describe those who are leading. In several cases it appears that the authors are using these words to refer to individuals who are exercising leadership in any aspect of kingdom life. So it seems that these words may include individuals who are neither elders nor traveling leaders. Some church assemblies had clearly identified elders, but based on these verses it seems there was a measure of fluidity associated with leadership in the New Testament. God may use any believer to provide leadership in a particular situation as He sees fit. He is not restricted to only leading through those with a particular title. In three verses the verb *poimaino* (to shepherd) is used to describe an activity of New Testament leaders.

All of these words support a range of translations, which indicate a corresponding range of leadership styles. All of these words can refer to a leadership style based on looking out for and influencing those who are being led (rather than directing them). This influence based leadership style includes helping people to connect with Jesus so that He can direct them. Some of these words for leaders can also refer to a decision-making and direction-giving leadership style. The few contexts that demand an authoritarian translation of a leadership word all explicitly refer to Jesus. Examples of this include Luke 19:44 (*episkopos*) and Revelation 2:27 (*poimaino*).

Having said this it is important to note that the predominant word for a local leader in the New Testament, *presbuteros* (elder), has the strongest connotations of the leader as an influencer, adviser and guide, rather than the leader as a decision-maker and direction-giver. The emphasis implicit in this word is on maturity, wisdom and watching over the community.

The numerous references to elders in the Old Testament show that elders were not decision-making and direction-giver leaders. [18] They were predominantly advisers and influencers. This is completely consistent with the role of elders within New Testament Christian assemblies. There are a few cases in the Old Testament where elders were appointed to a decision-making leadership position in the government, but this does not mean that all elders were decision-making leaders.

There are many fewer references to elders within the non-Christian Jewish community during the New Testament period, so it is harder to form a clear picture of their role. [19] It is highly plausible that the role of elders as advisers continued into the New Testament period within the Jewish community. Jewish elders had a strong role in protecting sound doctrine, which is also a role of Christian elders. It seems that Jewish elders during the period of the New Testament also had a role in legal processes acting as a combination of judge and jury in local and national courts known as Sanhedrin. This aspect of being an elder was not adopted by the Christian community. The New Testament teaches that decisions on church discipline are to be made by the whole church assembly. [20]

The second most common word for a leader within a local Christian assembly is *episkopos* (overseer). The focus of this word both in the Old and New Testaments is on looking out for others. The associated verb is used as a command to all believers. [21] This shows that the type of leadership implied by this word is a type of caring for others that should be part of the life of all believers. It is not describing a type of leadership that is defined by roles that only the leader may perform. The use of the terms “elder” and “overseer” to describe New Testament local leaders is consistent with the New Testament church being an organic community not an organization.

18. Appendix 3.1.6
19. Appendix 3.1.7
20. Subsection 1.1.4
21. Heb. 12:15, Appendix 1.17

Having a limited decision-making and direction-giving role does not imply that the opportunities for leaders to lead are limited. In fact, the house church model provides many opportunities for leaders to lead and help every member of the congregation continue to walk closely with Jesus and continue to grow spiritually and in ministry. It is reasonable to expect an elder to be active in many of the ministry areas discussed in Section 1.1 and Appendix 1. In fact there are specific verses linking elders to many of these activities. Elders also have a role in facilitating congregational decision-making.

Words for leader that only imply a decision-making and direction-giving leadership style: *e.g.*, *archon* (ruler) or *hegemon* (governor) are never used of church leaders in the New Testament. In several places *archon* is used of Jewish leaders.[22] Both *archon*[23] and *hegemon*[24] are used of civil authorities.

In the Greek of Titus 1:7 the overseer is described as a steward or manager of God's household. The steward is responsible for overseeing the smooth running of the household. When the master is absent the steward has complete control of the household, and may have responsibility for and control over any minor children.[25] Galatians 4:1-9 teaches that all believers are adopted children who have come of age. We are no longer under a steward, but are indwelt by the Holy Spirit and have direct access to our Father, who is not absent. When the Father is home and the children are of age, the steward does not make decisions concerning the children and he does not give them direction. He advises them and helps them do what the Father has asked them to do. Given this situation, it is not appropriate to assume that the use of the word steward in Titus 1:7 is describing a decision-making leader. Peter teaches that all believers are stewards of the grace of God.[26] When elders act as stewards they will typically be doing things that any believer may do.

In Matthew 23:8-10 Jesus commands believers to never use titles for another believer, which imply he has special status and rights. Special status and rights, including the right of unilateral decision-making and direction-giving are reserved for Christ. We are all brothers and sisters and God wants to teach and lead us directly.

---

22. Luke 8:41, 14:1, 23:13, 24:20, John 7:26, Acts 4:8
23. Matt. 20.25, Luke 12:58, Acts 16:19, Rom. 13:3
24. Matt. 27:23, Luke 21:12, Acts 24:1, 1 Pet. 2:14
25. Luke 12:42-48, Gal. 4:1-2
26. 1 Pet. 4:10

The strong link between the words for servant/service/to serve and Christian leadership is also significant in understanding church leadership during the time of the New Testament. [27]

A striking feature of the New Testament is the relatively few references to local leaders. This is another indicator that the life of each local New Testament assembly was not centered around decision-making and direction-giving leaders. Most of the letters included in the New Testament are addressed to the complete church in a city. Many of these letters address specific problems faced by the local church. In no case is an elder or overseer asked to solve the problem. The complete church was expected to address the issue. This supports the assertion that the leadership provided by elders to New Testament assemblies was radically different to the leadership provided by most current day church leaders.

In the pastoral epistles Paul does ask Timothy and Titus to address certain issues in the local churches they are visiting. Timothy and Titus were traveling leaders, so Paul's direction to them as individuals is an indicator of appropriate leadership for a traveling leader. [28] It is not necessarily an indication of appropriate leadership for a local leader. As discussed in Sections 3.7, 4.3 and 5.2, it seems that traveling leaders were expected to address issues in the churches they were visiting in a different manner than the elders of those churches. In particular, it seems that traveling leaders were expected to address sin and false teaching in a local church more bluntly than the local elders.

It is very hard to make a Biblical case for the office of pastor or priest as it exists in most churches today. Even in churches committed to congregational polity, pastors often exercise decision-making and direction-giving leadership over several aspects of ministry, especially services. The Scriptural emphasis on shepherding is predominantly on Jesus and not on human leaders. In the New Testament local church leaders are called elder (17 times) or overseer (6 times). There are at most four references to pastoring in the context of church leadership. Three of these references contain the verb "to pastor" and they emphasize pastoring as one activity of leaders–not a title or office, nor in the singular. Also all aspects of pastoring are open to all believers.

---

27. Section 1.4
28. Appendix 7

In some English translations the word "office" is sometimes used in the context of church leadership. [29] Some interpret this to mean that these leadership positions were organizational leadership positions similar to the role of pastors and priests in many churches today. The Greek does not support this. In fact the word "office" does not appear in the Greek of Acts 1:20, 1 Timothy 3:1, 3:10 and 3:13. The Greek word in Romans 11:13 is *diakonian*, which means ministry or service. The Greek word in Romans 12:4 is *praxin*, which means mode of acting or function. This verse is discussing every member ministry not a unique leadership office. These last two verses support the argument that the essence of Christian leadership involves acts of leadership performed by many individuals, not an office that grants authority to make decisions and organize what others do. This applies to leaders with titles (*e.g.*, elders) and to other believers who happen to be providing leadership at a particular time in a particular way.

The word "governments" is used in the KJV translation of the list of spiritual gifts given in 1 Corinthians 12:28. Some suggest that this is evidence of the existence of organizational leadership positions in the New Testament church. The Greek does not demand this. [30] It is more likely that Paul is listing a gift of being used to provide guidance. As noted in Chapter 1 and Appendix 1 there is no role mentioned in the New Testament, which could only be performed by recognized leaders within local Christian assemblies. These assemblies were a body, not an organization, so there was no place for a leadership or governing "office."

Some quote Psalm 105:15 that says "Do not touch my anointed ones; do my prophets no harm" (NIV) as a basis for assuming a single anointed leader within a church. This takes the verse out of its immediate context where it is clear that the "anointed ones" are the complete community. It also takes the verse out of our New Testament context where it is taught that all believers are anointed. [31] Unfortunately in some circles this verse is also used to teach that any suggestion that the pastor is less than perfect or has less than total authority is disobedience to God. This interpretation is a gross distortion of scripture and can lead to pastoral abuse.

---

29. *E.g.*, 1 Tim. 3:1 "The saying is trustworthy: If anyone aspires to the office of overseer, he desires a noble task."
30. Appendix 3.6
31. 1 John 2:20, 27

A major problem with the role of pastor as it exists in many churches today is that it places a totally unreasonable burden on the pastor. He or she is expected to perform roles that, in the New Testament, are reserved to God or distributed across the assembly of believers. It is not surprising that so many pastors burn out or fall into sin. The other side of this coin is that this leadership model also encourages laziness and passivity in the "laity." Neil Cole in his book Organic Leadership humorously captures the problem with leader-centric churches:

> Such Christian leaders behave as though Christ is on vacation and has put them in charge because they have special leadership abilities.[32]

Some well-managed corporations have done a better job of applying Biblical leadership principles than many churches. The fruit of applying these principles is to create a productive environment, which is also conducive to personal growth. Both in the church and in the work-place great things can be accomplished when the emphasis is on:

- Everyone using their talents to the best of their ability
- Everyone being encouraged to contribute and to use their initiative without needing to ask permission first
- Mentoring and coaching
- Everyone treating everyone else with respect

Unfortunately many churches choose the opposite approach, placing more emphasis on restricting participation and requiring individuals to ask permission before they act. In many cases leaders choose this approach out of a desire to protect individuals from well-meaning but inappropriate ministry. In a house church setting, where everyone is well known to one another, it is possible to protect individuals from this risk without having numerous rules and a permission-asking culture. Such a culture typically limits ministry fruitfulness and spiritual growth.

Even if a pastor does his best to create a culture of empowerment, where believers do not have to ask permission before engaging in ministry, the presence of a professional religious leader tends to inhibit individual spiritual initiative. Many believers believe that the paid professional can do ministry much better than they can, so they do not even attempt to do any ministry. This results in them not learning and growing.

---

32. *Organic Leadership*, pg. 25

## 2.2 Appointment of elders

In Acts 20:28 Paul says the elders in Ephesus were made overseers by the Holy Spirit. This is not explained. It could mean that over time it became obvious to the whole assembly that certain individuals had been raised up as elders by the Holy Spirit. The text could also imply a direction-giving prophetic word (*e.g.*, Paul's missionary call [33]). To be consistent with other scripture, the direction-giving prophetic word should be tested by the whole church.

Acts 14:23[34] addresses the appointment of elders in Lystra, Iconium and Antioch. Acts 14:23 is one of the less clear verses in the Bible due to the range of meanings of the key Greek word *cheirotoneo*. Bagster's *Analytical Greek Lexicon* offers the following three translations for *cheirotoneo*: to stretch out the hand (as in praying for someone); to constitute by voting; to appoint. If Luke had the first meaning of *cheirotoneo* in mind, then the verse is saying that Paul and Barnabas prayed for the elders. This provides no information as to how Paul, Barnabas and the church knew who should receive this prayer. The second potential meaning implies that Paul and Barnabas ran an election to select elders. The third potential meaning is that Paul and Barnabas had authority to appoint the elders. Even if this is the correct interpretation of this verse, the candidate elder would need the respect of the local congregation to be able to effectively serve it. This is because the leadership provided by New Testament elders was primarily relational and consensual.

There is a similar ambiguity in the Greek concerning Titus 1:5[35] that addresses the appointment of elders in Crete. The Greek word for appoint is *kathistemi*, which means to place or set or appoint, to make, render or cause to be. Does Titus appoint elders or does he facilitate a process that causes them to be? This Greek word is also used in Acts 6:3 concerning the appointment of seven men to serve food to widows. Acts 6:3-6 records that the complete community selected these men and that the apostles confirmed that selection by publicly praying for them and laying hands on them. It is probable that this balanced approach was used by Titus in Crete and was widespread in the appointment of elders.

---

33. Acts 13:4. 1 Tim. 4:14 may also be an example of this.
34. "And when they had appointed elders for them in every church, with prayer and fasting they committed them to the Lord in whom they had believed."
35. "This is why I left you in Crete, so that you might put what remained into order, and appoint elders in every town as I directed you."

Does Paul teach in 1 Timothy 5:22 that the laying on of hands is a part of the process of someone becoming a leader? Very likely yes, but this does not give much insight into the process. For example it gives no insight into whether or not the local body had any input into who was selected to receive such prayer. Acts 6:3-6 shows that in at least some cases the process of laying on of hands by established leaders was a public confirmation of an individual's role after the whole congregation had selected the leader. It is probable that this was a typical pattern in the New Testament church.

Acts 6 gives no hint as to what would have happened if the apostles had had reservations about one or more of the candidates. It is reasonable to assume that if an apostle (or other traveling leader) had a reservation about a local elder it would have been handled in the same way as other situations where a traveling leader had reservations about something in a local church assembly.[36]

Acts 14:23 and Titus 1:5 are examples of the importance of understanding the meaning of key Greek words used in verses about leadership. Some Bible translations occasionally select translations of key Greek words relating to leadership that do not reflect the full breadth of meaning associated with the Greek words.

In summary, the New Testament emphasis is on the primacy of the Holy Spirit in raising up individuals to serve as elders. This truth needs to be held in a delicate balance with the process (or processes) by which the church discerned this raising up. It is likely that in many cases individuals gradually grew into being elders and that at some point it became obvious to the whole assembly that this had happened. There are hints that in some cases the whole congregation nominated new elders. In other cases prophetic words may have played a part in identifying new elders. In these cases, to be consistent with other Scripture, it is reasonable to expect that the words were tested by the whole congregation. This implies that in these cases the whole congregation had a role in confirming new elders. It is very likely that this decision-making process would have been consensual, but it is possible that a vote was held. It is very likely that prayer with laying on of hands was a standard way of publicly confirming the new elders. It appears that in some cases a traveling leader may have helped facilitate the process of identifying and publicly confirming elders. It is possible that this assistance was most needed by relatively young churches.

---

36. Section 5.2

### *When were the first elders recognized in a new church?*

1 Timothy 3:6 teaches that elders should not be recent converts, because of the risk that immature elders may become conceited. Given the teaching contained in the parable of the sower, it also makes sense to wait and see who continues to walk closely with the Lord.[37] In the case of new church plants this means that it is necessary to wait a while before any elders are recognized.

1 Timothy 5:22 says, "Do not be hasty in the laying on of hands." The context does not demand that this passage is only talking about praying for someone to be an elder. Even if the application of this verse is broader, it supports the case that it is good not to rush into confirming anyone as an elder. Acts 14:23 and Titus 1:5 also imply that elders were not immediately recognized in new churches.

## 2.3 Qualifications of elders

The two key passages discussing the requirements to be an elder or overseer are 1 Timothy 3:1-7 and Titus 1:6-9. By my count, 1 Timothy 3:1-7 contains thirteen criteria associated with godly character, three related to family, and one each related to spiritual maturity and the ability to teach. Titus 1:6-9 contains twelve criteria associated with godly character, four related to family, and three related to doctrine and the ability to teach. So it can be seen that the predominant area of concern is godly character. Given that parental character is a factor contributing to the family-related criteria in these passages, the emphasis on character is overwhelming. This emphasis makes perfect sense for the type of leadership described in the New Testament. There is no mention in these passages of any formal training or education being required to serve as an elder.

Perhaps the most striking thing about these lists is the relatively low standard that Paul was setting. Many believers meet the character standard given in these lists. In fact many unbelievers would endorse and meet this character standard. Even the criteria related to spiritual maturity, knowledge of doctrine, the ability to teach and the ability to refute false teaching are met by many believers. So the standard set in these passages is compatible with each house church having a team of elders.[38]

---

37. Matt. 13:3-9, 18-23
38. Section 2.6

One potentially surprising character trait included in both of these lists is hospitality.[39] This character trait is the first positive trait listed by Paul in Titus 1:8. This character trait is important in several ways. In many cases elders hosted house church in their own home, and their home was a natural setting for many other meetings with church members (*e.g.*, for prayer, discipling, pastoral care etc.). Hospitality can be an excellent starting place for outreach. Elders would also have had opportunity to extend hospitality to traveling leaders during their visits.

### *Teaching and protecting sound doctrine*

1 Timothy 3:2 states that an elder must be able to teach and Titus 1:9 says that an elder must hold firm to sound doctrine, teach sound doctrine and refute those who contradict sound doctrine. As noted in Appendix 1.1 all believers are expected to teach. So teaching is not the exclusive preserve of elders. The role of elders and believers who are not elders in protecting sound doctrine is discussed in Appendix 1.21.

It does not take several years earning an M. Div. to meet Paul's standard for elders concerning teaching and protecting sound doctrine.[40] It is likely that some elders could not read and write. Normal house church participation with appropriate mentoring and in-depth study of the scriptures provides sufficient opportunities to grow into readiness to be an elder. This contributes to the ability of house church networks to grow exponentially.

### *The husband of one wife*

In both passages the first requirement is to be above reproach, which constitutes an excellent summary of all of the character related criteria. The second requirement in both lists is to be the husband of one wife. Some interpret this phrase as part of the argument that women cannot be elders.[41]

It is very unlikely that the requirement to be the husband of one wife is intended to exclude individuals who had remarried after the death of a first wife.[42] Similarly it is very unlikely that this passage is

---

39. All believers are commanded to practice hospitality in Rom. 12:13.
40. Sсction 7.4
41. Section 6.4
42. Luke 20:27-34, 1 Cor. 7:39-40, 1 Tim. 5:14

intended to exclude individuals who are single. Both Jesus and Paul recognized that some are called to singleness.[43]

The literal translation of the Greek is "the man of one woman." I believe Paul is saying that an elder may have only one wife at a time. Paul is excluding men with multiple wives or mistresses; *i.e.*, the sexually promiscuous.

It is, however, possible to also interpret this phrase to exclude individuals from leadership who have been divorced and then remarried. Given Paul's delight in the power of God to forgive and transform people,[44] and given that many church members (presumably including elders) had lived evil lives prior to their conversion, it seems to me unlikely that the only past sin that could prevent an individual from becoming an elder was divorce. Every other requirement in these two lists addresses the current behavior/ability/circumstance of the candidate elder, so it is in my mind very likely that this phrase also applies only to fairly recent behavior.

The key question concerning the criteria in these lists is not has the candidate elder always met all criteria? If this was the correct interpretation, then no one would be qualified, because as a young child no one can meet all of the criteria. The key question is does the candidate elder meet all criteria now? Obviously in considering such a question it is necessary to include a reasonable time period to ensure sufficient opportunities for all character traits to be observed. For divorce and remarriage it may well be appropriate to consider a somewhat longer time period than for other factors, as the process of relationship formation and failure tends to be drawn out. It is reasonable to interpret this phrase to exclude candidates who have a succession of wives or mistresses. It is not reasonable to interpret this phrase as an absolute exclusion of an individual, who had a divorce a long time ago and has experienced considerable character transformation in the intervening years.

### *An elder's children*

Titus 1:6 says that the children of an elder must be "*pista*." This Greek word can be translated faithful, trustworthy or believer.[45]

---

43. Matt. 19:10-12, 1 Cor. 7:7-8
44. *E.g.*, 1 Cor. 6:11
45. This Greek word appears in 62 verses in the New Testament. In the ESV translation it is translated "faithful" in 40 verses, "trustworthy" in 10 verses, "believe" or "believer(s)" in 10 verses.

Many English translations translate *pista* as “believer” in this verse.[46] This verse also says that the children must not “be debauched or insubordinate.” 1 Timothy 3:2-7 does not say that an elder’s children need to be believers. It does however say that a candidate elder’s management of his household is a criterion to be considered; a key piece of this is how his children respond to his leadership. Why were these criteria important and are they still important today? Also, do these commands only relate to minor children or do they include adult children?

The word used for child (*teknon*) in Titus 1:6 and in 1 Timothy 3:4 is a generic word for children that can be used for infant children, children around 12 years old and adult children.[47] The range of meaning of *teknon* is very similar to the range of meaning of the English word “child.” So it is not possible to restrict the meaning of these verses to only apply to children within a certain age range based on the meaning of *teknon*.

The word used for debauched (*asotia*) seems to apply to older teenagers and adults. The other two uses of this word in the New Testament include adults and older teenagers.[48] The word used for insubordinate (*anupotaktos*) can apply to individuals of any age. Other New Testament uses of this word appear to apply mainly to adults.[49]

The reference to household leadership in 1 Timothy 3:4 implies that Paul is considering households where the children were still living with their parents. In many cultures (including 1st Century culture) it was and still is common to have adult children living with their parents in multi-generational households.

The command that children of an elder must be faithful/believers is contained within the same sentence in which Paul says that elders must be above reproach, the husband of one wife and that the children should not be debauched or insubordinate. So it seems likely that in Paul’s mind this is all part of being above reproach. Some reasons underlying the importance of the children of elders being faithful/believers, who live reasonably moral lives include:

---

46. *E.g.*, ESV, NIV, NASV, NEB, GNB, RSV, NRSV, and KJV employ the word “faithful.”
47. *E.g.*, Matt. 2:18, Luke 2:48, 1 Tim. 5:4, John 8:39
48. Eph. 5:18, 1 Pet. 4:4
49. *E.g.*, 1 Tim. 1:9, Titus 1:10

- Firstly, in that culture (and in some current cultures) it was common to consider the behavior of children in forming an opinion on the character of their parents. Obviously if the children have moved to another city and no one in the local community knows their behavior this factor is not relevant.
- Secondly, in that culture (and in some current cultures) it was easier for an outsider to question the claims of Jesus if the children of a local leader, who no doubt have an excellent opportunity to observe Jesus' impact on their parents, have chosen to reject Jesus.
- Thirdly, our children are only with us for a short time. It is very easy to be so involved in church work that we do not give them the love, attention and support that God wants us to give them. If children, who are living at home, are going through a rebellious period (*e.g.*, teenage) there can be great wisdom in stepping back from church service to pour into our children while they are still with us. After they have left home it may be much harder to connect with them.

In summary, it is reasonable to interpret Titus 1:6 in the light of 1 Timothy 3:4 and assume that these commands apply to children still living with their parents. Even though the culture we live in has many differences from the culture Paul lived in, the final factor listed above is relevant to all cultures. There can be great wisdom in parents stepping back from church leadership and focusing on their children if they are passing through a rebellious phase. There may also be situations where a parent has a troubled child not living at home, and the parent needs to focus his energy on helping the child rather than on serving as an elder.

Wisdom is required in considering the age/maturity/attitude of children when evaluating the criterion that children need to be faithful /believers. Obviously this command is not intended to exclude individuals serving as elders when their children are still infants and are too young to have made a decision about Jesus. In many cases children in believing families participate in church life from birth and make a commitment to Jesus as teenagers.

Is an implication of 1 Timothy 3:5 that local church leadership should be similar to family leadership? Given the context of the rest of the New Testament, the answer to this question is a partial yes. Like fathers, elders should provide "training and instruction of the Lord" and elders must not exasperate church members. [50] Also church members should submit to elders, just as children should

---

50. Eph. 6:4 NIV

submit to their parents. However elders are required to submit to church members as part of the mutual submission of all believers. It is pushing 1 Timothy 3:5 too far to say it means that church leaders may expect obedience like a father.[51]

## 2.4 Training of elders

There is very little information in the New Testament about the training of elders. In at least some cases it seems that a visit by a traveling leader was the catalyst for the initial appointment of elders to new churches.[52] Given the number of towns being visited by Paul and Titus it is plausible that most of these visits were relatively brief (days or weeks, not months or years). So whatever training was given to these new elders it would also have been relatively brief.

As discussed in Section 3.4 it appears that most training of traveling leaders involved working with and being mentored by an existing leader. This happened in the context of on-going ministry. It is highly likely that most elders were also trained in this manner either by the current elders within a church assembly or by a visiting traveling leader. There is absolutely no hint in the New Testament of the existence of any dedicated training facilities comparable to current day Bible colleges and seminaries.[53]

In some cases God may raise up an elder without the individual realizing what is going on. The individual is focusing on following Jesus' lead in each situation. As he does this Jesus provides a series of circumstances that are the training he needs to become an elder.

## 2.5 Responsibilities and authority of elders

There are very few commands in the New Testament directed to elders. In Acts 20:28 Paul commands the elders of Ephesus to "keep watch over yourselves and all the flock of which the Holy Spirit has made you overseers. Be shepherds of the church of God, which he bought with his own blood (NIV)." In verse 31 he commands them to be "alert." In 1 Peter 5:1-3 elders are commanded to "shepherd the flock of God that is among you, exercising oversight, not under

---

51. Sections 4.1, 4.2, Appendix 5.
52. Acts 14:23, Titus 1:5
53. I am not saying that Bible colleges and seminaries are bad. There is value in theological study. I am saying that this type of training is not essential for all leaders. I am also saying that practical training is emphasized in the New Testament.

compulsion, but willingly, as God would have you; not for shameful gain, but eagerly; not domineering over those in your charge, but being examples to the flock." Similarly Hebrews 13:17 says "for they (those leading) are keeping watch over your souls." The word for leaders in this verse includes anyone who is moving in leadership at a particular time, not just elders. Elders, and others God raises up to lead, should watch over the souls of believers and over the dynamics of the local church assembly. They should care for the local Christian community. They should be a good example to the community and provide leadership without domineering. Elders seek to influence each believer and the whole local assembly to abide in Christ so that individually and corporately they bear much fruit. [54] Abiding in Christ places believers and the local assembly in the best position to hear the voice of Jesus as He directly leads each one. [55]

It is not the responsibility of the elder to organize the content of church meetings or to act as a permission giver/withholder for the ministry of other believers; Jesus wants to provide this leadership by communicating directly with every believer. Elders may of course encourage believers to be active in ministry. No verse in the New Testament mentions elders having any type of authority that is not available to non-elders. [56] Section 4.1 discusses whether believers were expected to obey New Testament leaders. Section 4.2 discusses submission of believers to New Testament leaders.

The vast majority of the responsibilities of an elder are activities which are also the responsibility of non-elders. Elders will be active in contributing to meetings, prayer, teaching, encouraging, admonishing, conflict resolution, challenging other believers about sin in their life, leading by example, providing love and care, evangelism and protecting unity. All believers are expected to contribute to these activities. Elders also have a responsibility to pastor and to protect sound doctrine. [57] In some cases elders administer charitable funds. [58] Non-elders may also contribute in these areas. The role of elder is not defined by tasks which only the elder is allowed to perform.

---

54. John 15:1-17
55. John 10:3
56. Section 1.3, Appendix 2. Protecting sound doctrine may be a partial exception to this general principle.
57. Appendix 1.20, 1.21
58. Acts 11:30, Subsection 6.7.1

Part of pastoring is to be alert to potential situations where someone might get hurt. This can easily happen as individuals learn how to move in the spiritual gifts. For example an individual may be so excited by the thought that he has a prophetic word for someone else that he delivers it in a disrespectful or hurtful manner. It is important not only to ensure that everyone is protected, but also to mentor and coach individuals so that their contributions are always edifying. God intends the house church community to be sufficiently close that our rough edges interact. He wants to use these interactions to provide the opportunity for us to develop godly character. Individuals with a pastoral heart will have plenty of opportunities to use this gift helping individuals work through these difficult interactions in a healthy manner.

Elders, and other believers, are responsible to lead by influence, not control. Effective leadership by influence is a form of authority, which grows out of mutual respect. Elders need to treat believers with respect and they need to earn the respect of each believer. Leaders need to live out mutual submission. [59] As elders lead in this way, they will have substantial authority to positively influence each believer. The other side of this coin is that each believer will choose to hold himself open to being persuaded by whoever is leading in a particular situation and the believer will choose to submit to the individual leading.[60]

An individual elder, just like any believer, may have authority in one or more ministry areas. [61] Elders do not have authority to direct the ministry activities of other believers. Elders do not have the authority to organize the main weekly meeting in a manner which prevents every member participation. Elders do not have the authority on their own to resolve issues of church discipline or to evaluate revelatory words for the church. This authority is reserved to the full congregation. [62]

Elders have an important role in facilitating the congregational process. Examples of this include:

---

59. Eph. 5:21
60. Heb. 13:17. See Sections 4.1 and 4.2 for a discussion of this verse.
61. For example, Matt. 10:1 says Jesus gave the twelve disciples authority over evil spirits and disease. Any believer or leader with an effective deliverance or healing ministry will have received this gift of authority. Similarly, authority can be associated with teaching (Luke 4:32).
62. Subsections 1.1.4, 1.1.5

- Encouraging quieter members to contribute to meetings and in other ways to the life of the church.
- Encouraging individuals who contribute a great deal to contribute slightly less to provide more opportunities for the quieter individuals to contribute.
- Stepping in when an inappropriate contribution may result in someone feeling disrespected or hurt. The art is to do this in a manner which not only protects the individual who may be being hurt, but also treats the individual who is contributing inappropriately respectfully. The goal is to coach each individual so that they learn to contribute in a way that builds up other believers.
- Facilitating consensus based decision-making. This includes making sure that everyone gets a chance to speak and that all opinions are treated with respect. It may include helping each individual to contribute to the process from a position of abiding in Jesus. It may also include seeking middle ground that everyone can agree on.

Elders also lead by protecting sound doctrine and by pastoring. Many of the roles described above are dimensions of pastoring. Pastoring also includes protecting, caring for and teaching believers. Protection is provided by helping each individual abide in Jesus, which is the one true place of safety and by protecting sound doctrine.

Elders have a significant leadership role without being the ones who make decisions in isolation from the rest of the assembly. The role of elders is not defined by things that only elders may do. An individual who is not an elder may provide leadership in any manner described in this section. In particular non-elders may also lead by influence in a manner similar to elders. Non-elders who do this consistently are likely to be recognized as elders in due course.

Hebrews 13:17 makes another important point about those who lead. They serve "as those who will have to give an account." Elders are accountable to God for how they serve Him in this role. It is plausible that elders, like teachers, will be judged with greater strictness than other believers. [63]

In many circles, even some Christian circles, leading only by influence as opposed to having authority to command is considered foolishness and weakness. This type of leadership may be despised by those who consider themselves to be wise and strong. In 1 Corinthians 1:27-29 Paul says:

---

63. James 3:1

> But God chose what is foolish in the world to shame the wise; God chose what is weak in the world to shame the strong; God chose what is low and despised in the world, even things that are not, to bring to nothing things that are, so that no human being might boast in the presence of God.

Is it possible that this passage is applicable to Christian leadership? Is it possible that God wants elders to lead only by influence to shame those who think they are wise and strong? Is it possible He has chosen this approach to ensure that no one can boast in His presence?

## 2.6 How many elders were there in each local assembly?

There is no statement in Scripture that definitively addresses the number of elders in each local assembly. Almost all of the general references to elders in the New Testament refer to them in the plural.[64] The few references to elders in the singular are for obvious reasons based on the context.[65] Some have suggested that each house church had only one elder and that the plurals refer to the group of elders in a particular town or region. It is possible that this was the case. However I see no benefit to limiting the number of elders to one per assembly and I see many benefits in having several elders in each assembly. The requirements to be an elder are relatively low, so it seems plausible that mature assemblies had several elders.

The New Testament expects elders to watch out for members of the assembly. To do this effectively each member of the assembly needs to have a good relationship with at least one elder. This is much easier to achieve if there are several elders within the assembly. Having several elders provides a wider range of giftings to address any issues that may arise and makes it less likely that someone will develop an inappropriate focus on a human leader. Having multiple elders helps the elders walk in humility and makes it easier to handle a situation where an elder enters into sin or doctrinal error.

It is implicit in Acts 14:23 that some new churches formed with new believers existed for a while without elders or traveling leaders. It is possible that in some of these assemblies, one person may have matured faster than the others and served for a season as the only elder in the assembly. Over time others would have matured to the point where they also were ready to serve as elders. So it is likely that some assemblies had periods of time with only one elder.

---

64. *E.g.*, Phil. 1:1, Acts 14:23, 15:4, Titus 1:5, James 5:14
65. *E.g.*, 1 Tim. 5:19, 1 Pet. 5:1, 2 John 1, 3 John 1

## 2.7 Was there a single senior elder in a church?

There is no statement in Scripture that definitively addresses whether one elder within a local assembly was recognized as the senior elder. As discussed in Appendix 3.8, the hints contained in Scripture support the assumption that in general each church assembly was led by a group of elders with no distinct senior elder. A possible exception to this pattern is Diotrephes, who may have been acting as a single senior elder. However 3 John makes clear that Diotrephes is not an example to follow.

The pattern of New Testament leadership described in Chapters 1 and 2 fits excellently with each church having a group of co-equal elders. These elders do not organize the content of the church meetings and do not tell other believers what ministry they should or should not be doing. So there is no role for a senior elder with particular authority to make these types of decisions.

In general elders lead by exercising influence and in general some individuals will have more influence than others. This does not necessarily make the individual with the most influence a senior elder. The beauty of leading by influence is that it requires no formal organization and it does not require leaders to have particular titles and roles.

Identifying a senior elder can be an impediment to the healthy flowing of influence within a church. If there is a senior elder, other members of a church may, out of respect for that individual's position, hold back from exercising the leadership (by influence) that God wants them to provide.

## 2.8 What to do when elders sin?

Unfortunately, the church needs to be willing to deal with sinful elders. No Christian leader is beyond the risk of falling into sin. For example Acts 20:30 records the prophecy that some elders at Ephesus will become savage wolves and in 1 Timothy 3:6-7 Paul mentions the risk of elders becoming conceited.

1 Timothy 5:19-21 provides a process to follow when elders fall into sin. This sin may be the teaching of false doctrine or a behavior issue. This process is written to Timothy as a traveling leader helping a local church at a difficult time. [66] Traveling leaders can be particularly

66. 1 Tim. 1:3-4, Appendix 7

helpful when local churches have problems such as elders falling into sin. [67]

The process given in 1 Timothy 5:19-21 should be considered in the context of Galatians 6:1, which teaches that a gentle (presumably private) attempt should be made to restore an individual who is in sin. The process in 1 Timothy 5:19-21 applies after the elder has rejected this invitation to repentance and has decided to continue in sin. The elder who continues in sin should be rebuked in the presence of the whole church so that the rest may stand in fear. The word for rebuke is in the singular and thus indicates a command to Timothy, a traveling leader. If the elder does not repent after being publicly rebuked it is reasonable to assume that the church discipline process will be initiated, which may result in the exclusion of the elder from the church.

This process is characterized by checks and balances. For example, evidence is required from two or three witnesses and this passage also teaches the importance of not prejudging a situation or person and of not showing partiality. The public setting for the rebuke provides an opportunity for others who are present to bring forward facts which may put a different spin on the situation. A wise traveling leader will want to check carefully to see if he is getting the full story from the witnesses who approach him. He will do everything he can to ensure that he has all of the relevant facts before he gives a public rebuke.

The process of dealing with a sinful elder becomes more complex if for any reason many members of the congregation either condone the elder's sin or are unwilling to address it. Timothy, as a traveling leader, is still commanded to rebuke the elder, but it may be easy for the sinful elder to ignore this rebuke if he has the support of the majority of the church. This topic is addressed in Section 5.2.

In the event that a local church is responding to the sin of an elder without the help of a traveling leader, it is reasonable to assume that they should follow the standard process for church discipline involving the full congregation as discussed in Subsection 1.1.4. The only difference between this process and the process in 1 Timothy 5:19-20 is the public rebuke in front of the whole congregation. Such public rebukes may have been the preserve of traveling leaders. [68]

---

67. Section 5.2
68. Section 4.3

## 2.9 Is it possible to be both an elder and an apostle?

Peter considered himself to be both an elder and an apostle. [69] It is possible that Paul referred to himself as an elder in Philemon 1:9; but he may just be calling himself an old man. Similarly in 2 John 1 and 3 John 1, John may be describing himself as an elder or as an old man.

It is possible that all three of these individuals had seasons of their life when most of their ministry was as an elder rather than as an apostle. For example, at the time Peter wrote 1 Peter he may have been serving as an elder in Rome. This hypothesis explains both 1 Peter 1:1, which reflects Peter's apostolic ministry to the Jews, [70] and 1 Peter 5:1 which may address a primary current role as an elder in Rome. So Peter may have been serving as an elder to the church in Rome while he remained an apostle to the churches he had previously planted. Similarly, at the time Paul wrote Philemon he may also have been serving (during house arrest) as an elder in the church in Rome. Based on 1 Corinthians 9:2 it is likely that Paul continued to consider himself an apostle to the churches he had planted.

It is possible that Peter, John and Paul chose to call themselves elders to maintain a distinction between their role at the time of their writing these epistles as elders of established churches and their apostolic role of planting, and providing ongoing support to, churches in regions where there were no churches. As noted in Chapter 3, almost all aspects of ministry performed by apostles may also be performed by individuals who are not traveling leaders. So if an individual serves as an apostle during one season of his life and as an elder in another season there may be very little difference in his day to day ministry. The only exception to this that I have found in the New Testament concerns rebuking. [71]

## 2.10 Deacons

As discussed in Appendix 3.7, the family of Greek words *diakonos/diakonia/diakoneo* that are typically translated servant/service/serve, is used many times in the New Testament to describe serving meals and providing financial assistance. This family of words is also extensively used to describe a wide range of spiritual service or

69. 1 Pet. 1:1, 5:1

70. Gal. 2:7-8. Peter may also have had an apostolic role in Pontus, Galatia, Cappadocia, Asia, and Bithynia (1 Pet. 1:1).

71. Section 4.3

ministry. It seems that the vast majority of these references are to practical serving and spiritual ministry which may be performed by any believer. There is also a strong linkage between this family of words and Christian leadership. This linkage reinforces the message that Christian leadership is about being a servant; it is not about being a church manager and decision-maker.

In two New Testament passages there are explicit references to deacons as a recognized group within a city-wide church. [72] A few other passages almost certainly refer to such a role. [73] Acts 6:1-6 describes the appointment of the seven to serve food to the widows in the community. The Bible never refers to these seven individuals as deacons, but it is possible that they were called deacons and that their role was similar to the role of the deacons mentioned in 1 Timothy and Philippians. Care is needed to differentiate between the general use of this family of words describing the servant lifestyle of all believers, especially leaders, and the occasional use of these words to refer to a recognized group of deacons with a particular role in the life of the church.

### *The role of deacons*

There is no clear statement in the New Testament as to the role of deacons as a recognized group within a church. It is very likely that Acts 6:1-6 is illustrating the role of deacons. If this is correct, we know that deacons were involved in serving food to widows. Also, the implication of Acts 4:34-5:2 and Acts 6:1-3 is that the Jerusalem network of house churches had a joint charity fund, which was initially administered by the apostles and later by the deacons. It is probable that the role of deacon was to serve a network of house churches in a community rather than a role within a single house church. Deacons could also be involved in spiritual ministry. [74]

### *Requirements to become a deacon*

The requirements for deacons given in 1 Timothy 3:8-12 are very similar to the requirements for elders given in 1 Timothy 3:2-7 and Titus 1:6-9. In all three lists the primary emphasis is on character issues and related family issues including being the husband of only one wife and managing their children and households well.

---

72. 1 Tim. 3:8-13, Phil. 1:1

73. *E.g.*, Acts 6:1-6, Rom. 16:1

74. *E.g.*, Stephen in Acts 6:8–10, 7:2-60 and Acts 8:5-40 shows that Phillip became a traveling leader.

Paul requires deacons to be dignified and not double tongued. These specific character traits are not mentioned for elders, [75] but are included in the requirement for elders to be above reproach. It is unlikely that Paul is seeking to create a meaningfully different character test for the two roles based on these minor differences.

However there are two potentially more significant differences between these requirements lists. One difference is that there is no mention of teaching and defending sound doctrine in the requirements for deacons. Deacons are however required to hold fast to the mystery of the faith with a clear conscience. This difference in requirements makes sense if deacons are focused on administering charitable funds, food distributions and similar activities.

The second difference is that the list for deacons includes specific character requirements for the deacon's wife or for female deacons. [76] These women are required to "be dignified, not slanderers, but sober-minded, faithful in all things." These character requirements are fully consistent with the character requirements for elders and deacons.

It is possible that in the case of elders the character of their wives is assumed to be included in the elder being required to be above reproach and to manage his household well. Certainly the behavior of other household members is in many societies a factor used to evaluate whether an individual is above reproach. It is also possible that deacons might have kept charity funds in their homes so the character of the wife as well as other household members is more important due to the risk of theft.

Some have suggested that 1 Timothy 3:11 is a specific character test for women deacons. As discussed in Section 6.4, I believe that there were women deacons in the New Testament church. Whether 1 Timothy 3:11 applies to women deacons or to the wives of deacons, it is unlikely that Paul is seeking to create different character tests for elders and for male and female deacons.

In Acts 6:3 the original seven "servers" (almost certainly deacons) were required to be men of good repute and full of the Spirit and of wisdom. This is a good summary of the requirements given by Paul for elders and deacons.

---

75. Except dignity in the context of dealing with children (1 Tim. 3:4).
76. 1 Tim. 3:11. The Greek word *gune* may be translated woman or wife. It is likely that Phoebe (Rom. 16:1-2) is an example of a female deacon (Section 6.4).

### *How were deacons appointed?*

Acts 6:1-6 records the appointment of seven men to serve meals to widows in the Jerusalem church. It is likely that these individuals were deacons. At the invitation of the apostles the whole community of believers in Jerusalem nominated seven men who were then prayed for by the apostles with laying on of hands. Based on verse 3, it appears that the process of the apostles laying hands on and praying for the deacons was interpreted as the apostles appointing them and thus publicly confirming their role. The word used in Acts 6:3 for appoint is the same Greek word used in Titus 1:5 for Titus appointing elders.[77] The process used by the believers to nominate the seven men is not described. It is likely that it was a consensus-based process.

It is plausible that the process for appointing deacons was similar to the process used for appointing elders. One potential difference between the two appointment processes may relate to the community involved in the selection process. Acts 6:1-6 records that all believers in Jerusalem were invited to participate in selecting the first deacons. This was the logical thing to do as the deacons would serve the whole city-wide church. It is likely that deacons in other cities also served the whole city-wide church, so it is possible that all believers within the city could be involved in their selection. It is possible that only the believers associated with a specific local assembly contributed to the selection of elders to serve that assembly.

### *Why are there so few references in the New Testament to Deacons?*

As noted in Appendix 3.7, the *diakonos/diakonia/diakoneo* family of words is used 95 times in the New Testament. But there are only five uses of this family of words that are explicitly linked to the position of deacon within a church. Four of these references occur in the passage which provides the qualifications for deacons. As noted above, a few other references almost certainly refer to such a role. There appear to be more links between this family of words and apostolic service than with a position of deacon.

It is possible that deacons were only appointed in cities with a large number of house churches. As noted above, it appears from Acts 4:34-5:2 and Acts 6:2 that the apostles administered the charity

---

77. Section 2.2

funds in the early Jerusalem church and that this role was only handed over to the deacons when the church became so large that the apostles did not have sufficient time to do it well. It is possible that in other communities elders administered charity funds until the church network became so large that it became appropriate to appoint deacons to focus on this role.[78] This may explain why deacons and financial assistance for widows are discussed in 1 Timothy, which was sent to Timothy while he was in Ephesus: a relatively large church.[79] It is possible that the churches in Crete, where Titus was ministering at the time of the writing of the epistle addressed to him, were smaller.

---

78. Acts 11:30
79. 1 Tim. 3:8-13, 5:3-16, Acts 19:26

# Chapter 3
# Leaders Who Travel Planting and Supporting Churches

## 3.1 Types of traveling leaders

Much of the material in the New Testament concerning the life of the early church is associated with leaders who traveled extensively. I call these individuals "traveling leaders." Their role is complementary to the role of local leaders (elders) who mainly serve in a single community. Some of these traveling leaders were called apostles. However this title was not used for all traveling leaders. [1]

The traveling leaders described in the New Testament went from city to city planting new churches and helping them to grow. Perhaps the best summary of the role of traveling leaders is given in 2 Corinthians 8:23 concerning Titus: "As for Titus, he is my partner and fellow worker for your benefit." Romans 16:21 provides a similar description for Timothy.

As we shall see, traveling leaders worked by influence based on mutual respect. Their assistance was not provided as part of an organizational hierarchy. New Testament traveling leaders did not hold a "management position" within a human organization. Nor was there any human organization with the authority to appoint anyone to such a position.

### *Apostles*

A primary focus of Jesus' earthly ministry was the selection and training of the initial apostles. These individuals played a key role in the development of the New Testament church.

---

1. The opening greetings of four of Paul's epistles (1 Cor. 1:1, 2 Cor. 1:1, Gal. 1:1-2, Col. 1:1) are written in a way that makes clear that he is an apostle and that his co-author(s) are not apostles. In two cases the co-author is Timothy, who was a traveling leader. See Appendix 4.1 for a further discussion of the use of the word apostle in the New Testament.

The root meaning of the word "apostle" is one sent as a messenger or agent, or the bearer of a commission. Being an apostle involved travel, which in the 1st Century was very dangerous.[2] Part of the secular connotation of the word "apostle" was "disposable slave;" one did not want to risk a valuable slave or employee on a dangerous journey. Of course being a slave was the lowest status role in the ancient world. Another secular meaning of the word "apostle" in 1st Century Greek is the "admiral" over a fleet of ships and/or the "fleet" itself. This meaning also has connotations of travel, risk and being sent to perform a task for a commander.

Jesus, Peter and Paul all explicitly link apostleship and serving like a slave. In John 13 Jesus models slave-leadership by washing the apostles' feet. In verses 14 and 15 He commands the apostles to wash one another's feet following His example. In verse 16 Jesus uses the words *doulos* (slave) and *apostolos* (apostle) in a parallel manner as He reinforces this message. This linkage would have been totally unremarkable in the 1st Century. Similarly, both Peter and Paul in a single phrase describe themselves as both a slave and an apostle.[3]

The first use of the word apostle in the New Testament is in Matthew 10:2. This passage describes Jesus' compassion for the crowds, His command for us to pray for laborers to go into the harvest and His selection of the twelve apostles. It also describes His commissioning of them to go from town to town preaching the kingdom, healing the sick, raising the dead, cleansing lepers and casting out demons. Jesus also taught that this ministry would involve a frugal lifestyle and would encounter strong opposition. The parallel passage in Mark says that Jesus appointed the twelve, "so that they might be with him and he might send them out to preach."[4] This brief summary beautifully captures two key dimensions of apostleship: the invitation to intimacy with Jesus; and being sent out to evangelize. As with all Christian ministry, healthy fruitfulness in apostolic ministry flows from abiding with Jesus.[5]

---

2. 2 Cor. 11:25-27
3. 2 Pet. 1:1, Rom. 1:1, Titus 1:1
4. Mark 3:14. The word "preach" in the New Testament refers to evangelistic proclaiming not to church sermons aimed at believers (Section 6.2).
5. John 15:4-5

Acts 1:8[6] also shows that apostleship is about evangelistic ministry, and by implication church planting in regions where there are no believers. The apostolic ministry of Paul and Barnabas is a good example of this. Apostles also provided ongoing care to the churches they had planted through personal visits, by encouraging other traveling leaders to visit and by writing letters.

Ephesians 2:20 and Revelation 21:14 make clear that the apostolic role is foundation laying.[7] In Romans 15:20 Paul states that his ambition is to preach the gospel in areas where it has not already been preached "lest he build on someone else's foundation." Taken together these passages indicate that the essence of apostleship is church planting in regions where there is no church. Paul's reference in Romans 15:19 to the part played by signs and wonders in the planting of the church from Jerusalem to Illyricum may, given 2 Corinthians 12:12,[8] be another indicator that he is considering his apostolic role in this passage. Similarly in 1 Corinthians 9:2 Paul describes the Corinthian church as "the seal of my apostleship in the Lord." In other words, the existence of the church in Corinth, which is an example of Paul's church planting work in a city where there had previously been no Christian community, is evidence that he is an apostle.

To summarize, the essence of apostleship is an itinerant, church-planting ministry accompanied by signs and wonders in regions where there is no church.[9] Apostles also provide ongoing support to these and other churches. Apostles typically encounter strong opposition.[10]

---

6. "But you will receive power when the Holy Spirit has come upon you, and you will be my witnesses in Jerusalem and in all Judea and Samaria, and to the end of the earth." Acts 1:2 makes clear that the you in this verse refers to the apostles. *Cf.* Matt. 28:16-20, which is also spoken to the initial eleven apostles.
7. Eph. 2:20 also mentions the role of prophets in foundation laying. It is possible that Paul had the role of the Old Testament prophets (and John the Baptist) in mind when he wrote this verse (*cf.* 2 Pet. 3:2). Jesus and the New Testament church based much of their message on what we now call the Old Testament, especially the prophetic books (Matt. 21:42, 22:29, 26:56, Luke 24:27, John 5:39, Acts 2:17-36, 17:2, 11, 18:28, Rom. 1:2, 1 Cor. 15:3-4).
8. "The signs of a true apostle were performed among you with utmost patience, with signs and wonders and mighty works."
9. Some suggest that this is too narrow a definition of apostleship. They suggest it is possible to be an apostle and to focus on evangelistic or teaching ministry in the context of established churches. Acts 3:1-8:1 is sometimes cited as an example of this type of apostleship. The time period associated with this section of Scripture is not definitely known, so

The New Testament says that false apostles existed in parallel with true apostles.[11] Paul says that these individuals are proud, deceitful workmen who teach false doctrine and disguise themselves as servants of righteousness. They make slaves of their followers, devouring them, taking advantage of them and mistreating them. In Revelation 2:2 Jesus commends the church in Ephesus for testing individuals who claim to be apostles and for rejecting the false apostles.

### *Other Traveling Leaders*

Several other types of ministry and gifting are mentioned in the context of traveling leaders and ministers in the New Testament:

- Prophecy: Agabus, Judas and Silas are all mentioned as prophets who traveled to minister.[12]
- Evangelism and preaching or proclaiming Jesus: Philip the deacon was an evangelist who spent at least some of his time in traveling ministry.[13] Paul commanded Timothy, who was a traveling leader, to "do the work of an evangelist."[14] Preaching and proclaiming are mentioned many times in the New Testament, often in the context of traveling leaders. As discussed in Appendix 4.4, these words refer to evangelistic preaching.
- Shepherding: John 21:16 mentions shepherding (pastoring) in the context of Peter, who was a traveling leader for much of his

---

the significance of this passage in this context is uncertain. Maybe the eleven apostles remained in Jerusalem about as long as Paul remained in Ephesus or maybe they remained in Jerusalem a little longer. The available Biblical and non-Biblical information concerning the activities of the initial group of apostles after Acts 8:1 is discussed in Appendix 4.1.3. This material supports my belief that the essence of New Testament apostleship was church planting in regions where there was no church. The fact that several apostles were in Jerusalem for the Acts 15 council may only indicate that God arranged for them to be there between ministry trips so that they could participate. Ancient tradition records that God supernaturally translated some apostles back from distant mission fields to participate in this council.

10. 1 Cor. 4:9-13
11. 2 Cor. 11:1-5, 12-15, 20, 12:11, Rev 2:2
12. Acts 11:27-28, 15:27-33, 21:10. See Section 6.3 for a discussion of the role of prophecy in the New Testament church and see Appendix 4.2 for a discussion of the Greek words associated with prophecy.
13. Acts 8:5, 26, 39-40, 21:8. See Section 6.2 for a discussion of preaching and evangelism in the New Testament church and see Appendix 4.3 for a discussion of the Greek words associated with evangelism.
14. 2 Tim. 4:5

life. Traveling leaders provided pastoral support to local church assemblies through visits and letters.

- Teaching: Paul considered himself to be a teacher and he commanded Timothy and Titus to teach as part of their role as traveling leaders. [15]

As discussed in Section 1.1 and Appendix 1 any believer may minster in any of these four roles. These roles are not exclusive to traveling or local leaders. [16] Some traveling leaders were so strongly gifted in one area that Luke refers to them by their ministry area (*i.e.*, prophet or evangelist). However, this should not be taken as implying that all traveling leaders neatly fit into one of these categories. Paul commanded Timothy to do the work of an evangelist and to teach. We have no record of Paul telling Timothy to provide pastoral care but this expectation is implicit in the two letters Paul wrote to Timothy. Paul says he is a preacher, apostle and teacher. [17] So some traveling leaders were active in several types of ministry.

## 3.2 Appointment of traveling leaders

The New Testament emphasizes the role of God in selecting individuals to serve as traveling leaders. For example, the original twelve apostles were appointed by Jesus after a night of prayer. [18] Paul is very clear in several places that he was appointed an apostle by God. [19] In Galatians 1:1 he emphasizes that humans were not involved in his appointment to apostleship. Visions and prophetic words played a key part in identifying candidate traveling leaders and in helping them to understand their future role. Paul had a personal vision of Jesus in which Jesus called him to apostolic service and others also received words that he was called to this service. [20] As with all revelatory words, words concerning traveling leadership roles should be tested, which in many cases will involve the candidate leader's local church. Paul teaches that the fruit of his

---

15. 1 Tim. 2:7, 4:11, 6:2, 2 Tim. 1:11, Titus 2:1. See Section 6.1 for a discussion of teaching in the New Testament church and Appendix 4.5 for a discussion of the Greek words for teaching.
16. Incidentally these four roles mentioned in the context of traveling leaders, along with apostleship, match the gifts listed in Eph. 4:11.
17. 1 Tim. 2:7, 2 Tim. 1:11.
18. Luke 6:12-13
19. *E.g.*, Gal. 1:1, 1 Cor. 1:1, 2 Cor. 1:1, Eph. 1:1, Col. 1:1, 1 Tim. 1:1, 2 Tim. 1:1. These scriptures are fully consistent with Acts 9:15, 13:2 and 26:16-18.
20. Acts 26:16-18, 9:15, 13:2. Acts 13:2 also records Barnabas' call to traveling leadership.

ministry confirmed the accuracy of these words. [21] Another test of the authenticity of an individual's apostolic calling is provided by 1 Corinthians 4:9-13, which describes the sufferings of apostles.

Similarly, Paul mentions multiple prophecies associated with Timothy's call to service as a traveling leader and Luke mentions the recommendation of the churches which knew him. [22] Prayer with laying on of hands by leaders and possibly non-leaders was part of the commissioning of local and traveling leaders. [23] The argument between Paul and Barnabas concerning John Mark indicates that each traveling team needs to reach consensus on who should join them. [24] Neither Paul nor Barnabas had the authority to make this decision without the agreement of the other. This passage also says that Paul chose Silas as his new partner and they went off on their missionary journey with the blessing of the local assembly. In Acts 18:24-28 Luke records that Apollos wished to minister in Achaia and went with the encouragement and assistance of the brothers.

In summary, it seems that in the New Testament traveling leaders were appointed by God and that prophetic words had a role in identifying candidates for this service. God's role in calling and appointing traveling leaders needs to be held in a delicate balance with the human role in this process. In the long term, the fruit of the individual's ministry is the evidence that he was appointed by God. In some cases it seems existing traveling leaders picked their partners. In some cases local assemblies recommended candidate traveling leaders and commissioned them with prayer and the laying on of hands. They may also have participated in evaluating relevant prophetic words. The New Testament mentions that there were false traveling leaders. So, local Christian assemblies need to test visitors who claim to be traveling leaders. [25]

## 3.3 Qualifications of traveling leaders

The key qualification to be a traveling leader is to be chosen for this role by Jesus. [26] It is clear from the New Testament that He chose

---

21. 1 Cor. 9:2, 2 Cor. 12:12
22. 1 Tim. 1:18, 4:14, 2 Tim. 1:6, Acts 16:2
23. Acts 6:6, 13:3, 14:23, 1 Tim. 4:14. 2 Cor. 8:19 uses the Greek word *cheirotoneo* to describe the appointment of traveling leaders. This word may mean stretching forth ones hands to pray for someone or to vote for someone (Section 2.2). It can also mean to appoint.
24. Acts 15:36-41
25. Rev. 2:2

individuals who would not seem to us to be well-qualified candidates. Paul was a primary persecutor of the church and Peter denied Jesus three times. As Paul says in 1 Corinthians 1:27-29:

> But God chose what is foolish in the world to shame the wise; God chose what is weak in the world to shame the strong; God chose what is low and despised in the world, even things that are not, to bring to nothing things that are, so that no human being might boast in the presence of God.

The context of these words indicates that they apply to the complete church in Corinth. However they are also extremely applicable to God's choice of apostles and other traveling leaders. He delights to change people in ways that bring glory to Him. The New Testament says that being an apostle was an exceptionally hard role. Paul provides a summary of this in 1 Corinthians 4:9-13:

> For I think that God has exhibited us apostles as last of all, like men sentenced to death, because we have become a spectacle to the world, to angels, and to men. We are fools for Christ's sake, but you are wise in Christ. We are weak, but you are strong. You are held in honor, but we in disrepute. To the present hour we hunger and thirst, we are poorly dressed and buffeted and homeless, and we labor, working with our own hands. When reviled, we bless; when persecuted, we endure; when slandered, we entreat. We have become, and are still, like the scum of the world, the refuse of all things.

Paul's personal testimony of these general truths about apostles is recorded in 2 Corinthians 11:23-28:

> Are they servants of Christ? I am a better one—I am talking like a madman—with far greater labors, far more imprisonments, with countless beatings, and often near death. Five times I received at the hands of the Jews the forty lashes less one. Three times I was beaten with rods. Once I was stoned. Three times I was shipwrecked; a night and a day I was adrift at sea; on frequent journeys, in danger from rivers, danger from robbers, danger from

---

26. Matt. 10:5, 28:19, Acts 9:15. Acts 1:21-22 mentions two qualifications the first 11 apostles considered in selecting someone to replace Judas Iscariot: traveling with Jesus throughout His public ministry and being an eye witness of the resurrection. Paul and Barnabas did not travel with Jesus, so this requirement is not applicable in all cases. It is not clear if the second requirement (seeing Jesus after his resurrection) applies to all candidate apostles. In 1 Cor. 9:1, 15:8-9 Paul may be implying that he thinks seeing Jesus is a qualification for being an apostle. It is possible that all apostles have a specific commissioning by Jesus similar to Paul's commissioning by Jesus. This does not mean that this commissioning is always part of a dramatic salvation experience. Selecting Matthias by lot to replace Judas is not recorded in Scripture as an example for us to follow in other apostolic appointments (Acts 1:24-26).

> my own people, danger from Gentiles, danger in the city, danger in the wilderness, danger at sea, danger from false brothers; in toil and hardship, through many a sleepless night, in hunger and thirst, often without food, in cold and exposure. And, apart from other things, there is the daily pressure on me of my anxiety for all the churches.

It takes exceptional character to walk the journey Paul describes in these passages. Only God's grace can qualify an individual for such a role. Not only do apostles need to be individuals of exceptional perseverance and endurance they also need to have the heart of a servant/slave. [27] Even though these two passages from the Corinthian epistles are specific to apostles, it is reasonable to assume that those called to other forms of traveling leadership will also lead challenging lives and will also need, by God's grace, to be individuals of godly character.

In 1 Corinthians 9:1-6 Paul is defending his qualifications as an apostle. The first qualification he mentions is freedom. From the context this appears to mean that the Corinthians had a narrow expectation as to how apostles should live. A couple of specific freedoms Paul mentions include the freedom for apostles to be married or single and the freedom for apostles to be financially self-supporting or to be supported by gifts. The text 2 Corinthians 12:12 indicates the marks of a true apostle include "signs and wonders and mighty works" that are performed with "utmost patience."

Being without sin is not a necessary qualification to be an apostle. Biblical examples of apostolic sin include Peter and Barnabas refusing to eat with the Gentiles and, most likely, the argument between Paul and Barnabas concerning John Mark. [28] I wonder whether the argument between Paul and Barnabas is recorded in Scripture in part as a warning to leaders. It is very easy for leaders to become so consumed with the importance of advancing the Kingdom that they forget to love and respect those around them, who may have a different opinion as to the best way to achieve this important goal.

### 3.4 Training of traveling leaders

The most complete picture in the New Testament of the training of traveling leaders is provided in the Gospels. In Mark 3:14-15 it says that Jesus chose the apostles so that "they might be with Him." This captures the foundation for all healthy Christian ministry, which

---

27. John 13:16, Rom. 1:1, Titus 1:1, 2 Pet. 1:1
28. Gal. 2:11-13, Acts 15:36-39

is intimate relationship with Jesus. How can we get with the program of "only doing the things I see the Father doing,"[29] if we are not in sufficient intimacy to have this insight? Jesus makes this explicit in John 15:15-16 where he says that the apostles are not His servants but His friends "for everything that I learned from my Father I have made known to you." In verse 16 He says that He has appointed them "to go and bear fruit—fruit that will last." This passage teaches that friendship with Jesus is a necessary precursor to receive insight into the activity of the Father. This insight is a necessary precursor for fruitful ministry. The other side of this coin is provided by the hard word of Matthew 7:21-23: 'I never knew you. Away from me, you evildoers!' (NIV).

In addition to the importance of developing intimacy there is a huge amount one learns by being with someone and observing how they live. A Biblical example of this is provided in John 13:3-17, which describes Jesus washing the feet of His disciples. The intentional teaching nature of this incident is emphasized in verses 14-15 where Jesus told His disciples to follow His example. Another example of Jesus revealing His true nature to some of the apostles is the transfiguration.[30] Obviously all believers can learn from both of these incidents by meditating on the relevant Scriptures. However, the learning impact is generally far greater when we experience something for ourselves than when we read about it. This is especially true for emotionally intense experiences. Owing to cultural changes over time, it is easy for modern day believers to be unaware of how shocking it was to the disciples to allow Jesus to wash their feet. We get a hint of this in John 13:8. Similarly Matthew 17:6 records that the disciples were terrified by the transfiguration. Paul also emphasized the importance of learning by observation.[31]

One of Jesus' primary goals was to develop faith in His apostles. He wanted them to have sufficient faith to be effective in ministry.[32] It seems that His primary teaching method for developing faith was to allow circumstances that severely tested the disciples' faith. Examples of this include: Peter walking on the water; the shekel in the mouth of the fish; Jesus stilling the storm; Jesus discussing the lesson of the

---

29. John 5:19
30. Matt. 17:1-8
31. 1 Cor. 4:16-17, 11:1-2, Phil. 4:9
32. Matt. 17:14-20

miraculous feeding of the crowds.[33] Most of these incidents involved the disciples experiencing strong emotions such as fear or a sense of inadequacy. Growth in faith happens as we walk through tough experiences with Jesus and find Him faithful. Listening to teaching and reading books can be helpful on this journey, but there is no substitute for personal experience of Jesus' faithfulness.

Another of Jesus' goals was to train the apostles in preaching, healing and deliverance ministry.[34] Again practical experience, including learning from our mistakes, is key to becoming effective in these areas. In the case of deliverance ministry and healing it is also necessary to receive authority.[35] So it is not surprising that Jesus' primary training method for these ministry areas was "on the job training." Jesus sent his disciples out in pairs to preach, cast out demons and heal.[36]

The apostles lived and traveled with Jesus for three years. During this time they heard Him teach the crowds many times. On at least some occasions he gave his disciples in depth explanations of his public teaching or provided them with other private teaching.[37] Jesus taught by storytelling (parables) and through informal dialog as various questions came up. This verbal teaching was a critical complement to the relationship building and the practical training concerning faith, preaching and deliverance/healing ministry, which Jesus provided the apostles. Verbal teaching in isolation from relationship building and practical training is of limited value.

It seems that Paul and Barnabas followed Jesus' pattern in training traveling leaders. They took John Mark with them on their first missionary journey, but he did not complete the trip with them.[38]

---

33. Matt. 14:28-33, Matt. 17:24-27, Mark 4:36-41, Mark 8:16-21
34. Matt. 10:1, 6-8, Luke 9:1-2
35. Mark 6:7, Matt. 10:1, Luke 9:1
36. Matt. 10:1-23, Mark 6:7-13, Luke 9:1-6, 10:1-20. The use of the phrase "began to send them out" in Mark 6:7 may imply that the apostles were sent on more than one preaching journey during Jesus' earthly ministry. The apostles also had opportunities to minister in these areas when they were not on preaching journeys (Matt 17:14-20).
37. *E.g.*, Matt. 13:36, Mark 4:10, John 14-16
38. Acts 13:5, 13, 15:38-39. It is likely that Barnabas continued to mentor John Mark as they ministered together. It appears that over time John Mark matured into a traveling leader and was reconciled with Paul (Col. 4:10, 2 Tim. 4:11, Phlm. 1:24). It seems that Barnabas was right about the divine potential for traveling leadership in Mark. In 1 Peter 5:13 Peter describes Mark as "my son." It is possible that Mark was also discipled by Peter.

While Paul was in Lystra on his second missionary journey, Timothy was recommended to him by the believers in Lystra and Iconium.[39] Paul invited Timothy to travel with him and Silas. They traveled together until Paul had to leave Berea in a hurry. Silas and Timothy stayed behind in Berea for a while before rejoining Paul in Corinth.[40] After this Paul sent Timothy on several trips to encourage/assist various churches[41] and Timothy co-authored six epistles with Paul.[42] The only definite evidence that Paul mentored Timothy are the two letters that Paul sent him. It is extremely plausible that Paul was intentionally mentoring and coaching Timothy in a similar manner to Jesus' mentoring and coaching of the twelve disciples. They formed a very strong bond, which Paul describes as being like a father/son relationship.[43]

It is likely that Paul also mentored various other individuals during his missionary journeys. By Acts 20:4-5 he had a team of helpers including: Sopater, Aristarchus, Secundus, Gaius, Timothy, Tychicus, Trophimus and Luke. Titus is mentioned as a partner and fellow worker to Paul in 2 Corinthians 8:23. He went to Corinth at Paul's urging and also served in Dalmatia and Crete where he received the epistle addressed to him.[44] Epaphras is mentioned in Col. 1:7 as a "fellow servant" with Paul and as "a faithful minister of Christ." Paul's command[45] to Timothy to "entrust [truth] to faithful men who will be able to teach others also" includes the mentoring of traveling leaders as well as local leaders. It is Jesus' strategy for raising up leaders.

In summary, it seems that Paul and Barnabas followed Jesus' example of raising up leaders by mentoring them as they went about their ministry. It is likely that the other apostles also did this. There is no hint in the New Testament of any training of leaders in a setting similar to modern day seminaries. Acts 4:13 says:

> When they [the Jewish leaders] saw the courage of Peter and John and realized that they were unschooled, ordinary men, they were astonished and they took note that these men had been with Jesus. (NIV)

---

39. Acts 16:1-3
40. Acts 17:14-15, 18:5
41. *E.g.*, Acts 19:22 (with Erastus), 1 Cor. 4:17, 16:10, Phil. 2:19, I Thess. 3:2, 6, 1 Tim. 1:3
42. 2 Corinthians, Philippians, Colossians, 1 Thessalonians, 2 Thessalonians, Philemon
43. 1 Cor. 4:17, 1 Tim. 1.2, 1 Tim. 1.18, 2 Tim. 1.2
44. 2 Cor. 12:18, 2 Tim. 4:10, Titus 1:5
45. 2 Tim 2:2

The most important preparation for Christian leadership is not schooling but being with Jesus. However, there is value in some leaders having formal theological training. For example, the theological depth of Paul's letters build upon his training as a rabbi.

## 3.5 Responsibilities and authority of traveling leaders

In Matthew 28:18-20 Jesus says:

> All authority in heaven and on earth has been given to me. Go therefore and make disciples of all nations, baptizing them in the name of the Father and of the Son and of the Holy Spirit, teaching them to observe all that I have commanded you. And behold, I am with you always, to the end of the age.

These words were spoken to the eleven remaining apostles. They are Jesus' ongoing commission to all traveling leaders, and they provide a high level definition of their responsibilities.

Almost all of this commission also applies to all believers. The promise "I am with you always, to the end of the age" applies to all believers. [46] All believers are expected to be involved in teaching other believers and any believer may baptize a new believer. [47] The Greek verb translated "make disciples" is only used four times in the New Testament. None of these references is explicitly addressed to all believers, but none of them imply that this role is restricted to leaders. Two key elements of discipling are evangelism and teaching. All believers are expected to have at least some involvement in both of these roles. [48]

The only aspect of Matthew 28:18-20 that does not apply to all believers is the command to "go [to] all nations." Most believers remain in their community and minister to those around them. As described in the book of Acts and the epistles, traveling leaders go to places where there is no church in order to plant churches. They also support existing churches by teaching, encouraging, advising, evangelizing and assisting as needed. [49]

Matthew 28:18 makes clear that all authority has been given to Jesus. Jesus delegates authority over evil spirits and sickness. [50]

---

46. *E.g.*, Heb. 13:5 is addressed to all believers and says "I will never leave you nor forsake you."
47. Appendix 1.1, 1.10
48. Appendix 1.8
49. Section 3.7
50. Mark 6:7, Matt. 10:1, Luke 9:1

Jesus was careful to teach that the authority of the apostles and other Christian leaders is totally different to the authority of leaders within the government. Christian leaders are not to lord it over other believers nor are they to exercise authority over them; they are to be servants. [51] Key elements of governmental authority are the authority to decide who does what [52] and controlling the legal system that allows them to punish those they wish to punish. [53] This authority is not given to Christian leaders. God does not delegate to Christian leaders the authority to decide who contributes to meetings of a local Christian assembly or who may minister in particular ways. [54] Christian leaders do not have the authority to implement church discipline. This authority is given to the full community of faith. [55] Traveling leaders have authority to build up local believers, not to organize and control them. [56]

The authority to write scripture is perhaps the most significant delegation of authority by Jesus to human leaders. 2 Peter 3:15-16 shows that Peter considered at least some of Paul's writings to be Scripture. It took the church until the 4th Century to complete the process of evaluating the various documents written in the 1st Century. They then decided which books should be included in the Bible. Selected apostles and other traveling leaders were used by God to write the New Testament. [57] Some of Paul's epistles were co-authored with other traveling leaders. Obviously modern day traveling leaders do not have the authority to write scripture.

To summarize, traveling leaders planted new churches and helped existing church assemblies as needed. New Testament missions strategy is inextricably linked with New Testament church support strategy. The interactions between traveling leaders and other traveling leaders are further discussed in Section 3.6. The interactions between traveling leaders and local churches are further discussed in Section 3.7. These sections provide more details concerning the responsibilities of traveling leaders and their associated authority to carry out these responsibilities.

---

51. Matt. 20:25-26, Mark 10:42-43, Luke 22:25-26, 2 Cor. 1:24, 1 Pet. 5:3
52. *E.g.*, Matt. 8:5-10, Luke 7:1-9 where the centurion notes his authority to command his soldiers and servants.
53. John 19:10-11, Acts 9:14, 26:10
54. Subsections 1.1.2, 1.1.3
55. Subsection 1.1.4
56. 2 Cor. 10:8, 13:10
57. 2 Tim. 3:16

## 3.6 How did traveling leaders work together?

In general, traveling leaders worked in teams. Jesus sent out the twelve and the 72 in pairs.[58] Peter and John went as a team to Samaria.[59] On Paul's first missionary journey he traveled with Barnabas and for the first portion of the trip they were accompanied by John Mark.[60] On Paul's second missionary journey he partnered with Silas, an experienced leader.[61] While they were in Lystra, Timothy joined the team as a trainee and Luke also briefly joined the team.[62]

As Paul's ministry grew he began to lead a larger team.[63] It is likely that this team included both experienced traveling leaders and less experienced leaders who were being mentored. It seems that this team did not always travel together.[64] Paul's partners often visited various churches either alone or in pairs.[65] It appears that Philip was alone when he went to Samaria, when he met the Ethiopian eunuch and for his preaching tour from Azotus to Caesarea.[66]

### *Leadership within teams of traveling leaders*

In some cases, it seems that teams had a clear leader. For example, Paul on his second and third missionary journeys and Barnabas at the start of Paul's first missionary journey.[67] In other cases it appears that there was no single clear leader. Examples of teams with no clear leader include Peter and John in Acts 8:14-25 and Paul and Barnabas during the second half of Paul's first missionary journey.[68]

Even though the New Testament records that some teams of traveling leaders had a definite leader, there is no explicit statement as to how much authority this leader had to direct the activities of the other team members. I am aware of one place where Scripture

---

58. Mark 6:7, Luke 10:1
59. Acts 8:14
60. Acts 13:5, 13
61. Acts 15:22, 27, 32, 40
62. Acts 16:1-3. Luke's participation in the team is indicated by the use of the word "we" in Acts 16:11-16.
63. *E.g.*, Acts 20:4-5
64. Acts 20:5, 6, 13, 14
65. *E.g.*, Acts 19:22, 1 Cor. 4:17, 16:12, 2 Cor. 12:17-18
66. Acts 8:5, 26, 40. Paul traveled alone to Athens and Corinth. But this is a special case as it was a result of a need to escape persecution. Silas and Timothy joined Paul in Corinth as soon as possible (Acts 17:4, 18:5).
67. Acts 13:2, 7
68. Acts 13:43, 46, 50, 14:12, 14, 20, 15:2, 12

records Paul giving a command to team members.[69] But in some senses this was not much of a command as he only told Silas and Timothy to join him as soon as possible. No doubt they were still fully committed to continuing to work with Paul, who had to leave Berea suddenly because the Jews were stirring up the crowds. The phrase "as soon as possible" left Silas and Timothy with the freedom to decide, no doubt guided by the Holy Spirit, when the church in Berea was stable enough to flourish without traveling leaders present.

There are several verses that record Paul sending various team members to various cities and several other verses record Paul urging team members to go to various cities.[70] It is possible to interpret all of these references to Paul sending traveling workers to various cities as indicating that Paul had authority to direct the activities of his co-workers. An alternative interpretation is that the phrase "I sent" indicates that Paul took the initiative in suggesting that these trips be made. The individual concerned, and the team as a whole, were expected to prayerfully consider the appropriateness of the suggestion. This seems to be the best explanation of the use of the singular ("I sent") in 1 Thessalonians 3:5 and the plural ("we sent") in 1 Thessalonians 3:2. This interpretation also fits well with Acts 17:10, 14, which records that the brothers sent Paul away from Thessalonica and Berea to escape the Jews. Given all that we know about Paul, it is implausible to suggest that he would allow the brothers to decide to send him to another city without him having the opportunity to prayerfully consider the decision for himself. These verses also show that sending other believers is not a particular right of an apostle. Any brother can be involved in sending another believer.

The interpretation of the word "sent" as indicating who suggested the trip also seems to be a better fit to the references to Paul urging individuals to make certain trips. If Paul had authority to order his team members to make certain trips there would be no need to urge them—unless their reluctance was due to sin. Given the number of cases where Paul urged his co-workers to make certain trips and the positive references to the co-workers it seems unlikely that he was urging them to overcome sinful reluctance. 2 Corinthians 8:16-17 seems to capture the delicate balance between Paul urging Titus to go to Corinth and Titus having the freedom to decide for himself if he would go. Similarly 1 Corinthians 16:12 records that Paul strong-

69. Acts 17:15

70. Appendix 2.2 provides a more detailed discussion of this topic.

ly urged Apollos to go to Corinth and that Apollos chose not to go. There is no hint in this passage, or anywhere else in Scripture, that this choice was wrong. Obviously Paul was disappointed. However, that is not evidence that Apollos was wrong. In at least one case Paul seems to use the words "sent" and "urged" interchangeably. [71]

In summary, it is not possible to make a definitive Biblical case that leaders of teams of traveling leaders had authority to direct the ministry of their team members. The texts we have discussed permit an interpretation that is fully consistent with broader Scriptural teaching on leadership. It is reasonable to assume that the leadership style within teams of traveling leaders was consistent with these broader teachings. In other words, Paul and other team-leaders led by influence and example, not by command.

Ultimately Paul had no authority to enforce any command he might wish to give to another traveling leader. An example of this is the split between Paul and Barnabas. [72] Neither apostle had the authority to force the other to do it his way. So they split up, with Barnabas forming a team with Mark and Paul forming a team with Silas.

### *Stability of membership of teams of traveling leaders*

It appears that there was a measure of fluidity in the membership of traveling leadership teams. For example 2 Timothy 4:9-12 says:

> Do your best to come to me soon. For Demas, in love with this present world, has deserted me and gone to Thessalonica. Crescens has gone to Galatia, Titus to Dalmatia. Luke alone is with me. Get Mark and bring him with you, for he is very useful to me for ministry. Tychicus I have sent to Ephesus.

It is clear from these verses that several individuals who had been working with Paul were no longer working with him or were working at his request in other cities. It is possible that Crescens and Titus were doing valuable ministry, but that this ministry had matured to the point where it had grown separate from Paul's ministry.

Other potential examples of individuals moving between traveling leadership teams include Silas who was with Paul for the second missionary journey but seems to have worked with Peter later. [73]

---

71. 2 Cor. 9:3, 5
72. Acts 15:36-40
73. Acts 15:40, 16:19, 25, 29, 17:4, 10, 14, 15, 18:5, 1 Pet. 5:12. Silas and Silvanus are generally considered to be the same person.

Mark served with Barnabas, Paul and Peter.[74] Timothy may have served with the author of Hebrews.[75] It also appears that at times Luke ministered with Paul and that at other times he did not.[76]

### *Relationships between teams of traveling leaders*

There is very little specific information in the New Testament about the relationships between teams of traveling leaders. Based on Galatians 2:7-10, it seems that there was a relationship of mutual respect and encouragement, but not of control, between the team centered on Paul reaching out to the Gentiles and the team centered around Peter reaching out to the Jews.

## 3.7 How did traveling leaders work with local churches?

Most new churches mentioned in the New Testament were planted by traveling leaders.[77] These leaders provided continuing support and assistance to the churches they planted, through visits and letters. Paul often arranged for other traveling leaders to visit church assemblies he had planted. No doubt one reason why Paul did this was his busyness, but it is likely that another reason for doing this was to bring each church into relationship with several traveling leaders. The significance of this strategy is discussed in Chapter 5.

In 2 Corinthians 11:22-33 Paul describes the many trials and persecutions he had endured as an apostle. Within this list he includes the daily pressure he felt due to his anxiety for the churches. He implies that this pressure was as much of a burden as the other trials and persecutions. Clearly he cared deeply for the churches.

Based on the analysis of Paul's travels in Section 3.8, it is plausible that Paul typically stayed a few months in each city when he planted a church. Presumably one of his goals was to stay long enough to disciple the new believers so that a healthy church would remain after he left.[78] This was balanced with a desire to move on as soon

---

74. Acts 15:39, 2 Tim. 4:11, Philem. 1:24, 1 Pet. 5:13
75. Heb. 13:23
76. Acts 16:10-16, 20:6-21:17, 27:1-28:16, Col. 4:14, 2 Tim. 4:11, Philem. 1:24
77. Some churches were planted by believers who moved to a different town or by individuals, who came into contact with the Gospel while traveling (Acts 2:5-11, 8:4, 26-39). In at least some cases these churches were supported by traveling leaders (Acts 8:14, 9:32).
78. On several occasions Paul was driven out of cities by persecution (*e.g.*, Acts 13:50, 14:6, 20, 16:40, 17:10, 14, 20:1). It is likely that Timothy and

as possible to spread the gospel to other cities. It is also plausible that Paul was sensitive to the risk of new believers becoming inappropriately dependent on him. Hints of this are contained in 1 Corinthians 1:10-16.

Ephesians 4:11-16 provides an excellent summary of the goals of traveling leaders when visiting churches.

> And he gave the apostles, the prophets, the evangelists, the pastors and teachers, to equip the saints for the work of ministry, for building up the body of Christ, until we all attain to the unity of the faith and of the knowledge of the Son of God, to mature manhood, to the measure of the stature of the fullness of Christ, so that we may no longer be children, tossed to and fro by the waves and carried about by every wind of doctrine, by human cunning, by craftiness in deceitful schemes. Rather, speaking the truth in love, we are to grow up in every way into him who is the head, into Christ, from whom the whole body, joined and held together by every joint with which it is equipped, when each part is working properly, makes the body grow so that it builds itself up in love.

Leaders are responsible to equip believers so that they may enter into their full potential. This passage emphasizes the responsibility of all believers (the saints) to do the work of ministry, which includes equipping one another. This work is not reserved to leaders. This passage also emphasizes the direct connection of believers to Jesus as the head and the primacy of Jesus' headship in causing the body to grow as each part works properly under his direct command.

The following verses state the purposes Paul had in sending various colleagues to visit particular church assemblies:

- Timothy was sent to Corinth "to remind you of my ways in Christ, as I teach them everywhere in every church."[79]
- Tychicus was sent to Ephesus so "that you may know how we are, and that he may encourage your hearts."[80]
- Paul hopes to send Timothy to Philippi soon so "that I too may be cheered by news of you."[81]
- Tychicus was sent to Colosse "for this very purpose, that you may know how we are and that he may encourage your hearts."[82]

---

Silas remained in Berea after Paul was driven out to complete the initial discipling of the new believers (Acts 17:13-15).

79. 1 Cor. 4:17
80. Eph. 6:21-22
81. Phil. 2:19
82. Col. 4:7-9

- Timothy was sent to Thessalonica "to establish and exhort you in your faith, ...when I could bear it no longer, I sent to learn about your faith, for fear that somehow the tempter had tempted you and our labor would be in vain."[83]

### *What roles did traveling leaders play when visiting the church in a city?*

The pastoral epistles were written by Paul to Timothy and Titus while they were serving as traveling leaders. These epistles contain much of the New Testament teaching that is specific to traveling leaders. In these epistles Paul provides clear directions as to the roles he expects traveling leaders to perform when visiting a church. These roles include:

- Example of speech, conduct, love, faith and purity: 1 Timothy 4:12, Titus 2:7.
- Preach/do the work of an evangelist: 2 Timothy 4:2, 5.
- Role in appointment of elders: Titus 1:5.
- Public reading of Scripture: 1 Timothy 4:13. The key verb in this verse is *anagnosei,* which means reading. The Greek does not include the words "public" or "scripture," even though several translations add these words.
- Teaching: 1 Timothy 4:6, 11, 13, 6:2, Titus 2:1.
- Teach teachers: 2 Timothy 2:2.
- Exhortation/Urging: 1 Timothy 4:13, 6:2, 2 Timothy 4:2, Titus 2:15.
- Command/Insist: 1 Timothy 4:11, 5:7, Titus 3:8. From the context of these three verses it appears that they are addressing issues of doctrine and behavior, not ministry. These verses do not provide a mandate for a traveling leader to control the ministry being performed by the believers in the church he is visiting. An exception to this is silencing false teachers.
- Protection of sound doctrine by silencing false teachers: 1 Timothy 1:3-4, Titus 1:10-14.
- Rebuke those who persist in sin: 1 Timothy 5:20, 2 Timothy 4:2, Titus 1:13, Titus 2:15.
- Ensure a good process is followed when there are charges against an elder: 1 Timothy 5:19.
- Have nothing to do with a person who stirs up division: Titus 3:10.
- Titus 1:5 says "This is why I left you in Crete, so that you might put what remained into order." The phrase "put what remained in order" is open to a wide range of interpretations. It is most plausible to

---

83. 1 Thess. 3:2, 5

interpret it as a summary introduction to all of the other directions Paul includes in this epistle. This phrase is not a mandate for traveling leaders to take over the organization of ministry while visiting a church.

Almost all of these roles were open to all believers. So the vast majority of ministry performed by traveling leaders could also be performed by any mature believer. This is the same as the situation with elders who also perform ministry that may be performed by any mature believer.

Paul uses stronger language in his commands to Timothy and Titus concerning the protection of sound doctrine and rebuking those who persist in sin than he uses when discussing these topics with elders and believers who are not traveling leaders. These commands are in the second person singular indicating that they are individual commands to Timothy and Titus, who were traveling leaders. [84] So it is likely that traveling leaders were expected to play a more robust role in these areas than other believers. I believe that one reason why traveling leaders could be more forceful in addressing these areas was that they typically interacted with the local believers as temporary visitors not as permanent members of the community.

### *What relationship was expected between traveling leaders and elders/local believers?*

The same teachings that address how believers relate to one another also apply to the relationships between traveling leaders and local believers including elders. In both of Paul's letters to Timothy he emphasizes the need to treat people well. [85] This is fully consistent with Scriptures such as Ephesians 5:21, which commands mutual submission, and Luke 22:25-26, which commands leaders not to lord it over their followers. As noted above rebukes should only be given in response to established sin or false teaching. See Section 4.3 and Appendix 6 for further discussions of rebuking.

### *What authority did traveling leaders have when they visited local churches?*

Traveling leaders have authority to build up local believers. They are not to use this authority to tear down or destroy. [86] Obviously the

---

84. Appendix 7
85. 1 Tim. 5:1-3, 2 Tim. 2:24-25
86. 2 Cor. 10:8, 13:10

authority to build up believers is not restricted to apostles. Traveling leaders build up believers by encouraging, teaching and when necessary correcting them. Traveling leaders have a very limited ability to force others to follow their direction.[87] As with all believers, their authority flows from who they are in Christ. If they are walking closely with Jesus, this will be obvious to spiritually mature local believers, who will then be open to receiving from them. Spiritually mature local believers will also recognize unhealthy traveling leaders and respond accordingly.

Paul commands Titus to teach, exhort and rebuke with all authority.[88] This command is relevant to all traveling leaders, who should lead with the confidence that as they abide with Jesus, He will give power to their words, just as Jesus gave authority to the twelve disciples to heal and cast out demons.[89] Authority flows out of relationship not titles. Obviously Titus 2:15 should be held in balance with 2 Timothy 2:24-25 that says "And the Lord's servant must not be quarrelsome but kind to everyone, able to teach, patiently enduring evil, correcting his opponents with gentleness. God may perhaps grant them repentance leading to a knowledge of the truth."

## 3.8 How long did traveling leaders stay in one place?

The book of Acts and the epistles make it clear that traveling leaders such as Paul, Timothy and Titus traveled a great deal. The New Testament mentions visits varying in length from a day to three years.[90] Paul focused his two longest stays on two critical cities: Ephesus where he stayed three years and Corinth where he stayed 18 months.[91] It seems that visits to encourage existing churches may often have been very brief.

Paul's first missionary journey may have lasted about two years and involved ministry in at least seven towns, three of which were visited twice during this trip.[92] So the average length of stay in any one town was around three months.

Paul's second missionary journey may have also lasted about two years and included strengthening the churches in Syria and Cilicia

87. Section 5.2, Appendix 2.3
88. Titus 2:15
89. Mark 6:7, Matt. 10:1, Luke 9:1
90. Acts 20:14-17, 31
91. Acts 18:11
92. Acts 13:1 – 14:28

prior to church planting in Philippi, Thessalonica, Berea, Athens and Corinth. [93] If all of this was accomplished in about two years and Paul spent eighteen months in Corinth many of the other visits must have been very brief, perhaps a month or less.

Paul's third missionary journey may have lasted about four years. [94] It included an overland trip from Antioch to Ephesus strengthening the churches on the way. Paul stayed three years in Ephesus. He then traveled through Macedonia and Greece, where he stayed three months before returning to Tyre. [95] On this journey he had various brief stops to encourage churches, two of these lasted a week. [96] Given that the whole trip lasted about four years of which three were spent in Ephesus, and that he traveled more than a thousand miles, much of it overland, most of the other visits must have been about a week or just a little longer. Details of the travels of Timothy and Titus are provided in Appendix 7.

In almost all of the cities they visited it is likely that the traveling leaders interacted with the local believers as temporary visitors not as permanent members of the community. As will be discussed in Chapter 5, I believe that this is a key element of the balance of power within the early church.

---

93. Acts 15:36-18:22
94. Acts 18:23 – 21:16
95. Acts 20:3
96. Acts 20:6, 21:4

# Chapter 4
# Obedience, Submission and Rebuking

## 4.1 Do Christians have to obey their leaders?

The ESV translates Hebrews 13:17 "Obey your leaders and submit to them, for they are keeping watch over your souls, as those who will have to give an account. Let them do this with joy and not with groaning, for that would be of no advantage to you." This translation is representative of most English translations. This verse is the closest the New Testament comes to commanding believers to obey their leaders.

The Greek verb *peitho* is translated "obey" in this verse by most English translations. In this verse the Greek uses the second person plural imperative of the middle voice of this verb. Bagster's lexicon gives the following translations for this word in the passive and middle voices: to be persuaded of, to be confident of, to yield to persuasion, to be induced, to be convinced, to believe, to listen to, to obey, to follow, to be assured, to be confident, to confide in, to trust, to rely on, to place hope and confidence in. This verb occurs in 55 verses in the New Testament. The KJV translates this verb as "persuade" in 22 places, as "trust" in eight places and as "obey" in only seven places. A much stronger Greek verb (*upakouo*) is more commonly used to mean "obey."[1]

Another key Greek word in this verse is the verb *hegeomai*.[2] This verb may be translated "to lead the way" or "to take the lead." The form of the verb in Hebrews 13:17 is a plural present participle so it may be translated "those who are leading." This word describes the individual or individuals who are leading in a particular situation. This is broader than local and traveling leaders and may include any believer, who is providing leadership in response to the leadership of

1. *E.g.*, Mark 1:27, 4:41, Eph. 6:1, 5, Col. 3:20, 22
2. Subsection 2.1.5

the Holy Spirit. Is it possible that the author of Hebrews deliberately chose to use a verb to identify those leading (as opposed to a noun) to emphasize that this verse is not a blanket release of authority to recognized local or traveling leaders? Instead, this verse reinforces the authority of an individual (not necessarily a formal leader) who has been prompted by the Spirit to provide leadership in a particular context.

The first portion of Hebrews 13:17 may be translated "Be persuaded by those who are leading and submit to them" or "Listen to those who are leading and submit to them." Both of these translations fit the context of Hebrews 13:17 and as will be seen in the following paragraphs are a much better fit with other New Testament teachings on the relationship between individual believers and their leaders. On this basis I conclude that these translations are more likely to reflect the intent of the author of Hebrews than the traditional translation.

Several passages, including Luke 22:25-27, command all Christian leaders not to lord it over other believers. [3] The same Greek word (*hegeomai*) is used for those providing leadership both in Hebrews 13:17 and in Luke 22:26. This is one of the less common New Testament words for leaders. Did God guide both Luke and the author of Hebrews to use this less common word in these verses to emphasize that Hebrews 13:17 should be understood in the context of Luke 22:26?

Servanthood is a key dimension of spiritual leadership. [4] Clearly part of this servanthood includes looking to Jesus as master. These passages also teach that Christian leaders are expected to have the attitude of servanthood towards other believers. Servants do not tell those whom they are serving what to do.

In Ephesians 5:21 Paul commands all believers to submit to one another, which in turn requires leaders to submit to non-leaders. So it can be seen that there are several passages which unambiguously teach that Christian leadership does not include taking broad authority over another person's life. Our understanding of Hebrews 13:17 needs to be consistent with these scriptures. This is why I conclude that "Be persuaded by those who are leading and submit to them" is a much more plausible translation of this verse than "Obey your leaders and submit to them."

---

3. Matt. 20:25-28, Mark 10:42-45, Luke 22:25-27, 1 Peter 5:3
4. Matt. 20:25-28, 23:11, Mark 10:42-45, Luke 22:25-27. See also Appendix 3.7.

What does it mean to be persuaded by those who are leading? Implicit in the use of this word is that the one who is leading is expected to give good reasons for his position. He is not to give orders with no explanation. The listener is expected to consider carefully the leader's perspective with an expectation that he will find it to be compelling. The process of persuasion often includes dialog. The one being led is free to ask questions and respectfully challenge the one leading. The individual leading has a duty to take these questions and challenges seriously. This is part of moving in mutual submission. The one leading may end up changing his direction as a result of this dialog. In the majority of cases being persuaded by the individual leading will result in following his lead after any appropriate dialog and fine tuning of the direction.

It may be helpful to paraphrase Hebrews 13:17 to say, "Expect to be persuaded by those who are leading and submit to them." This wording emphasizes that the believer should enter the dialog with whoever is leading expecting that the one leading has good reasons for his perspective and that the believer will end up being persuaded. A further benefit of this paraphrase is that it is consistent with the reality that no human leader is always right. Occasionally the believer will not be persuaded by the one leading and it will be appropriate to respectfully disagree. [5]

Regardless of the appropriate translation of the first part of Hebrews 13:17, this verse begs a key question: in what areas did an individual providing leadership have authority to seek to persuade or to expect obedience? The author of Hebrews and the first readers of Hebrews would have had an understanding of the realm of authority of leaders in the New Testament church. They would have all interpreted this command as being limited to that sphere of authority. This text gives no insight as to the extent of that sphere of authority. To discover this sphere of authority we need to look at many other passages in the New Testament. As discussed in Chapter 1, especially Subsection 1.1.3, in the New Testament church individual believers were free to minister as led by Jesus. It is reasonable to assume that the author of Hebrews and the original readers of Hebrews took this for granted. It is very unlikely Christians in the New Testament period would have

---

5. Timothy Willis provides a more detailed discussion of the appropriate translation of *peitho* in his paper "Obey your leaders: Hebrews 13 and leadership in the church," *Restoration Quarterly,* 36, no. 4, 1994, pp. 316–326.

interpreted Hebrews 13:17 as supporting elder control of meetings and ministry.

The New Testament makes it clear that elders have authority to teach. [6] The content of Jesus' teaching and of the epistles show that the teaching of doctrine, the teaching of how to minister and the teaching of appropriate behavior are all important parts of Christian teaching. The first part of Hebrews 13:17 applies to these three categories of teaching. Individual believers have a great deal of freedom to find the specific ways Jesus wants them to live and minister within the broad context of these teachings.

In some places the New Testament records that Paul sent individuals to particular towns. At first glance these passages may look like examples of individuals being expected to obey Paul concerning where they should minister. However, there are other passages which indicate that Paul did not have the authority to direct the travel of his coworkers. [7]

1 Timothy 5:17 refers to elders "who rule well" (KJV, ESV) or "who direct the affairs of the church well" (NIV). This verse is discussed in Subsection 2.1.6, which concludes that these translations imply a style of leadership that is not demanded by the Greek. The Greek refers to elders "who lead well." The Greek does not indicate the nature of this leadership.

Matthew 23:8-11 teaches that Christian leadership is not about individuals having special titles with associated special rights. [8] We are all brothers and sisters and it is not appropriate to demand obedience from a sibling. We should all be in direct relationship with God who wants to teach and lead us. Believers have only one teacher and leader: Jesus. He is the only individual we should always obey. To give the honor of total obedience to any other human is idolatry. [9] Interpreting Hebrews 13:17 as giving broad authority to leaders to direct the lives of other believers is an abuser's charter.

Subsection 1.1.4 and Appendix 1.6 make the case that church discipline and the final stage of conflict resolution between believers are a matter for the full congregation. These teachings imply a limit

---

6. Titus 1:9
7. Section 3.6, Appendix 2.2
8. Section 1.4
9. Idolatry is giving a piece of the created order (in this case the other person) honor which is due only to God.

to the range of any appropriate obedience to an elder. If someone disagrees with direction given by an elder and the elder insists on obedience, he or she can bring the matter up with the full congregation. This moves the focus from obeying the elder to submitting to the full congregation.

There is a seed of pride contained within the assumption by a leader that he has the right to expect obedience from the people he leads. Once this seed has been embraced it can be hard for humans to prevent its growth. In some cases this seed grows into a level of pride and hypocrisy similar to that addressed by Jesus in Matthew 23:2-7, 13-33. Unfortunately in some Christian communities, both the leader and the individuals being led believe that this is godly leadership.

Having said all of this, it is important to remember that elders are expected to provide significant leadership working by influence and example rather than controlling meetings and ministry. Working by persuasion and influence it is both possible and appropriate for Christian leaders to greatly help other believers to grow spiritually and to become more effective in ministry.

## 4.2 Submission to Christian leaders

Biblical teaching concerning submission is a huge topic. It is a component of our relationship to God, to civil authorities, to our bosses, which in New Testament times often meant a slave master, to Christian leaders, to our parents, to other believers and of wives to their husbands. Appendix 5 provides a brief introduction to this topic addressing all of these dimensions. In this section I will summarize the conclusions of this appendix as they apply to the relationship between believers and leaders.

The primary Greek word which is translated "submit" (*hupotasso*), may also be translated "to bring under influence" or "to yield to one's admonition or advice." [10] When believers submit to their leaders they are choosing to place themselves within the circle of influence of the leaders. This is completely consistent with the conclusion reached in other sections of this book that New Testament leadership is about leading by influencing not by commanding.

There is a great deal of overlap between the command in Hebrews 13:17 to "be persuaded by those who are leading" and the command in

---

10. Appendix 5.1.1

the same verse to "submit to those who are leading." As discussed in the previous section, the dynamics of being persuaded by those who are leading may include extensive dialog. It is healthy for believers to submit ideas to their leaders and to ask them questions. If the leader is in a healthy place he will welcome such dialog and in many cases this dialog will result in them reaching agreement. Sometimes this process will result in the leader changing his mind. In general the outcome of this process is for the one being led to follow the leader.

Given the clear teaching in the New Testament that each believer is expected to follow Jesus' personal lead in specific ministry matters, it is unlikely that the command for believers to submit to leaders is giving leaders the right to direct their ministry. To be consistent with the rest of the New Testament it seems likely that submission to leaders primarily applies to doctrine and general ethical teaching. Obviously if a discussion of a specific ministry matter comes up the believer should have a gracious and submissive attitude towards the leader. However the believer has freedom in this area to respectfully differ with the leader. Leaders must never forget that the command for mutual submission between all believers means that leaders need to submit to all believers including those who are not elders or traveling leaders. [11] The whole community must work to create and maintain an environment of mutual trust and respect. Healthy submission is an expression of strength not weakness.

1 Corinthians 7:1-5 teaches that consensual decision-making has a place within marriage, which is a relationship where the Bible commands submission. This particular passage addresses decisions between a husband and wife concerning sexual relations, but it is reasonable to assume that consensual decision-making also has a place in other relationships where the Bible commands submission. In particular it is reasonable to assume that consensual decision-making has a place in the relationship between Christian leaders and individual believers.

As noted in Appendix 5, research into the use of the Greek word "to submit" (*hupotasso*) in papyri from the New Testament period indicates that it can also mean "to support." This meaning is a dimension of healthy submission between believers. Believers should support their leaders, and leaders, as part of the mutual submission

---

11. Eph. 5:21

commanded in Ephesians 5:21, should support other believers including those who are not elders or traveling leaders.

Appropriate submission to leaders who are not in a healthy place requires a great deal of wisdom. 1 Timothy 5:19-20 shows that it can be appropriate for an individual who is not a leader to challenge an elder about sin in his life. The command to submit to elders is consistent with being free to challenge an elder about sin in his life.

Paul says in Galatians 2:5 that he chose not to submit to false brothers. It is reasonable to assume that some believers considered these false brothers to be leaders.[12] So, just as Peter teaches in Acts 4:19, 5:29 that we must obey God rather than men, Paul is providing an example of not submitting to Christian leaders when they are in doctrinal error.

Paul and Barnabas sometimes left the city where they were ministering to avoid persecution.[13] However both Jesus and Paul both went to Jerusalem knowing they would be arrested. These incidents demonstrate that godly submission to civil authorities sometimes includes getting a safe distance away from them. This principle is directly applicable to other relationships of submission, including the relationship between leaders and believers. If a leader is behaving abusively or teaching false doctrine, godly submission may involve leaving or it may involve staying. Just as with decisions concerning abusive civil authorities, case-by-case wisdom and guidance is needed concerning leaving or staying in a church with unhealthy leaders.

## 4.3 Rebuking

The two Greek words most commonly used in the New Testament for rebuking are *elegcho* and *epitimao*.[14] As with many key words in the New Testament, both of these words support a range of meanings. It appears that in general *epitimao* describes a more severe rebuke than *elegcho*.

In the New Testament *elegcho* is almost always associated with sin and is occasionally associated with false doctrine or convincing individuals of the truth about Jesus. We should seek to correct others

---

12. Gal. 1:6-9
13. *E.g.*, Acts 13:50-51, 14:5-6
14. See Appendix 6 for additional discussion of New Testament teaching related to rebuking.

gently first and only consider the possibility of a rebuke if gentle correction is rejected.[15] Everything we say should be to build others up and to benefit the listener.[16] We should never rebuke someone to get our own back or as an outflow of our anger towards them.

Most Biblical teaching on how to bring correction to another believer applies equally to all believers. There is only one verse in the New Testament, Titus 1:9, which directly links rebuking to elders.[17] The focus in this verse is on responding to false teaching. It is almost certain that individuals who are not elders may also be involved in responding to false teaching.[18]

It appears from the context of the passage and the New Testament as a whole that a relatively soft translation is appropriate in Titus 1:9.[19] Thus NRSV, NASV and NIV are most likely appropriately translating *elegcho* as "refute" in this verse. Similarly RSV and NEB with "confute" and KJV with "convince" may be appropriate. The implication of "refute," "confute" and "convince" is that the elder is focused on the content of the incorrect teaching. ESV with "rebuke those who contradict it" may be unduly strong. This translation implies the elder is addressing the teacher rather than the teaching. The softer translations seem to me to be more consistent with the style of leadership that the New Testament expects from elders (and individuals who are not elders). In the event that a false teacher rejects correction the elder is free to bring the matter to the full congregation as a matter of church discipline. There is no Biblical basis for suggesting that elders should rebuke differently from individual believers.

In four passages *elegcho* is associated with traveling leaders.[20] In all of these verses the verb form is second person singular. This shows that these commands are a specific word to Timothy and Titus

---

15. Gal. 6:1
16. Eph. 4:29
17. This verse uses *elegcho*. The New Testament never mentions *epitimao* rebukes in the context of elders.
18. Appendix 1.21
19. *Elegcho* may be translated: Put to proof, test, convict, refute, detect, lay bare, expose, reprove, rebuke, discipline, chastise. There is a huge difference between detecting and laying bare a false teacher/teaching and rebuking, disciplining or chastising the false teacher.
20. 1 Tim. 5:20, 2 Tim. 4:2, Titus 1:13, 2:15. In 2 Tim. 4:2 Paul commands Timothy to *epitimao* and to *elegcho*.

both of whom were traveling leaders at the time they received these letters. [21] Both 1 Timothy 5:20, "as for those who persist in sin, rebuke them in the presence of all, so that the rest may stand in fear," and Titus 1:13, "rebuke them sharply," are describing strong rebukes, which are focused on the person as well as their sin. So there are some circumstances where it is appropriate for traveling leaders to issue strong rebukes. This is consistent with 1 Corinthians 4:14-21, which discusses Paul's authority related to the Corinthian church. [22] This appears to be in contrast to the appropriate level of rebuke to be given by an elder or by an individual who is not a leader. Some pastors and priests take these Scriptures, which apply to traveling leaders and assume that they as local leaders have the same authority to rebuke. There is no Biblical support for this assumption. In general, I think that a visitor may speak a harder word than a local person, because it is easier to reject a word from a visitor if it is inappropriate.

The majority of uses of *epitimao* are associated with Jesus. Obviously all Jesus' rebukes/commands were appropriate. Most of the other *epitimao* rebukes/commands recorded in the Gospels are inappropriate. [23] There is only one appropriate *epitimao* rebuke given by an individual other than Jesus recorded in the New Testament. [24] This is a reminder of the need for wisdom in deciding if it is appropriate to rebuke someone.

In Luke 17:3 Jesus commands believers to both rebuke (*epitimao*) and forgive the brother who sins against us. The next verse implies that this command is particularly relevant in cases of repeated sin where the individual knows that they are sinning.

In 2 Timothy 4:2 Paul uses *epitimao* in the second person singular. So this verse is a command to Timothy as an individual not a broad command to the church as a whole to *epitimao*. To be consistent with Luke 17:3, 1 Timothy 5:20 and other relevant Scriptures, it is likely that this verse applies to situations of repeated sin or teaching of false doctrine. A potential difference between 2 Timothy 4:2 and Luke 17:3 is that Luke 17:3 only gives the individual who is sinned

---

21. Appendix 7
22. Appendix 2.3
23. Matt. 19:13, 20:31, Mark 10:13, 48, Luke 18:15, 39
24. Luke 23:40 where the "good" criminal rebukes the "bad" criminal for being disrespectful to Jesus, while all three were being crucified.

against permission to rebuke the person committing the offense. Luke 17:3 does not tell individuals to take up the offense of others. Paul commands Timothy, as a traveling leader, to rebuke (with patience and teaching) as part of his broader ministry to the church assembly he is visiting. This may include situations where the sin was not directed towards Timothy.

With the exception of rebukes related to the teaching of false doctrine, there is no hint in Scripture that leaders may rebuke individuals over ministry matters. Leaders do not control ministry. An example of the inappropriateness of rebuking individuals with different ministry priorities is the situation where parents were bringing their children to Jesus. [25] The disciples rebuked the parents for bringing their children to Jesus for prayer. Presumably they thought Jesus had more important things to do with His time. Jesus did not agree with the disciples, He wanted to spend time blessing the children.

---

25. Matt. 19:13, Mark 10:13, Luke 18:1

# Chapter 5
# Balanced Power in The New Testament Church

Power and influence may be used both for good and for bad. The intended good uses of power and influence by elders and traveling leaders are discussed in Sections 2.5, 3.5 and 3.7. The focus of this chapter is the approach taken by the New Testament church to protect against bad uses of power. Some of the trickiest issues associated with the use of power within the church relate to dealing with sin and doctrinal error. So this chapter discusses the approach taken by the New Testament church to address sin and doctrinal error.

There were three possible centers of power in the New Testament church: believers acting jointly as a local church assembly; elders; and traveling leaders. The New Testament is clear that all three of these possible centers of power are vulnerable to sin and doctrinal error.[1] So a balance of power is required to handle the variety of potential problems that might occur. The first section of this chapter addresses the balance of power within a local church *i.e.*, the balance between elders and the believers who are not elders. The following section addresses the balance of power between local churches and traveling leaders.

## 5.1 How is power balanced in a local church?

### *Leadership of Holy Spirit*

A goal of the New Testament church is to let God be the one who sets the direction. The approach taken by the New Testament church to achieve this goal was to allow God's leadership to flow through a wide range of individuals who speak or act in response to

1. Churches: Gal. 1:6, 2 Tim. 4:2-4, Rev. 2, 3; elders: Acts 20:30, 1 Tim. 5:19-20, 3 John 1:9-10; apostles: Gal. 2:11-14, 2 Cor. 11:3-5, 13, Rev. 2:2. The problem may be a brief lapse, such as Peter ceasing to eat with Gentiles, or it may be a longer term issue, such as the ongoing efforts of the circumcision party.

His prompting. For example in meetings of New Testament churches every member is expected to contribute to the flow of each meeting as led by the Holy Spirit. The meetings, and ministry outside of meetings, are not organized and controlled by a single leader or a small group of leaders.

The role of elders includes helping each believer remain close to God so that each believer is well positioned to receive direction from God. This focus for the leadership provided by elders encourages humility, and mutual submission. It discourages dominance by a single person and thus discourages the abuse of power. This model also provides an open door for individuals led by the Holy Spirit to correct someone who is using power inappropriately.

### *Every believer involved in church discipline process*

Decisions related to church discipline are made by all of the believers in the local assembly.[2] Neither individual leaders nor groups of elders are free to punish believers without the involvement of the full congregation. This provides a measure of protection to the church assembly from a dominant individual riding roughshod over the rest of the congregation. It is harder for a dominant individual to control the whole church, than to control a small group. Obviously, if a significant portion of the congregation is inappropriately influenced by a particular individual, it may be possible for him to dominate the church.

Having the full church assembly involved in the discipline process makes it more likely that all relevant facts and viewpoints will surface. Matthew 18:17 implies that the full congregation acts both as judge and jury in the final stage of the conflict resolution process described in that passage. There is of course the risk that the congregation will make poor decisions, especially if they are not walking closely with Jesus. Elders need to provide leadership during the discipline process to help everyone to keep close to Jesus. 2 Corinthians 10:6 implies that it is only appropriate to undertake church discipline when the bulk of the congregation is walking in obedience to Jesus.

### *Every believer involved in testing revelatory words*

Revelatory words (*e.g.*, prophetic words, visions) were sometimes used in the New Testament to set ministry direction.[3] The New Testament practice was for the whole church assembly to test poten-

---

2. Subsection 1.1.4
3. Section 6.3

tial revelatory words that apply to the whole church.[4] This protects against inappropriate control by those with prophetic gifts.

### *Multiple co-equal local leaders*

It is likely that most local churches had a team of co-equal leaders.[5] Co-equal elders act as a check and balance to each other as they move in mutual submission to each other and to the rest of the congregation. This protects the church in several ways.

Firstly, an individual who is part of a co-equal leadership team is at less risk of becoming proud or controlling than an individual leader. Secondly, it is less likely that a complete group of elders will enter into sin or doctrinal error at the same time than that a single leader will enter into sin or doctrinal error. Thirdly, if there is a team of elders and only one is in sin or doctrinal error, it is easier for appropriate individuals to work to restore that elder.

### *Role of elders in helping the local assembly and its members remain in a healthy place*

Elders have a key role in maintaining a healthy balance of power within a local church assembly. They are responsible to watch over believers and watch over the dynamics of church life.[6] They encourage quieter members to participate and protect meetings from being dominated by more talkative individuals. They use their influence to help ensure that decisions are made by consensus in a healthy manner. Another primary responsibility of elders is to help each believer maintain their focus on Jesus. This positions the believers to make good decisions. Elders are responsible to teach sound doctrine and refute those teaching error.[7] This includes providing moral teaching. Individuals who are not elders are free to contribute in these areas alongside the elders.

## 5.2 How is power balanced between a local church and traveling leaders?

### *Local churches were in relationship with several traveling leaders*

Several of the local Christian assemblies, which are mentioned in the New Testament, were in relationship with multiple traveling

4. Subsection 1.1.5
5. Section 2.6
6. Heb. 13:17
7. Titus 1:9

leaders.[8] There are many references to Paul asking other traveling leaders to visit churches he had planted to help build them up and/or to address specific problems. There are also passages that indicate that traveling leaders operating independently of Paul visited churches he planted. Similarly, John in 3 John 1:5-8 commends Gaius for his hospitality to visiting brothers who are strangers to him. Verse 7 states that these individuals travel "for the sake of the Name." The implication is that they are traveling leaders.

False apostles and teachers troubled some of the churches that were planted by Paul.[9] Paul's response is to teach these churches how to discern the false teacher. He does not instruct them to only relate to him and his teammates. He appears to want them to be open to relationship with all good traveling leaders.

At different times churches have different needs. These highly diverse needs are much more likely to be effectively met if each church is in relationship with multiple traveling leaders.

### *Relating to several traveling leaders protects local churches when a traveling leader is in sin or doctrinal error*

Relating to several traveling leaders helps each local church assembly to develop an understanding of the nature of healthy traveling leadership. This makes it easier for a local church to notice when a traveling leader becomes compromised doctrinally or morally or becomes inappropriately controlling. Also, if the failure in the traveling leader is such that the local church needs to reject the ministry of that traveling leader, either for a season or permanently, they still have other traveling leaders to whom they can turn. They do not need to fear isolation or a total loss of support from traveling leadership if they distance themselves from a compromised traveling leader.

Part of the New Testament balance of power to protect churches from compromised apostles is the pattern of apostles and other traveling leaders not staying a long time in any one place.[10] This reduced the risk of personality cults and sycophantism.[11] Local

8. Appendix 2.2, 4.1.3. For example, traveling leaders with a relationship to the church assembly in Corinth include: Paul; Apollos (1 Cor. 1:12, 3:6); Timothy (Acts 18:5, 1 Cor. 4:17, 2 Cor. 1:19); Titus (2 Cor. 8:16-17, 12:17-18); Silas/Silvanus (Acts 18:5, 2 Cor. 1:19).
9. 2 Cor. 11:3-4, 13, Gal. 1:7, 9
10. Section 3.8
11. 1 Cor. 1:12

assemblies need to test individuals who claim to be apostles and reject those who are not godly. [12]

A further benefit with this model is that a traveling leader, who ministers in local churches as one of several traveling leaders connected to each church he visits, is at less risk of becoming proud or controlling than a traveling leader who is the only traveling leader in relationship with a particular group of local churches.

### *Benefit to local church of relating to several traveling leaders when the local church is in sin or doctrinal error*

The personality type and gifting of the traveling leader best suited to help depends on the issue troubling the local church. So being in relationship with multiple traveling leaders makes it more likely that one will be available with the appropriate gifting and personality to address the issue. In some cases, a church may be more willing to accept that it is in the wrong if multiple traveling leaders all give the same rebuke.

### *Correction provided by traveling leaders to churches in sin or doctrinal error*

Part of the role of traveling leaders was to bring correction to local churches with problems. [13] For example, Timothy was asked by Paul to remain in Ephesus to deal with teachers teaching false doctrine. [14] Paul expected Timothy to rebuke individuals who continued in sin. [15] Similarly, Paul commands Titus to protect sound doctrine by silencing false teachers and to rebuke those who persist in sin. [16] Paul brought correction to churches with doctrinal and moral problems through his letters. Paul also uses letters to call churches back to the pattern or style of church life that he had taught them. [17]

### *Approach used by traveling leaders to bring correction to a local church in sin or doctrinal error*

In most circumstances the best way for a traveling leader to bring correction to a local church is to work with whatever portion of the church is still walking with God, seeking to draw the rest of the church

---

12. Rev. 2:2, Acts 17:11, 1 Thess. 1:5
13. Section 3.7
14. 1 Tim. 1:3
15. 1 Tim. 5:20, 2 Tim. 4:2
16. Titus 1:11, 13, 2:15
17. 1 Cor. 4:16-17, 11:1-2, 16, Phil. 4:9, 2 Thess. 2:15

back to this good place. He can use existing relationships from prior visits to reach out to those who are in sin or doctrinal error. The primary approach available to the traveling leader is to use influence. As commanded in Galatians 6:1 initial attempts to address sin and error should be undertaken gently.

When gentle attempts at correction are ignored, it may be appropriate for traveling leaders to rebuke those in sin or teaching error. The commands to Timothy and Titus to do this appear to call for a more forceful level of rebuke than elders are taught to provide. [18] It may also be appropriate to use the church discipline process in concert with the rest of the church. Rebuking is only appropriate to address sin and doctrinal error. Rebukes are not appropriate in situations where a leader does not like the ministry being performed by another believer. Leaders may of course seek to influence other believers to improve the quality of their ministry. This may include giving advice, making recommendations and providing teaching.

This approach to bringing correction does not succeed in all cases. Some individuals become hardened in their sin and ignore rebukes. In these cases it may be appropriate to initiate the church discipline process. As discussed in Subsection 1.1.4, the church discipline process involves the whole congregation and exclusion is the only form of church discipline mentioned in the New Testament. 2 Corinthians 10:6 says "being ready to punish every disobedience, when your obedience is complete." My interpretation of this verse is that the church discipline process should only be initiated when the bulk of the congregation is walking in obedience to Jesus.

Apostles and other traveling leaders may participate in the church discipline process for a church they are visiting. [19] It also seems that in circumstances where a traveling leader has a strong link with a church he can participate in the church discipline process by letter. [20] The exact nature of Paul's role in this case is not explicit. Paul may be saying that he is still spiritually connected to the church and through that connection he is casting an absentee vote for the punishment.

---

18. These commands (1 Tim. 1:3, 1 Tim. 5:20, 2 Tim. 4:2, Titus 1:11, 13, 2:15) are in the second person singular which indicates that they apply to Timothy and Titus as individuals and that they are not broader commands to the whole church. They were both traveling leaders at the time that they received their letters (Appendix 7). See Section 4.3 and Appendix 6 for a more detailed discussion on New Testament teaching related to rebuking.
19. 1 Tim. 5:19
20. 1 Cor. 5:2-5

Obviously as the founding apostle of the church in Corinth his lead would be highly influential on other church members and it seems to me that he intends this.

It is clear from the New Testament that there is a tension within Paul concerning the best way to bring correction to churches he has founded. Paul prefers to work by influence and persuasion with gentleness. He often beseeches when he might command and his pattern was to warn with tears. [21] He chooses "not to lord it over" the Corinthians and he chooses to avoid "another painful visit." [22] Paul claims spiritual authority to build up the Corinthians, not to destroy them, and he does not want to frighten them. [23] In contrast to this, in 1 Corinthians 4:21 he mentions the possibility of coming to them with a "rod" (KJV, ESV) or a "whip" (NIV). As discussed in Appendix 2.3, it is extremely unlikely that the "rod" or "whip" is describing some kind of human authority structure by which Paul could force the Corinthians to do things his way. It is likely that it refers to a supernatural power demonstration authenticating a rebuke and call to repentance. Even with the mention of the "rod" or "whip" the primary tone of this passage is one of beseeching the Corinthians to change. [24]

Zechariah 4:6 says "Not by might, nor by power, but by my Spirit says the Lord." This spiritual principle is a good summary of the approach New Testament traveling leaders are expected to use in seeking to bring correction to local congregations. In particular we have seen in the preceding discussion that New Testament traveling leaders primarily worked by influence and persuasion. They may also rebuke individuals and they may initiate the church discipline process. In some cases God may choose to validate the authority of the traveling leader with some kind of supernatural power demonstration. In some cases, even after a power demonstration, hardened individuals will ignore rebukes and will have sufficient congregational support to make the church discipline process ineffective. The New Testament strategy in these circumstances is to leave these congregations to Jesus. [25]

Jesus often works through human leaders to call individuals and churches to repentance. These human leaders are only responsible

21. Acts 20:31, 1 Cor. 1:10, Philem. 1:8, 9
22. 2 Cor. 1:24, 2:1
23. 2 Cor. 10:8-9
24. 1 Cor. 4:14-21
25. Rev. 2:16, 3:3, 16

to give the message that has been entrusted to them. [26] They are not responsible to enforce a particular outcome. Jesus is the head of the church and He is responsible for the health of churches. It is His responsibility to deal with sin and doctrinal error. He will discipline each church as He sees fit. Jesus taught in the parable of the tares that He will not remove all of the "tares" from His church until the final judgment. [27] He does this to maximize the growth of the good fruit in His church. He is often willing to let His discipline play out over longer time scales than we might choose. For example, churches that reject critical doctrine may gradually die over a period of decades.

### 5.3 Summary

The New Testament acknowledges that any leader or group of believers can become compromised morally or doctrinally. The New Testament leadership model to protect the church from this risk contains the following key elements:

- Commitment to leadership based on mutual submission rather than leaders "lording it over" non-leaders. Another way of expressing this is: leadership based on the principle of doing unto others as you would have done unto you.
- Leaders understand that they are the servants/slaves both of Jesus and of the believing community. Leaders are expected to move in gentleness and humility.
- Decisions concerning church discipline and the testing of revelatory words relevant to the whole church assembly are made consensually by the full congregation. This approach provides substantial protection from abuse of power by any member of the church.
- Typically each church has a team of co-equal elders. Sharing leadership within a team of co-equal elders helps each elder remain humble and in an attitude of mutual submission. Also if an elder does fall into sin or doctrinal error, the other elders are available to help handle the situation appropriately.
- Elders do not have decision-making authority and power over the members of the congregation they serve. They mainly work by influence seeking to help each believer to walk closely with Jesus.
- It is helpful for each church to be connected to multiple traveling leaders. This provides two-way protection. If the local church slips into doctrinal error or sin, a group of traveling leaders is available to help restore them. If a local church is in relationship with several

---

26. Ezek. 3:16-21
27. Matt. 13:24-30, 36-43, Section 1.4

traveling leaders, it is easier for the church to notice when one of these leaders becomes compromised. Also, it is much easier to disconnect from a compromised leader if an assembly has continuing relationships with several good leaders.

- In general traveling leaders have no decision-making authority and power over the congregations they serve. They are expected to teach and if necessary correct with gentleness and humility. They mainly work by influence. They may participate in the church discipline process and they may rebuke individuals as appropriate. In some cases God may choose to provide a power demonstration to underline His opinion concerning a conflict.
- Jesus is the head of the church and He is responsible for the health of churches. It is His responsibility to deal with sin and doctrinal error. He will discipline each church as He sees fit. Jesus is often willing to let His discipline play out over longer time scales than we would choose.

There was plenty of sin and doctrinal error in the New Testament church just as there is today. The early church could have chosen to concentrate hierarchical power in elders and traveling leaders to protect the body from this sin and doctrinal error. It is likely that many believers would have welcomed this approach just like the Israelites wanting a king. It is significant that the early church did not choose this route. The early church intentionally chose to limit the power given to leaders.

# Chapter 6
# Other New Testament Church Practices

## 6.1 Teaching

Teaching is mentioned many times in New Testament and it is clear that teaching was highly valued. [1] However, very little information is provided describing how it was done in New Testament churches. All believers were encouraged to teach one another, however, it is possible that the bulk of teaching was done by individuals with the gift of teaching. [2] Elders were expected to be able to teach and to be able to protect sound doctrine. [3]

Teaching was a regular part of New Testament house church assembly meetings. [4] In addition to this, teaching also took place one-on-one or in small groups in homes. [5] In Jerusalem and in Ephesus a traveling leader taught in larger meetings. [6] Acts 15:35 shows that teaching was not restricted to apostles even when they were in town.

Given that the essence of New Testament church meetings was every member participation, it is highly plausible that teaching involved interaction. This format provides opportunity for questions, which helps ensure the relevance and clarity of teaching. This format also provides opportunity for several individuals to contribute their understanding of a topic rather than restricting the teaching to the insights of a single individual. This is good because some individuals find one person's teaching style helpful and other individuals are best helped by someone else's teaching style.

---

1. Appendix 1.1, 4.5
2. 1 Cor. 12:28, 29, Eph. 4:11
3. 1 Tim. 3:2, 5:17, Titus 1:9
4. 1 Cor. 14:26
5. *E.g.*, Aquila and Priscilla teaching Apollos (Acts 18:24-26).
6. Acts 5:42, 19:9, 20:20. It is possible that the primary focus of the meetings in the hall of Tyrannus was evangelistic.

Another benefit of encouraging wide participation in teaching is that many of us learn best when we attempt to teach others. When we listen to others teach it is easy to avoid thinking deeply about what they say. Also it is very common for much of what they say to end up only in our short-term memory. Attempting to teach should challenge us to think deeply about the topic and it is more likely that some of the material will reach our long-term memory. Attempting to teach others is one of the best ways to learn. Not only do we learn from the preparation, we also learn from questions and comments resulting from our teaching.

The main example of teaching we have in the New Testament is Jesus. A key feature of His teaching technique was the use of parables. These brief stories capture an important spiritual truth and are easy to remember. He engaged in dialog with his disciples in response to questions they asked and things that happened as they traveled together. He also asked questions as part of his teaching technique. He emphasized learning-by-observation (following His example) followed by learning-by-doing as He mentored and coached the 12 disciples. [7] Another key feature of Jesus' teaching style is His humility. [8] It is likely that teachers in the New Testament church embraced Jesus' example as a teacher.

In Jesus' personal teaching as recorded in the Gospels and in His complete word, the Bible, we are not given a book of systematic theology. Also we are given very few teachings that take more than a few minutes to read. Spiritual truth is commonly presented in small snippets using a wide variety of formats including history, laws, genealogies, parables, miracles, speeches, letters and poetry. Biblical poetry includes psalms, proverbs, prophecy and other wisdom literature. It is reasonable to assume that teaching within New Testament churches was as varied in style as the Bible. It is implausible that New Testament church meetings contained anything resembling a modern-day sermon. [9] Recent research into the most effective ways to teach adults has shown that extended monologues

---

7. Section 3.4
8. Matt. 11:29
9. See Chapter 2 of *Pagan Christianity* by Frank Viola for a detailed discussion of the origin of sermons. See also *To Preach Or Not To Preach* by David Norrington, who concludes that sermons became widespread in the 3rd Century and became a standard element of services in the 4th Century (pg. 177 of Ekklesia Press edition).

similar to a sermon are relatively ineffective. The methods used by some corporations to train and teach their employees are substantially identical to the methods Jesus used to train and teach His disciples during his public ministry.

In 1 Corinthians 4:16-17, 11:1-2 and Philippians 4:9 Paul emphasizes the importance of following his example as one way of learning from him. In this manner we can learn good priorities for our lives, appropriate ways to treat other people and how to do ministry. For example, Paul says that he worked making tents to teach, by example, the importance of working to support oneself and to provide money to help those in need. [10]

In 1 Timothy 5:17 Paul mentions giving double honor to elders "who labor in the word" (KJV). This indicates the value Paul placed on careful preparation before teaching. Some modern translations (*e.g.*, NIV, ESV) use the word "preach" to translate this phrase. This is an unfortunate translation as it may lead readers to think that the sermon format was used in New Testament house churches.

In Acts 20:7-9 Luke twice uses the Greek word *dialegomenous* to describe Paul's teaching. This word may be translated as discourse, argue, reason, address, speak to, contend, dispute. In the New Testament this word is often used to describe evangelism. [11] This word was also used of arguments, [12] and in Hebrews 12:5 of Scriptural teaching. The use of this word in Acts 20:7-9 is consistent with teaching in New Testament house churches including extensive dialog. [13]

In John 6:45 Jesus says "It is written in the Prophets: 'They will all be taught by God'" (NIV). It is possible that Jesus had Isaiah 54:13 and Jeremiah 31:33-34 in mind when he said this. He may also have been considering various other verses, which refer prophetically to

---

10. Acts 20:33-35, 2 Thess. 3:8-9
11. Acts 17:2, 17, 18:4, 19, 19:8-9, 24:25
12. Mark 9:34, Acts 24:12, Jude 1:9
13. This is the incident where Eutychus fell to sleep as he listened to Paul and then fell out of a window and died. The passage emphasizes that Paul was the predominant speaker. This does not necessarily mean that he was giving a multi-hour monologue. Luke uses the Greek word *homileo,* which means to talk or have a conversation, to describe the dialog after the incident with Eutychus. It is likely that at least some of this conversation included teaching.

God teaching.[14] In Matthew 23:10[15] Jesus says that He is our only teacher. This is reaffirmed by both Paul and John, which indicates that the New Testament church experienced Jesus as their only teacher.[16]

Jeremiah 31:33-34 says:

> But this is the covenant that I will make with the house of Israel after those days, declares the LORD: I will put my law within them, and I will write it on their hearts. And I will be their God, and they shall be my people. And no longer shall each one teach his neighbor and each his brother, saying, 'Know the LORD,' for they shall all know me, from the least of them to the greatest, declares the LORD. For I will forgive their iniquity, and I will remember their sin no more.

This passage makes clear that the essence of the New Covenant is a profound change to our hearts. There are three aspects of this change mentioned in this passage: forgiveness of sins; relationship with God/knowing the Lord; and having God's law written on our hearts.

In this passage the phrase "know the Lord" does not mean filling our head with facts about God, it means knowing God like we know a close friend or family member. Both of the key elements of teaching mentioned in Jeremiah 31:33-34 (the writing of God's law on our hearts and relationally knowing the Lord) involve God touching our hearts. Only He can write His law on our hearts and only He can reveal Himself in direct relationship with each believer. You cannot develop relational knowledge of an individual second hand. It has to come from direct personal interactions.

Similarly in Isaiah 54:13[17] it is implied that part of the result of being directly taught by God is great peace. When He writes His truth on our hearts, deeply rooted lies and fears are displaced bringing great peace to our hearts. Jesus makes a very similar point in Matthew

---

14. *E.g.*, Isa. 2:3, 30:20, Micah 4:2. About another 20 verses in the Old Testament acknowledge God as teacher and more than 20 other Old Testament verses record prayers requesting God to teach. Neh. 9:20 links the Holy Spirit to teaching.
15. "Nor are you to be called 'teacher,' for you have one Teacher, the Christ." (NIV).
16. 1 Cor. 2:10-13, 1 John 2:27
17. "All your children shall be taught by the LORD, and great shall be the peace of your children."

11:29[18] where He offers to personally teach us and promises that part of the fruit of this personal teaching will be "rest for our souls." God's primary focus in teaching us is on transforming our hearts by revealing Himself, His character and His truth to our hearts.[19] As we enter into relationship with God and become yoked with Him we are positioned to learn from the humble Teacher. As we allow Him to write His love and truth onto our hearts, we respond in love and obedience.[20] This leads us to "present [our] bodies as a living sacrifice...that results in the renewing of our minds."[21] We develop the "mind of Christ" by allowing the Holy Spirit to impart the wisdom of God to us.[22] God wants to teach us and transform our minds by writing on our hearts.

God uses a wide variety of ways to reveal Himself to us and to write His law on our hearts. Personal study and meditation on Scripture are important, as are personal worship, prayer, listening to God and devotional times. God also delights to touch His children as they appreciate the beauty of His creation, participate in group worship, as we pray for one another and through various life experiences. Specifically, praying for a deeper and more personal heart-level revelation of our Trinitarian God is particularly powerful.

God also sometimes uses dreams and visions to reveal Himself to His children and to write His law on our hearts. Sometimes this is how He chooses to draw individuals to Himself.[23] Jesus also sometimes uses visions to heal an area of deep wounding in our soul. This is a beautiful example of the fulfillment of Isaiah 54:13. Through a vision He teaches us truth about Himself, which brings great peace to an area of deep emotional pain. Commonly this kind of emotional healing frees the individual to live more righteously. So the vision results in us both knowing God more intimately and also results in His law being written on our heart.

---

18. "Take my yoke upon you and learn from me, for I am gentle and humble in heart, and you will find rest for your souls." (NIV)
19. See also Psalm 51:6 and Luke 24:32. Head knowledge of key doctrines and what is right and wrong is also important.
20. John 14:15, 23
21. Rom. 12:1-2. Mind renewal results from God writing His truth on our hearts. Whatever is written on our hearts flows to our heads.
22. 1 Cor. 2:12-16
23. *E.g.*, Paul in Acts 9:1-18

Obviously, sometimes God also chooses to use words spoken or written by a human as part of the process of His teaching us in a way that transforms our hearts. Part of the spiritual gift of teaching[24] is that God takes the teacher's words that would otherwise only touch our minds and He miraculously uses them to touch our hearts. In this process God remains the only true teacher. So even though the New Testament church did use the title teacher as an abbreviated way of referring to individuals with the spiritual gift of teaching,[25] there is no conflict with Matthew 23:8-10, which says that Jesus is our only teacher.[26]

## 6.2 Preaching and evangelism

The prominence given to preaching in the Book of Acts shows that preaching was a high priority of the New Testament church. Many references to preaching are associated with Jesus and traveling leaders, especially the apostles. However, any believer may participate in evangelism and preaching.[27]

Two groups of Greek words are commonly translated preach in English Bibles: *euaggelizo*, which means to proclaim/preach good news or to evangelize, and the related noun *euaggelion*, which means good news or the preaching of good news; and *kerusso*, which means to proclaim or preach, and the related noun *kerugma*, which means proclamation or preaching.[28] All four of these words mainly apply to evangelistic preaching and the proclaiming of Jesus. The focus of preaching in the New Testament is on reaching unbelievers. New Testament preaching has nothing to do with the primary modern meaning of the word: the preaching of sermons aimed at believers, who are attending a church service.

In order to reach unbelievers, New Testament preachers went wherever there were people prepared to listen. Most preaching and proclaiming of Jesus took place in public places such as the Jerusalem temple, synagogues, open air gathering places for prayer, market places, Mars Hill, an open air court/meeting place in Athens,

---

24. 1 Cor. 12:28, 29, Eph. 4:11
25. Acts 13:1, 1 Tim. 2:7, 2 Tim. 1:11
26. Of course, within the unity of the Holy Trinity, there is also no conflict with John 14:26 which emphasizes the role of the Holy Spirit in teaching and reminding us of the words of Jesus. Section 1.4 provides a more detailed discussion of Matthew 23:8-10.
27. Appendix 1.8, 1.9
28. See Appendices 4.3, 4.4 for a detailed discussion of these words.

the lecture hall of Tyrannus, in law courts, and while traveling.[29] Jesus was also proclaimed in homes.[30] Most examples of preaching in the New Testament involve preaching to groups of people, but the same word was also used for one-on-one evangelism.[31]

The book of Acts records several evangelistic speeches.[32] New Testament preachers usually started with what the listeners would consider to be truth. Messages preached to Jews contained many quotes from the Old Testament. Peter's address to Cornelius and his friends and relatives started with their knowledge of the public ministry of Jesus. Paul's speech to the Athenians started with their belief in an unknown God and included a quote from a Greek poet. From this starting point these evangelistic presentations typically move to Jesus' death and resurrection and end with a call to repentance with the offer of forgiveness. Paul also sometimes used his testimony in evangelistic preaching.[33]

There are many references to evangelistic preaching in the Gospels especially to the preaching of the Gospel of the Kingdom.[34] Similarly Matthew 4:17 and Mark 1:15 record the command to repent for the Kingdom of Heaven is at hand. But, unlike the book of Acts, there are no examples of evangelistic preaching recorded in the Gospels. Luke emphasizes the continuity of the preaching of the Kingdom of God between the Gospels and Acts.[35] The good news of the Kingdom of God is that God is King and that He wants us to come to Him in repentance to receive forgiveness, so that we may enter into a love relationship with him.

All of the examples of evangelistic preaching recorded by Luke in Acts are very brief. In Acts 2:40 Luke mentions that he has only recorded a portion of what Peter said. It is possible that the other evangelistic speeches recorded in Acts are also only a portion of the full speech. All of the evangelistic speeches in Acts (except Acts

---

29. Luke 20:1, Acts 3:8-12, 5:42; Matt. 9:35, Mark 1:39, Luke 4:44, Acts 9:20, 13:5, 14, 14:1, 17:1, 10, 17, 18:4, 19, 19:8; Acts 16:13; Acts 17:17; Acts 17:22; Acts 19:9-10; Acts 26; Acts 8:35-36
30. Acts 5:42, 10:22-48, 28:23, 30-31. This is implicit in the command to seek "the man of peace" (Luke 10:5-9).
31. Acts 8:26-38
32. Acts 2:14-36, 3:12-26, 10:34-43, 13:16-41, 17:22-31
33. Acts 26:1-29
34. *E.g.*, Matt. 4:23, 9:35, 24:14, Mark 1:14, Luke 8:1, 16:16
35. Acts 8:12, 19:8, 20:25, 28:23, 31

2:37-38) are a monologue given by the preacher. However, it is likely that much of the preaching that took place during the New Testament period included dialog. In fact, Luke also uses the word *dialegomai*[36] to describe preaching. This word may be translated to discourse, to argue, to reason, to address, to speak to, to contend or to dispute. NIV and ESV commonly translate this word "reason." Obviously it is possible to provide a reasoned argument in the form of a monologue,[37] but it is likely that in many cases individuals who became interested in Jesus after hearing a brief evangelistic presentation would then enter into dialog with the preacher.[38] Dialog permits the preacher to focus on each individual's specific questions.

Both in the Gospels and in the Book of Acts preaching is strongly linked with healing and deliverance.[39] Mark 16:20 states that accompanying signs confirmed the apostle's preaching. These signs not only included healings and deliverances but also other supernatural events such as occurred on the day of Pentecost and the angel visiting Cornelius.[40] Sometimes people get the wrong message from a miraculous healing. For example in Acts 14:8-18 it is recorded that the people of Lystra thought that Paul and Barnabas were gods after a crippled man was healed. Even so it appears that some people came to faith in Lystra.

Philip and the Ethiopian eunuch is one of the relatively few examples of personal evangelism recorded in the book of Acts. However, there are several examples of personal evangelism recorded in the gospels and there are several references to Jesus being proclaimed in homes. So it is likely that the New Testament church was active in personal evangelism as well as evangelistic proclaiming to groups.[41]

It is almost certain that the New Testament church considered evangelism to be a spiritual gift.[42] It is likely that an aspect of this spiritual gift is that God takes the words of the gifted evangelist and writes

---

36. Acts 17:2, 17, 18:4, 19, 19:9, 24:25
37. *E.g.*, Stephen's defense Acts 7:2-53
38. *E.g.*, Acts 2:37, 17:11, 26:24-29, 28:23, *cf.*, John 3:1-21, 4:4-25
39. *E.g.*, Matt. 4:23, 9:35, Luke 7:22, 9:2,6,11, 10:9, Mark 1:39, Acts 3:1 – 4:4, 14:3, 19:10-20
40. Acts 2:1-41, 10:30-33
41. Acts 8:27-38 Phillip and the Ethiopian; John 3:1-21 Nicodemus; John 4:4-25 Samaritan woman; Acts 5:42, 10:22-48, 11:12, 28:23, 30-31 proclamation of Jesus in homes.
42. Eph. 4:11

them on the heart of the individual hearing. In this respect the gift of evangelism may be similar to the gift of teaching. Another aspect of the gift of evangelism is that God sets up divine appointments with individuals whose hearts are ready to receive the Gospel.

As I have already noted, evangelism and preaching are strongly emphasized and highly valued in the New Testament. Given this context, it is slightly surprising that there is only one verse that unambiguously commands all believers to be active in evangelism.[43] A possible explanation for this seeming disconnect may be that most of the evangelism and preaching was done by individuals with the gift of evangelism.

## 6.3 Prophecy and other revelatory gifts

Prophecy and other revelatory gifts[44] are mentioned many times in the New Testament.[45] It appears that their use was widespread within the life of the New Testament church. In some cases these gifts were given at conversion. They were not reserved to mature believers and leaders.

Spiritual gifts, including revelatory gifts, are given for the common good by the Holy Spirit, who distributes gifts to each one as he chooses. These gifts are analogous to the organs and limbs of a human body.[46] All are needed and all must work together in a humble and loving manner for the body to be healthy and complete. Paul encourages the use of prophecy in assembly meetings "so that all may learn and all be encouraged" and prophecy "speaks to people for their upbuilding and encouragement and consolation."[47] Prophecy may also be used by God to bring individuals to faith. All prophecies and revelations should be tested.[48]

There are several examples in the New Testament of prophecy and visions being used to guide ministry. For example, God used a

43. Jude 1:23. Appendix 1.8

44. Revelatory gifts are gifts of the Holy Spirit which reveal a message from God. Examples of this category of spiritual gift include prophecy, visions, dreams, interpretation of tongues, words of knowledge and discernment of spirits.

45. Matt. 1:20, 2:12-22, Luke 1:22, Acts 2:17, 9:10-17, 10:3, 17, 19, 11:5, 27-30, 12:9, 13:1, 15:32, 16:9-10, 18:9-10, 21:9-10, Rom. 12:6, 1 Cor. 11:5, 12:7-11, 13:2, 14:1-5, 24-39, 2 Cor. 12:1, Eph. 4:11, Col. 2:18, 1 Thess. 5:19-21 , 1 Tim. 1:18, 4:14, 1 John 4:1-3

46. 1 Cor. 12:12-26

47. 1 Cor. 14:3, 31

48. 1 John 4:1-3, 1 Thess. 5:19-21, Subsection 1.1.5

vision to tell Ananias to go and pray for Saul so that he might recover his sight. Similarly God used a vision to guide Paul and his team to go to Macedonia. The church in Antioch collected financial aid for the church in Judea following a prophecy predicting a famine. God also used prophetic words and visions to identify future leaders and to help these individuals understand their calling. [49]

Throughout the New Testament there is a strong sense of the continuity of the role of prophetic ministry from the Old Testament to the New Testament. In both the Old and New Testaments prophets made predictions about what God would do in the future. They taught people about God and how we should live in response to His character. A third role of Old Testament prophets was to anoint individuals to the leadership role God had selected for them. [50] Similarly New Testament prophets were used to reveal to individuals the ministry role to which God was calling them.

Ephesians 2:20 states that the church is being built on the foundation of the apostles and prophets. Numerous New Testament references indicate that the early church considered the fulfillment of Old Testament prophecy in the life and ministry of Jesus a primary argument for the truth of the Gospel. [51] The New Testament church turned to the Old Testament prophets to address doctrinal issues. [52] The apostles and prophets have a joint role in bringing the revelation of God to the world. [53] So, it is almost certain that Paul has the full continuity of Old Testament and New Testament prophetic ministry in mind in Ephesians 2:20.

The New Testament includes examples of partially accurate prophecies. For example, in Acts 27:10 Paul predicts the loss of the ship and cargo with heavy loss of life if they continue their voyage to Rome. In the event God spared everyone traveling with Paul. [54] Similarly, the respected New Testament prophet Agabus prophesied that Paul would be bound by the Jews if he went to Rome. When Paul got to Jerusalem he was bound by the Romans. [55]

---

49. Section 3.2
50. 1 Sam. 10:1,16:13, 1 Kings 1:34,19:15-16, 2 Kings 9:3-6
51. Matt. 1:22, 5:17, Mark 1:2, Luke 18:31, John 12:38, Acts 3:18, 13:23-41, 26:22-28, 28:23
52. Acts 15:15-17, 2 Pet. 1:19-21
53. Eph. 3:5
54. Acts 27:22-24, 44
55. Acts 21:10-11, 33

As noted in Subsection 1.1.5, 1 John 4:1, 1 Thessalonians 5:19-22 and 1 Corinthians 14:29 teach that potential prophetic words should be submitted to the whole church for evaluation. This command is a specific implementation of the broader principle that potential prophetic words should be submitted to the individual or group to which they apply. An example of this principle is given in Acts 16:9-10, which relates Paul's vision of the Macedonian. The phrase "concluding that God had called us" implies that the traveling ministry team evaluated this vision, which applied to their joint ministry. The principle that a prophetic word should be submitted to the individual or group to which it applies, is implicit in Ephesians 5:21. Submitting potential prophetic words protects against manipulation and inappropriate control.

Acts 21:11-14 is a good example of how prophecy should be used. Agabus provided a prophetic warning of Paul's arrest in Jerusalem and the people pleaded with Paul to stay away from Jerusalem. None of them wanted Paul to be arrested. But Paul was allowed to make his own decision as to the accuracy of the prophecy and as to what God wanted him to do. This is also a good example of mutual submission. Agabus submitted his word to Paul and let Paul decide if it was true and how he should respond.

Learning to handle revelatory gifts in a healthy manner is a major opportunity to develop godly character. Maybe this is one of the reasons God likes to give these gifts. When handled well, these gifts can be a huge blessing and can bring much encouragement and edification.

## 6.4 Did New Testament house churches place any limits on the participation of women?

### *Could women speak in New Testament house church meetings?*

In Section 1.1, I have argued, based on 1 Corinthians 14:26-33 — and other Scriptures—for the participation of every member in house church assembly meetings. An obvious interpretation of the next two verses is to limit this participation to men only. [56] Similarly 1 Timothy 2:11 may be interpreted as commanding women not to speak during teaching including teaching in house church meetings.

1 Corinthians, like all of the New Testament letters, was written to be understood by its original readers. It is unlikely that Paul would

---

56. 1 Cor. 14:34-35

have expected believers who had never participated in a New Testament style house church to be reading this letter. So it may have never occurred to him that certain things he said might be unclear to individuals who have never participated in a New Testament style house church. In particular, it may have never occurred to him that later generations would interpret these passages as a total ban on women speaking during meetings. It may have been obvious to the original readers that Paul was reminding them not to indulge in distracting speech during meetings.

To protect against this type of potential misunderstanding, 1 Corinthians 14:34-35 needs to be understood in the context of other Scriptures such as 1 Corinthians 11:2-16, 14:29 and 1 Timothy 2:9. 1 Corinthians 14:29 says let two or three prophets speak. We know that there were female prophets in the New Testament church [57] and 1 Corinthians 12:7 states that spiritual gifts are given for the common good. So it is natural to assume that women spoke prophetically in church meetings for the benefit of both the men and women who were present. Revelation 2:20 says that a woman (Jezebel) was teaching and prophesying in the church at Thyatira. While the church was reprimanded for allowing her to teach, the basis for this reprimand was not her gender but the content of her teaching. It is also implied that she was not a true prophet.

The first Greek word in 1 Timothy 2:9 is *hosautos*, which means "likewise" or "in like manner." So it is plausible that this verse is continuing the topic of appropriate spoken prayer in church meetings from the preceding verse. This is particularly likely given that 1 Timothy was written to Timothy by Paul while Timothy was in Ephesus. [58] Ephesus was the center of the cult of Artemis. [59] In this female-dominated cult, women prayed to Artemis wearing elaborate clothing and with adorned braids of hair. Men prayed to Artemis with their hands raised slightly above waist level and with palms turned upwards. [60] So it seems that 1 Timothy 2:8-9 is directly addressing individuals who were praying in church meetings in the same manner as they had prayed to Artemis. Men prayed to Artemis for aid in war and Paul commands them to pray for peace. [61] Women prayed to Artemis

---

57. Acts 2:17, 21:9
58. 1 Tim. 1:3
59. Acts 19
60. *What's with Paul and Women*, Jon Zens, Appendix 1
61. 1 Tim. 2:2

for safety in child birth and Paul promises safety in child birth based on faith in Jesus, love and holiness. These are further indications that in this chapter Paul is addressing specific corruptions that were entering the Christian assemblies in Ephesus due to the influence of the cult of Artemis. In summary, 1 Timothy 2:9 is almost certainly addressing spoken prayer by women in church assemblies, which is another indication that women were free to speak in these meetings. Similarly 1 Corinthians 11:2-16 is very likely to be discussing women praying and prophesying in church meetings.

Several other Scriptures indicate that women were free to prophesy, pray and speak in tongues in the presence of men. [62] For example in Luke 2:36-37 Anna prophesied and prayed in the temple in the presence of both men and women. Similarly in the Old Testament, Deborah appears to have worshipped, prophesied and judged in front of both men and women. [63] Huldah prophesied in front of men. [64] Miriam was recognized by Micah as a co-leader with Moses and Aaron. She also led in worship almost certainly in front of both men and women. [65]

Romans 16:7 refers to Junia, which is a woman's name, as an apostle. [66] Given the broad role of apostles in the New Testament

---

62. Acts 1:14, 2:1-4, 15-18, 10:24, 44-46. Some English translations include the word "men" in Acts 2:15. This word is not present in the Greek. The Greek uses the masculine form for the word "these" in this verse. But this does not prove that Peter was only referring to men. This exact Greek word is used in 77 verses in the New Testament. In many of these verses it is clear that both men and women are included when the masculine form of the word "these" is used.
63. Judges 4-5
64. 2 Kings 22:14-20
65. Exod. 15:20-21, Micah 6:4
66. This verse is subject to much scholarly debate. This debate addresses two primary points: firstly is the Greek name Junia or Junias that are respectively female and male names? Secondly was this individual a distinguished apostle or well known to the apostles? Eldon Jay Epp, a prominent New Testament scholar, has published the most in-depth study available on Romans16:7, *Junia: The First Woman Apostle*. Joel Comiskey provides this summary of some of the key points in this book. Epp documents that "(a) there are over 250 1st Century inscriptions in Rome alone with the female name "Junia," (b) there is no evidence whatsoever in the Greek or Latin literature of the day for the existence of the male name "Junias," (c) there is no evidence whatsoever that the known male name "Junianus" was ever shortened to "Junias" or any other type of nickname, (d) the construction of the Greek wording in this verse should not be translated as "well known to the apostles," and (e) virtually all bible scholars and

church it is exceptionally unlikely that an individual could serve as an apostle without speaking, including teaching, in house church meetings. In Romans 16 Paul commends 7 women and 5 men for their spiritual service. In verse 3 Prisca (short for Priscilla) is mentioned, before her husband, as a fellow worker. Also in Philippians 4:2-3 Paul refers to Euodia and Syntyche as women and as fellow workers. The title "fellow worker" is used of individuals who worked with Paul to plant churches. Again it is exceptionally unlikely that these women could have been co-workers with Paul and not spoken and taught in house church meetings.

In some English Bibles, 1 Timothy 2:11 is translated "Let the woman learn in silence" (KJV). The key Greek word in this verse and the following verse is *hesuchia*, which may be translated, rest, quiet, tranquility, a quiet tranquil life, silence, silent attention. There is nothing in the context of 1 Timothy 2:11-12, which demands that *hesuchia* be translated silence in these verses. These verses could equally well be commanding a heart attitude of peace and tranquility. In fact to be consistent with other scriptures, which indicate that women did speak in house church meetings, it is more plausible to translate these verses as addressing the women's heart attitude rather than whether or not they could speak in meetings. It is also good for men to have a heart attitude of peace and tranquility while listening to teaching. [67]

Given all of this, it seems that the command for women to be silent in 1 Corinthians 14:34 cannot be a general prohibition against all female speech during meetings. It must be something more specific. In my mind the most plausible interpretation of these verses is that they refer to speech that would distract from the flow of the meeting rather than a prohibition on speaking to contribute to the flow of the meeting.

theologians up to about 1300 AD acknowledged that "Junia" was indeed a female name" (Comiskey, Joel, *Biblical foundations for the cell-based church*, pg. 131). Epp also notes that almost all editions of the Greek New Testament published prior to 1927 show Junia; for the next 75 years almost all Greek New Testaments show Junias and in 1998 the highly influential Nestle-Aland/UBS editions reverted to Junia. The preponderance of Bible translations (*e.g.*, KJV, NIV, RSV, NRSV, NASV and NEB) say that Junia(s) was a distinguished apostle. The ESV translation says that she is well known to the apostles.

67. It is possible that Paul only mentions women needing to learn with an appropriate attitude because some of the women in the church assembly may have had an inappropriate attitude due to their prior involvement in the cult of Artemis.

So, if the focus of 1 Corinthians 14:34-35 (and 1 Timothy 2:11) is on speech that would distract from the flow of a meeting, why does Paul emphasize the application of this command to women? Presumably he does this because the problem of distracting speech was predominantly associated with women. Given the restrictions on women in the Roman Empire, it is plausible that some women inappropriately exploited their freedom in the church.

An alternative understanding of 1 Corinthians 14:34-35 is that these verses are a quote from a letter sent to Paul by the Corinthians.[68] In this interpretation verse 36 is Paul's incredulous rejection of this position. Interpreting verses 34–35 as a quote from the Corinthians and verse 36 as Paul's rebuttal is attractive, because it deals with four issues[69] in this text:

- Firstly, v. 36 appears to be a rebuttal of a position taken by the Corinthian church. A very natural interpretation is that it is a rebuttal of vv. 34 - 35. If v. 36 is not rebutting these verses what is it rebutting?
- Secondly, the law may say that women should be in submission to their husbands.[70] But being in submission has nothing to do with requiring individuals to be silent in church or anywhere else. Ephesians 5:21 requires all believers to be in mutual submission. So, if part of being in submission is a requirement to be silent then all believers should be silent. I can find no text in the law or any other part of the Old Testament, which suggests that women should be silent during services. In fact, several Old Testament passages imply that women were free to speak during services.[71] There are indications that some Jewish traditions during the New Testament period commanded women to be silent during services.[72] These traditions were later collected as the Talmud. Some Jews treated these traditions as having greater authority than the Old Testament.[73] So it is seems that the reference to the law in 1 Corinthians 14:34 is actually a reference to Jewish traditions.

---

68. *Cf.*, 1 Cor. 7:1
69. These issues are among the reasons why some scholars suggest that these verses are an interpolation into the text (*e.g.*, Eldon Jay Epp *Junia: the first woman apostle*, Chapter 2).
70. Gen. 3:16, Eph. 5:22, Col. 3:18, 1 Pet. 3:1
71. Exod. 15:20-21, 38:8, Num. 5:18-31, 6:2, 30:3, 30:9, Judges 5:1, 1 Sam. 2:22, 2 Chron. 35:25, Ezra 10:1-5, Neh. 8:1-6, 12:43, Ps. 68:11
72. *What's with Paul and Women*, Jon Zens, Appendix 2. This book contains a lot of other useful information related to the role of women in the New Testament church.
73. Matt. 15:3-6

Both Jesus and Paul strongly rejected these traditions when they conflicted with the Gospel. It is extremely implausible that Paul would cite a Jewish tradition and refer to it as "the law." So this is a strong indicator that these verses are a quote from a letter sent by the Corinthians.

- Thirdly, the word for shame *(aischron)* in v. 35 is a very strong word. Its literal meaning is "deformed." Metaphorically, it means indecent, dishonorable, vile or disgraceful. The same word is used in 1 Corinthians 11:6 where it has connotations of sexual indecency. Given the high respect that Jesus, Paul and the other New Testament authors had for women, it seems extremely implausible that Paul would pick such a word to describe women speaking in a house church meeting. The Talmud does describe female speech as shameful. So this word is another hint that Paul is quoting the Corinthians who may have been making a point based on Jewish tradition.
- Fourthly, as discussed above there are many indicators in the New Testament that women were free to speak in house church meetings.

### *Could women teach in New Testament house churches?*

In 1 Timothy 2:12a Paul says that he is not allowing (present tense, not an imperative) a woman to teach a man. The second half of the verse goes on to discuss his not allowing a woman to have authority over a man. I will discuss the second half of this verse in the next subsection. The Greek words for man and woman in 1 Timothy 2:12 are both in the singular. If Paul was thinking about teaching in the local church assembly it would seem reasonable to expect him to use the plural especially for men as several men would typically have been present at each local church assembly meeting. This verse appears to be addressing one-on-one discipling and mentoring. [74]

To reduce the risk of inappropriate relationships being formed, many churches discourage long-term one-on-one ministry between a man and a woman, who are not married to each other. This may be what Paul has in mind in 2 Timothy 2:12a. The reference to the exercise of authority also makes sense in the context of one-on-one

---

74. An example of two-on-one discipling is given in Acts 18:26 which records that Priscilla and Aquila jointly taught Apollos. Note that in this verse Priscilla is mentioned first. It is possible that one-on-one discipling was a common part of the discipling of new believers. One-on-one discipling and mentoring appear to have been an important part of the training of traveling leaders (Section 3.4).

discipling, as this relationship is vulnerable to inappropriate use of authority.

1 Corinthians 12:7 states that the gifts of the spirit are given for the common good, which implies for the good of both the male and female members of the body. Teaching is listed in 1 Corinthians 12:28 as a gift. It is reasonable to assume that women who receive the gift of teaching were expected to use it to benefit both men and women. 1 Corinthians 14:31 links prophecy to learning and encouragement. If women may prophesy in Christian assemblies, which may result in both men and women learning, why can't they teach both men and women in other ways?

As noted in the discussion of women speaking in church, women leaders almost certainly taught both men and women in New Testament church assemblies. In summary, I believe that women were free to teach in New Testament church assemblies.

### *Could women lead in New Testament house churches?*

1 Timothy 2:12 says that a woman may not have authority over a man. Some interpret this verse as meaning that women cannot be elders or other types of Christian leaders. This presumes that part of the role of an elder is to have authority over members of the church. This concept is totally unbiblical. The clear teaching of scripture, as documented in many places in this book, is that being an elder is not about having authority over people, especially not the kind of dominating authority described by the Greek word *authenteo*, which is used in this verse.[75] Also if Paul was intending to say that women could not be elders why does he say "man" instead of "men"? Being an elder involves providing leadership to the whole local assembly not just to one man. So whatever Paul may be talking about in this verse, I do not think it is a ban on women serving as elders or in other leadership roles.

As noted in the discussion of women teaching in New Testament churches this verse is almost certainly discussing one-on-one ministry.

---

75. The Greek word for "have authority" in this verse (*authenteo*) has a very forceful meaning. Strong offers the following translations: one who with his own hands kills another or himself; one who acts on his own authority, autocratic; an absolute master; to govern, exercise dominion over one. Similarly, Bagster offers the following translations: one acting by his own authority or power; one who executes with his own hand; to have authority over; to domineer. This verb is only used once in the New Testament. Other references in the New Testament to having authority use different words.

Also, as noted in the discussion of women speaking in church it is likely that the Greek word *hesuchia* in this verse is referring to a heart attitude of rest or tranquility, not to being silent. I believe this verse is saying that a woman should not use the opportunity of one-on-one ministry to form a controlling relationship over a man. Paul is also saying that in one-on-one ministry relationships the one leading should minister from a place of rest and tranquility.

Given that Christian leadership both in group settings and in one-on-one ministry is not about leaders having authority over other believers, why does Paul emphasize a woman not having authority over a man in this passage? I have already noted that 1 Timothy was written by Paul to Timothy while he was in Ephesus and that Ephesus was dominated by the female-centered cult of Artemis. Within this cult women had authority over men. So it is plausible that certain women who had come to faith in Jesus out of the cult of Artemis were continuing their practice of dominating men. 1 Timothy 2:12b is an example of a command that applies both to men and women, where Paul chooses, for reasons associated with the specific circumstances of the recipients of his letter, to mention the application to women.

Some individuals suggest that 1 Timothy 2:13-14 are inconsistent with the interpretation of 1 Timothy 2:12 given in the previous paragraphs. In 1 Timothy 2:13-14 Paul says that the basis for the preceding teaching is related to the order of creation and the fall. Many interpret these verses as teaching that men are superior to women because Adam was created before Eve and Eve fell into sin before Adam. They treat this assertion of male superiority as Paul's justification for teaching in the previous verse that women should not teach or lead in local Christian assemblies.

The Greek used in 1 Timothy 2:13 does not demand that this verse be interpreted as teaching the superiority of men over women. The two key Greek words (*protos* "first" and *eitai* "then") need only imply a sequence of events. These Greek words appear together in only four verses in the New Testament. In two cases the words are definitely used to describe a sequence of events. [76]

1 Timothy was written to Timothy while he was serving in Ephesus. Given this context, it is plausible that Paul is only intending to make a chronological point in 1 Timothy 2:13-14. Many Greeks believed that

---

76. Mark 4:28, 1 Tim. 3:10. 1 Cor. 12:28 may be an example of the use of these words to describe a ranking.

Artemis and Apollo were the twin children of Zeus and Leto. The cult of Artemis, which was centered in Ephesus, argued for its superiority over the more widespread cult of Apollo based on the belief that Artemis was born first. It is plausible that in 1 Timothy 2:13-14 Paul is countering this argument for women dominating men by emphasizing the order of the creation of Adam and Eve and by pointing out the order in which they first sinned.

In summary, it is likely that the Greek of 1 Timothy 2:13-14 is only addressing the order of events in creation and the fall. It is unlikely that these verses are teaching a general superiority of men over women. So these verses do not support the interpretation of 1 Timothy 2:12 as a general prohibition of women leading or teaching in New Testament Christian assemblies based on their inferiority to men.

Another potential reason for believing that elders must be men is the phrase "the husband of one wife," which is included in the lists of qualifications to be an elder.[77] The exact same phrase is used in the list of qualifications for deacons.[78] We know from passages like Romans 16:1 that some deacons were women so the phrase cannot imply a ban on female deacons or elders.[79]

Furthermore, given the New Testament usage of gender specific words it is hard to make a compelling case from the phrase "the husband of one wife" that elders must be men. The Greek word for husband (*aner*) used in this phrase is used in 193 verses in the New Testament. From the context of these verses it is clear that many references are specific to men. However, in several cases it appears that it is used to mean person rather than man as distinct from woman.[80] This word is also used, in the plural, to address groups of people that almost certainly included women.[81] For this same reason the fact that all references to elders use a masculine word ending is

---

77. 1 Tim. 3:2, Titus 1:6
78. 1 Tim. 3:12
79. Some may argue that the word for deacon in this verse is a generic reference to servanthood rather than the specific leadership role of a deacon. This is unlikely given the formal wording of the verse specifying the church assembly where Phoebe served. Also the next verse describes Phoebe as a *prostatis*—a female leader (Appendix 3.5).
80. Acts 10:28, Rom. 4:8, Eph. 4:13, James 1:8,12 ,20, 23, 3:2
81. Luke 11:31, Acts 2:14, 22, 13:16, 26. The Greek word for brother (*adelphos*) is another example of a word with a gender specific meaning, which is also used generically.

not the basis of a compelling argument to restrict the role of elder to men.

As noted above there is a reference to a female apostle, to a female deacon/leader and there are several references to female prophets, which was seen as a significant leadership role in the New Testament church. [82] Paul mentions at least three female "fellow workers:" Priscilla in Romans 16:3-4; and Euodia and Syntyche in Philippians 4:2-3. Some of the other fellow workers mentioned by Paul include Timothy, Titus and Luke. Fellow workers were traveling leaders who planted and supported churches. It seems hard to make an argument that women can serve in these four leadership capacities and not as elders. Ann Nyland in her paper, *Papyri, Women and Word Meaning in the New Testament,* provides references for about ten examples of female elders being mentioned in inscriptions. [83]

In summary, it is not possible to make a compelling case from scripture for women to be barred from serving as elders. This is consistent with Galatians 3:28, which states that our unity in Christ transcends gender. However, given the prevailing culture of the New Testament period it is likely that the majority of elders were men.

### *Do women need to cover their heads in house church meetings?*

1 Corinthians 11:2-16 teaches that women should cover their heads when they pray and that men should not cover their heads. This passage also teaches that women should not cut their hair and that men should. Paul's argument to support these teachings is based on the following factors: the God given complementary roles between men and women that go back to creation; an understanding of what constitutes a disgrace, which he states is based in what nature teaches (this aspect of the argument is specific to hair length); the traditions/practices of all New Testament churches; a concern for the angels.

The key question in considering this passage is to what extent it constitutes an example of applying a timeless Biblical principle (gender complementarity) in a culturally specific manner. If the application is specific to a particular culture then it is possible that

---

82. Rom. 16:1-2, 7, Eph. 2:20
83. Priscilla Papers, Volume 17, Number 4, Fall 2003, pp 3-9, published by Christians for Biblical Equality (www.cbeinternational.org).

the application of the underlying Biblical principle will be different in other cultures.

In passages such as Matthew 15:10-20, 23:25-28, Jesus teaches that it is what comes out of our heart that makes us unclean. Externals (such as clothing) do not make us unclean. In Matthew 6:25-33 Jesus specifically downplays the importance of clothing while acknowledging that it is something we need and that God will provide. Based on these passages it is reasonable to conclude that what we wear has no impact on how God sees us. This teaching needs to be balanced by 1 Timothy 2:9 which says that modesty in clothing is important. This verse is consistent with the teaching in Matthew because modest clothing is only relevant in circumstances where we expect to be seen by others and the choice of what we wear in public is an out working of heart attitudes.

Similarly in Romans 14 where Paul discusses food offered to idols and the particular honoring of certain days, which were divisive issues at that time, he concludes in v. 23 by saying that "whatever does not proceed from faith is sin." So again the heart attitude is more important than the external practice.

Numbers 6:2-21 describes the regulations concerning Nazarite vows. Both men and women could take this vow, if they wanted to have a period of special consecration to God. During the period of the vow, haircuts were forbidden. For men this would result in long hair. At the end of the vow, the individual shaved his/her head and burned his/her hair. For a woman this would result in her having very short hair for a while. The most famous Nazarite in the Old Testament is Sampson. In his case the Nazarite vow was intended to apply to his whole life.[84] So in the case of the Nazarite vow God commands individuals who want to have a season of particular dedication to Him to do the exact opposite concerning hair length to the standard set in 1 Corinthians 11:2-16. This is further evidence that what matters is one's heart attitude towards God, which can be expressed in some situations by one's hair length.

Based on these passages, it is reasonable to consider the teaching of 1 Corinthians 11:2-16 in the context of heart attitudes. It seems reasonable to assume that in the setting of the New Testament church Paul assumed a strong link between head covering/hair length and heart attitudes towards gender roles and/or moral behavior. In many

---

84. Jud. 13:5-7

modern societies the thought that there might be a link between these topics has been completely lost. In these societies the importance of honoring the Biblical truths associated with gender complementarity and moral behavior in the specific manner discussed in 1 Corinthians 11:2-16 has ended. It seems to me be that in such societies this issue has become like those discussed in Romans 14. [85]

## 6.5 Where and when did New Testament churches meet?

In four places Paul refers to church assemblies which meet in homes. [86] It is likely that Romans 16:23 implies that a church met in Gaius' home. Similarly it is possible that a church regularly met in the home of Mary the mother of John Mark and in Lydia's home. [87] Also the setting for the incident in Acts 20:7-12 appears to be a church meeting held in a multi-story apartment building. Three verses reference teaching/meeting in public places and house-to-house and two verses reference meetings in public places. [88]

Jesus' training of his disciples in outreach emphasized using the home of a man of peace as the base of outreach. [89] The initial context of these passages is the sending out of the 12 and of the 72, but the flow of Matthew 10 links this training trip to ministry after Pentecost. So it is plausible, based on these passages to assume that apostles and traveling evangelists in the New Testament period planted churches, which met in the home of the man or woman of peace. Some possible examples of this may include Acts 16:13-15, 40, 17:5, 18:7. This is also consistent with the significant portion of Jesus' ministry, which took place in homes.

It appears that the primary meeting place for New Testament church assemblies was private homes. This is consistent with the emphasis on close relationships within New Testament churches and with the New Testament model of participatory church meetings and participatory decision-making. This participatory style of church works

85. Some argue that the mention of angels in this passage implies that the command applies to all societies equally. This argument pre-supposes that angels are not aware of and sensitive to the unique aspects of various societies. It is reasonable to assume that angels are aware of and sensitive to each society where they minister. So I do not think that the mention of angels invalidates my conclusions concerning this passage.
86. Rom. 16:5, 1 Cor. 16:19, Col. 4:15, Philem. 1:2
87. Acts 12:12, 16:40
88. Acts 2:46, 5:42, 20:20, 5:12, 19:9-10
89. Matt. 10:12-14, Mark 6:10, Luke 9:4, 10:5

best with groups of up to about twenty people. As groups get larger than this it is no longer possible to have fully participatory meetings and decision-making. It is also much harder to be connected to everyone in larger groups. Groups of more than twenty people can meet in larger homes. [90] They do not need to meet in a public building. It is likely that as a church grew it would divide so that each church would remain small enough to maintain a participatory style. Dividing also means that churches can continue to meet in a house. In some cases a church may divide into two (or more) new churches of roughly equal size and in other cases a church may divide by sending out a team of church planters to start a new church.

Some have suggested that New Testament churches only met in homes because they could not afford buildings or to avoid persecution. However there were many periods in the first two centuries of the life of the church when there was very little persecution and there was sufficient prosperity for the churches to have been able to afford buildings. There are almost no examples of churches having buildings during this period. It appears that meeting in homes was the positive choice of the early church. [91]

The majority of New Testament believers came from religious backgrounds (either Jewish or pagan) which were centered on religious meetings in religious buildings (synagogues or temples) led by some form of trained religious leader (typically a rabbi or priest). So these believers would have known from personal experience that the dynamics associated with participatory meetings in homes are very different to the dynamics associated with meetings in a religious building led by a religious professional. Presumably this experience with both types of meeting was a factor in the choice of the New Testament church to embrace participatory meetings in homes. This is consistent with the New Testament understanding that the people of God are the temple which God is building. [92] Often we use the term

---

90. According to David Norrington, the largest rooms in the very largest homes in Corinth and Pompeii could accommodate about 50 people (p. 56 of Ekklesia Press edition of *To Preach Or Not To Preach*).
91. Steve Atkerson, Were Persecution, Poverty, and Progression the Real Reasons for First Century House Churches?, this essay is published as Chapter 12 in *Nexus, The World House Church Movement Reader*, edited by Rad Zdero. Norrington, ibid. pg. 52 mentions a church building in Edessa around 200 AD. He also mentions that some homes may have been adapted for church meetings at an earlier date.
92. 1 Cor. 3:16, 2 Cor. 6:16, Eph. 2:21-22, 1 Pet. 2:5

church to refer to a building where Christians meet for services. This use of the word church is completely different to its use in the New Testament.

The large public meetings mentioned in Acts are associated with apostles and are mentioned as occurring in the Jerusalem temple and a public lecture hall in Ephesus. [93] Based on Acts 5:42, 19:10 and 20:20 it seems that the purpose of large meetings was outreach and teaching. These passages all mention the role of apostles in public meetings. This does not prove that the content of these meetings was organized by the apostles in a manner similar to many current day church services. It is possible that the larger public meetings were structured in a similar manner to house church meetings: anyone could contribute as led by the Holy Spirit. This would result in "many others" teaching and preaching alongside the apostles as mentioned in Acts 15:35. There is no definite mention in the New Testament of large meetings being held when there was no traveling leader in town. However, such meetings may have taken place when the level of opposition permitted. [94]

It is interesting to note the gender balance in the four scriptures which explicitly name the hosts/hostesses of house churches. There are two references to the same married couple hosting a house church. In one case the man's name is listed first and in the other the woman's name is listed first. There are also two references to a house church being hosted by one person. In one case this is a man and in the other it is a woman.

There is very little information in the New Testament as to the day and time of house church meetings. [95] Acts 20:7 mentions an evening

---

93. It is possible that Acts 21:4-5, 7 and similar passages are implicit references to other larger public meetings.

94. It is possible that the Greek word *olos* (whole) in 1 Cor. 14:23 indicates that this passage refers to joint meetings of all of the house churches in Corinth. However this verse could equally apply to a single house church being fully assembled. The teaching in the following verses is equally applicable to meetings of individual house churches and joint meetings of multiple house churches. If this passage does apply to joint meetings of multiple house churches, it is evidence that these larger meetings were based on every member participation as led by the Holy Spirit.

95. Acts 2:46, 19:9 mention daily meetings. In Acts 19:9-10 it is clear that this reference is to public meetings most likely for outreach. In Acts 2:46 it is possible that the reference to daily meetings only applies to the meetings in the temple (*e.g.*, NIV translation of this verse). It is possible that the second half of this verse is referring to the daily meals for widows mentioned in

meeting on the first day of the week (Sunday). It is possible that this was a special meeting scheduled around Paul's travel plans or it may have been the regular meeting time for this church. It is possible that 1 Corinthians 16:2 is a hint that church meetings in Corinth typically occurred on Sundays. Romans 14:5 says that "One man considers one day more sacred than another; another man considers every day alike" (NIV). The primary point of this passage is the importance of respecting the opinions of others and not disputing over secondary matters. This variety of opinions as the relative importance of various days may have impacted when some churches met.

A further uncertainty relates to the length of a week. The Jewish week had seven days including a day for rest. The pre-imperial Roman week had eight days. The Roman Empire gradually transitioned to the seven-day week over the first three centuries AD. The Roman calendar also included large numbers of holidays. Some churches may have chosen to meet on holidays as more people would have been off work. Given that the whole tenor of the New Testament church is to give as much freedom as possible to believers, it is possible that there was no preferred day for church meetings. It is reasonable to assume that the meeting place, day and time were decided by consensus in a similar manner to other church decisions. Justin Martyr, in the mid-2nd Century mentions churches holding their meetings on Sundays. It is possible that a transition to a standard meeting day occurred in parallel with the transition to more leader-centric meetings which occurred over the second and third centuries.

Bread was the staple food of ordinary people during this era. The word bread was often used as a generic word for all food. [96] So the references to the church breaking bread together are likely to refer to full meals. [97] 1 Corinthians 11:17-34 indicates that the Corinthian church assembly meetings included a full meal. Paul criticizes the Corinthian Christians for allowing these meals to be an expression of their lack of love and respect for one another. He says that it is better to eat at home than to eat together in a manner that dishonors the body and results in judgment. So, having a full meal together was not required.

---

Acts 6:1-3. It is unlikely that individual house churches met daily on a regular basis.

96. Matt. 6:11, Mark 6:8, Luke 15:17, 2 Thess. 3:8

97. Acts 2:42, 46, 20:7, 11

## 6.6 Cooperation between local churches

### *Cooperation between churches in the same town*

New Testament church assemblies were relatively small to maintain intimacy and to permit participatory meetings and decision-making. So it is likely that in many towns and cities it did not take long for there to be several individual house churches. Given the emphasis in the New Testament on the importance of relationships between believers, it is reasonable to assume that most believers (including the elders) would be committed to a specific house church community.

New Testament churches provided financial assistance to members in need. [98] In Jerusalem this money was administered jointly for all of the house churches in the city, first by the apostles and later by the seven who most likely were the first deacons. There is no clear statement in the New Testament as to the approach used in other places to administer money collected to provide financial assistance. It is possible that in communities with only a few house churches these funds were jointly administered by the elders and that in communities with many house churches these funds were jointly administered by a group of deacons.

Acts 15 records the elders of the city-wide church of Jerusalem meeting, along with the apostles who were in town, to address the doctrinal concern raised by the church in Antioch. Another area of cooperation between house churches in the same town involves ensuring that letters from traveling leaders were read to all believers in the town. [99] We also know that in Jerusalem and Ephesus public meetings were held in the temple and the lecture hall of Tyrannus. [100] These meetings were used to teach and proclaim Jesus and may also have included worship. These meetings included the participation of believers from several house churches. Similar meetings may have taken place in other cities.

John records in Revelation 1:11 that Jesus directed him in a vision to send the book of Revelation to the seven churches of seven named cities. An implication of this verse is that Jesus considers that there is only one church in each city. Similarly, Paul addressed his letters

---

98. Acts 2:44-34, 4:34-35, 6:1-3, 1 Tim. 5:3-16. See Subsection 6.7.1 for a more complete discussion of this topic.

99. 1 Thess. 5:27, Col. 4:16, Rom. 1:7, Phil. 1:1

100. Acts 2:46-47, 5:12, 42, 19:9-10, 20:20

to the Corinthians and to the Thessalonians to the church (singular) in the town.[101] He refers in Colossians 4:16 to the church (singular) of the Laodiceans and in Romans 16:1 to the church (singular) at Cenchreae. Luke also uses the word church in the singular to describe the whole church in various cities.[102] It is very likely the church in several of these cities had grown to the point where it consisted of many house churches. Even so in some meaningful way they remained the single church of the town or city.[103]

The understanding that there is a single church in a town with several house churches implies cooperation and fellowship between the house churches in the town. It is reasonable to assume that this cooperation extended beyond the specific areas of cooperation that are mentioned in the New Testament. It is possible that local house churches gathered together for joint worship, teaching and/or outreach when there were no traveling leaders in town and it is highly plausible that individuals from various house churches maintained fellowship with one another and cooperated in various types of ministry. Given that New Testament style house churches are relatively small, the encouragement of being in fellowship and/or joint ministry with believers in other house churches can be greatly appreciated. It is also possible that as the house churches within a community became more numerous and mature they provided support to each other in some of the ways that the New Testament mentions in the context traveling leaders.[104]

The existence of an organic unity between the house churches within a town does not imply the need for a formal organizational unity between these house churches. The model of church and church leadership discussed in this book is consistent with a network of mutually supporting autonomous house churches within a town. The available evidence indicates that each house church made decisions related to the house church by consensus of the house church. It is possible that some decisions that impacted several house churches

---

101. 1 Cor. 1:2, 2 Cor. 1:2, 1 Thess. 1:1, 2 Thess. 1:1

102. Jerusalem Acts 8:1, 11:22, 15:4, Antioch 13:1, 14:27, 15:3, Caesarea 18:22, Ephesus 20:17

103. The word church (assembly) in the singular is also used in some passages to refer to an individual house church (*e.g.*, Col. 4:15, Philem. 1:2) even in cities where there are likely to have been several house churches. The word church is also often used in the New Testament to describe the universal church.

104. Section 3.7

were made by consensus of the house churches jointly. For example the phrase "when you are assembled" in 1 Corinthians 5:4 may refer to the assembly of a single house church or to a meeting of all of the house churches in Corinth. Given that the topic in this passage is applying church discipline, in particular exclusion from the spiritual community of an individual living in sexual immorality, it is possible that all local house churches needed to understand the situation and agree to the discipline. Otherwise, the situation might arise where one house church disciplines an individual, who then joins another local house church that is totally unaware of the issue.

There is no evidence in the New Testament of the existence of local leaders with authority to make unilateral decisions concerning a single house church or group of house churches. The concept of a local leader or group of local leaders running a network of house churches without consensual decision-making of everyone involved is alien to the New Testament. A partial exception to this is the protection of sound doctrine, which is particularly mentioned in the New Testament in the context of elders and traveling leaders. However it is likely that individuals who were not elders or traveling leaders were free to contribute to the protection of sound doctrine. [105]

Groups of leaders associated with various house churches may get together to encourage one another, pray together and organize a special event such as an outreach, a worship event or a prayer meeting. Any group of believers is free to meet together for any of these purposes. Acts 20:17 records Paul meeting with the elders of Ephesus. 1 Timothy 4:14 records a group of elders praying for Timothy. Acts 13:1-3, which describes the call of Barnabas and Paul to missionary service, may be an example of prophets and teachers from various house churches within the city-wide church of Antioch gathering to fast and worship.

### *Cooperation between churches in different towns*

In 1 Thessalonians 4:9-10 Paul commends the Thessalonian believers for their brotherly love, which extends "to all the brothers throughout Macedonia." He goes on to encourage them to do this even more. The primary outworking, mentioned in the New Testament, of this brotherly love between church assemblies in different towns was financial. In Acts 11:27-30 it is recorded that the church in Antioch collected money to aid the brothers living in

105. Appendix 1.21

Judea during a period of famine. In Romans 15:25-26, Paul says "At present, however, I am going to Jerusalem bringing aid to the saints. For Macedonia and Achaia have been pleased to make some contribution for the poor among the saints at Jerusalem." This is an example of Paul responding to the request of James, Peter and John that he remember the needs of the poor in other churches. [106] It also seems that churches in various towns jointly contributed to the financial support of traveling leaders. [107]

Another area of cooperation between churches in different, but nearby towns, was sharing letters from traveling leaders. [108] Over time the sharing and copying of letters and other New Testament documents was not limited to churches in nearby towns. In due course this led to the development of the New Testament. Colossians 4:16 indicates that the churches in Colosse and Laodicea, a pair of nearby towns in modern-day Turkey, maintained contact with each other.

### *Did one church ever have control over another church?*

Chapter 5 discusses the delicate balance of power between traveling leaders and local churches to help individuals, local churches and traveling leaders all remain in a healthy place. This delicate balance of power is based on influence and not on control. Acts 15 is the only passage that may possibly be interpreted as an example of one church having control over another church.

Acts 15:1 records that some men came from Judea (v. 24 implies Jerusalem) to Antioch and taught what at least Paul and Barnabas considered to be false doctrine: the need to be circumcised. After much debate on this topic at Antioch, the church in Antioch sent Paul, Barnabas and some others to Jerusalem to resolve this issue. They met with the apostles and elders to address this contentious issue. Verse 22 hints at the whole church also having some say. At minimum, the whole church was involved in the decision to send representatives with Paul and Barnabas to Antioch. The letter sent after the meeting records that the reason they were writing was because the individuals who were teaching that circumcision was

---

106. Gal. 2:9-10. Judea was a poorer region of the Roman Empire than several of the areas where Paul ministered. Collections are also mentioned in Acts 24:17, 1 Cor. 16:1-4 and 2 Cor. 8-9. These texts may be referring to the same collection as is mentioned in Rom. 15:25-26.

107. 2 Cor. 11:8-9, Subsection 6.7.3

108. Col. 4:16

necessary came from Jerusalem. The elders of the Jerusalem church are responsible to protect sound doctrine within the Jerusalem church. So, it was important for these elders to be involved in dealing with a case of false doctrine being taught by some of their members. Similarly, it was important for the apostles to be involved as they have a broad role in protecting sound doctrine. [109] Acts 15 is an example of one church asking a second church to issue a public correction of false teaching that originated in the second church. As will be discussed below, Acts 15 is not an example of a church determining correct doctrine and behavior for other churches.

The teaching in Acts 15:23-29 concerning food offered to idols is only partially consistent with Romans 14 and 1 Corinthians 8, 10:23-32. This shows that Paul felt free to provide teaching, which was different to the direction provided by the Acts 15 council. It implies that these churches did not need to follow the direction given by the Acts 15 council. [110]

On what basis did Paul teach what he taught? In Galatians 1:11-2:14 Paul says that he received by direct revelation the Gospel he preached as the apostle to the Gentiles. Claims concerning direct revelations are to be tested against Scripture by the individual or church or group of churches to which the revelation is relevant. [111] Paul's visit to Berea is a good example of this. In Acts 17:11 Luke commends the Bereans for checking this message against the Scriptures. Each church should look to the Bible as the final authority concerning matters of doctrine and practice. If a traveling leader or another church teaches something contrary to the Bible we should reject the teaching. Obviously there can be value in discussing matters with other churches and other leaders. Paul's visits to Jerusalem which he mentions in Galatians 1:11-2:14 are an example of this.

In Romans 14 and 1 Corinthians 8, 10:23-32 Paul discusses the eating of meat offered to idols and other potentially divisive topics. In these chapters Paul is very careful to respect the consciences of his readers. He does not pressure them to conform to his lifestyle choices on secondary matters. Unless something is unambiguously

---

109. 1 Tim. 1:3-4, Titus 1:10-14

110. The other side of this coin is that it took the church more than two centuries to decide which documents should be included in the New Testament. This process eventually resulted in the church concluding that Romans and 1 Corinthians are not just Paul's opinion but part of the inspired word of God.

111. Sections 1.1.5, 6.3

taught in Scripture, one church (or individual, even an apostle) should not pressure another church (or individual) to believe or behave in a certain way. In the cases where something is unambiguously taught in Scripture, leaders are responsible to counter the teaching of false doctrine or false moral teaching. The New Testament shows that this is to be done by influence and spiritual authority and possibly by using the local church discipline process. No other organizational or administrative authority existed.

## 6.7 Money and the New Testament church

### 6.7.1 Charity fund to benefit local community

New Testament church assemblies provided financial assistance to members of their own community who were in need.[112] In cities where there were a large number of house churches, these funds may have been jointly administered by a group of deacons. In other cases they may have been administered by the elders.

The early Jerusalem church assisted all of the members of their fellowship with financial needs. However, by the time Paul wrote his first letter to Timothy it seems that church practice had changed. In 1 Timothy 5:3-16 Paul commands Timothy, and by extension the whole church in Ephesus, to honor widows who are truly widows. He makes the following points concerning financial assistance:

- Financial assistance is focused on widows who have no children or grandchildren. Widows with relatives are expected to be supported by their relatives.
- Widows receiving financial assistance are expected to have set their hope on God and to be committed to prayer.
- They are expected to live selflessly.

The primary reason this passage focuses on financial assistance to widows was that women were usually financially supported by their husbands. Men were expected to work to provide for themselves and their families.[113] There may have been fewer opportunities for paid employment or self-employment for women than for men. It is possible that in some cases men also received financial assistance if they became unable to work and had no family to support them.[114]

---

112. Acts 2:44-45, 4:34-35, 6:1-3, 11:29-30, 1 Tim. 5:3-16

113. 2 Thess. 3:6-12

114. Verses 17, 18 of this chapter may refer to financial assistance to elders/ old men who have contributed significantly to the life of the assembly (Subsection 6.7.4).

Verse 8 seems to be a turning point in the passage. It introduces a specific list of widows. The nature of the list is not specified. Some have suggested that the widows on the list were paid church workers. The balance of the New Testament evidence does not support the suggestion that local church leaders were paid. [115] Another possibility is that the individuals on the list received long-term financial support whereas other widows only received temporary support. This interpretation seems to fit better with the following verses, which discuss the risks associated with providing long-term financial support.

The requirements to get on the list are much more stringent than the requirements to receive financial assistance listed in verses 3-7. The widows on the list must be over 60 years old and must be well known for their good deeds and their service to other believers. It is likely that the standard set in verse 10 would make it hard for recent converts to be included on the list. It is possible that the widows on the list made some kind of pledge that included remaining single. [116] Paul encourages younger widows to remarry.

There are parallels between the character traits for widows on the list and the character traits required for elders and deacons. In my mind it is completely reasonable to expect a proven track record of godly character from an individual before committing to long-term financial support. This applies regardless of whether the financial support provided to the widows on the list was pay for being a church worker or a long-term support commitment not linked to specific church work. Individuals receiving financial assistance would be expected to contribute to the life of the church just like all other church members.

Widows on the list must have "been the wife of one husband." The requirement to only have one husband is similar to the requirement for elders and deacons to only have one wife. [117] The interpretation of this requirement was discussed in Section 2.3, where it was concluded that this requirement addresses sexual promiscuity and the ability to form healthy long-term relationships. It is reasonable to extend this interpretation to this passage. It is not preventing individuals who have never married or who have remarried after the death of their partner from being on the list.

---

115. Subsection 6.7.4
116. v. 12 NIV
117. 1 Tim. 3:2, 12

Verse 13 states, "Besides that, they learn to be idlers, going about from house to house, and not only idlers, but also gossips and busybodies, saying what they should not." In this verse Paul addresses the potentially corrupting effect of receiving long-term financial support. I believe this is why he directs Timothy to restrict long-term support to individuals with demonstrated Christian character.

Some details associated with this passage may be specific to the cultural and historical situation. All churches should be generous to those in need within their own community. Great wisdom is needed in handling these charity funds. Support should be provided to those genuinely in need without creating an environment where they become more vulnerable to falling into sin. Particular care should be taken before committing to provide long-term support to an individual. The church should not subsidize people who are being lazy or who become lazy because the opportunity to do so is provided to them. Paul also makes this point in 2 Thessalonians 3:10-12 where he states that those who do not work should not eat. The pattern of financial support commanded in 1 Timothy 5:3-16 and 2 Thessalonians 3:10-12 seems more cautious than the practice of the early Jerusalem church.

### 6.7.2 Charity fund to benefit other communities

Galatians 2:9-10 records that James, Peter and John asked Paul and Barnabas to remember the needs of the poor in other churches as they took the gospel to the Gentiles. At least two collections by churches to aid members of other churches in financial need are recorded in the New Testament. In Acts 11:27-30 it is recorded that the church in Antioch collected money to aid the brothers living in Judea during a period of famine. In Romans 15:25-26 Paul says "At present, however, I am going to Jerusalem bringing aid to the saints. For Macedonia and Achaia have been pleased to make some contribution for the poor among the saints at Jerusalem." [118]

### 6.7.3 Financial support to traveling leaders

For the most part, the material needs of Jesus and his disciples were met by the gifts of various supporters. [119] On at least a few occasions they benefited from supernatural provision. Examples of this

118. Collections are also mentioned in Acts 24:17, 1 Cor. 16:1-4 and 2 Cor. 8-9. These collections may be the same collection as the one mentioned in Rom. 15:25-26.

119. Luke 8:3

include the feeding of the 5,000, the feeding of the 4,000 and the fish with a shekel in its mouth. [120]

When Jesus sent the 12 and the 72 on their ministry trips he commanded them to take no money or moneybag and to rely on the hospitality of a man of peace for the provision of food and shelter. [121] Jesus assures them of provision saying, "the laborer deserves his wages." The context shows that Jesus' understanding of wages in this passage is very different from ours. God is committed to providing for the needs of those engaged in ministry that He has initiated. But He is not promising payment of a pre-agreed amount on a regular basis as we assume when we use the word "wages."

It appears that the command to carry no money or moneybag on these ministry trips was specific to these particular trips. Luke 22:36 shows that there are situations where it is appropriate to have a moneybag. Similarly John 12:6 and 13:29 record that Judas had a moneybag that was used to provide for the needs of Jesus and the party that traveled with Him. It is likely that it was also used to provide for the needs of the poor. It appears that the command to not carry money on the ministry trips of the twelve and of the seventy two was given to provide an opportunity for them to see God's provision and thus strengthen their faith. [122]

The pattern of support of traveling leaders in the New Testament church is similar to the support of Jesus and the disciples. In 1 Corinthians 9:1-18 and 2 Thessalonians 3:6-12 Paul teaches that as an apostle he has the right to receive financial support for the work of church planting. It is likely that other traveling leaders also received financial support for church planting. In 1 Corinthians 9:11, 12a and 2 Thessalonians 3:7-8 he says that the churches he planted have a particular duty to support him. He also states that, "Nevertheless, we have not made use of this right, but we endure anything rather than put an obstacle in the way of the gospel of Christ." [123] Paul often chose to work as a tentmaker rather than receive financial support, which could be misinterpreted and thus become a barrier to the advance of the Gospel. Similarly, in Acts 20:33-35 and 2 Thessalonians 3:8-9 he says he supported himself by working to be an example of hard work to the congregation he

120. Matt. 14:15-21, 15:32-38, 17:24-27

121. Luke 9:1-5, 10:1-8

122. Luke 22:35

123. 1 Cor. 9:12b

was planting. In Acts 20:35 Paul also says that he wanted to earn so that he would be able to give, and so that he could provide an example of generosity. Paul did on occasion receive financial support. For example in 2 Corinthians 11:8-9 Paul says that he received financial support from the churches in Macedonia while working in Corinth. John in 3 John 1:5-9 tells his readers that they ought to support traveling leaders.

Traveling leaders often worked a considerable distance from their supporters. At least in Paul's case his support came from multiple churches spread over a considerable area. The risks and difficulties associated with travel in the 1st Century make it likely that supporters sent gifts relatively infrequently. It also means that there may have been limited human coordination between supporters living in different areas. So it is unlikely that the financial support received by traveling leaders came in the form of a fixed payment paid on a regular basis.

There are some indicators that teams of traveling leaders shared their money. For example in Acts 20:34 Paul states that his work not only provided for his own financial needs but also for the needs of those who were with him.

### 6.7.4 Financial support to local leaders

The use of the word "we" in Acts 20:34-35 indicates that Paul expected the elders of Ephesus to be working hard in secular employment so that they would be able to help the weak just like he did. Similarly in 2 Thessalonians 3:6-12 Paul reminds the Thessalonians that he and his companions worked to provide for their own needs. He explicitly states that they chose to do this to be an example to the Thessalonian church assembly. This passage sets a clear expectation that all believers will work. There is no hint in this passage of the elders being paid by the church. Why would elders be paid if Paul, Silas and Timothy were not paid?

Galatians 6:6 commands individuals to share all good things with their teacher. Presumably this includes money and hospitality, including hospitality for traveling teachers. Teaching is not restricted to elders so it is hard to use this verse to argue for elders receiving a salary. In fact it may imply the opposite. If in a particular case the teacher was an elder and the elder was receiving a salary funded through the donations of church members, it seems duplicative to expect the church member receiving teaching to share directly "all good things" with the elder.

It is likely that church members, acting as individuals, gave gifts and extended hospitality to elders from time to time—especially if they were in financial need. It is also plausible that some elders after receiving a gift would work fewer hours in secular employment and more hours in ministry.

Some people interpret 1 Timothy 5:17-18 as teaching that at least some elders were paid. I believe that to correctly understand this passage it is necessary to interpret it in the context of the preceding section. It is highly plausible that in Paul's mind 1 Timothy 5:3-18 is a single topic in two parts. The first part (vv. 3-16) is about the appropriate honor (v. 3) for widows especially elderly widows, and the second part (vv. 17-18) is about the appropriate honor (v. 17) for old men/elders especially those who "labor in preaching and teaching."

The Greek word for honor in v. 17 is *time*, which may be translated estimate of worth, price, value, precious things, careful regard, honor, state of honor, dignity, observance, veneration, mark of favor and consideration. This word occurs 43 times in the New Testament. In 33 places the KJV translates it "honor" and in eight places the KJV translates it as "price." It is never used to describe a salary or wages. The related Greek verb (*timao*) is used in v. 3. It is reasonable to assume that Paul has the same meaning in mind in both verses. As Paul's use of this word is spelled out in more detail in vv. 3-16 we have an opportunity by looking at these verses to gain additional insight into his meaning in vv. 17-18. Honoring widows, who are truly widows, only includes providing financial assistance if no family member is available to help. [124] In most cases it seems that only short-term financial assistance was provided. It seems that only widows over 60 with no family received long-term financial assistance.

Given this context it is reasonable to presume that honoring elders included short-term financial assistance to meet a particular need when no family was available to help. It is plausible that if an elder became permanently unable to work, long-term financial assistance might be provided if no family was available to support him.

---

124. Subsection 6.7.1

The quotes in 1 Timothy 5:18 may sound like pay to modern readers. Even if this is the correct interpretation, which as will be seen in the following discussion is questionable, it does not mean that elders should be paid. Paul is making the point that elders deserve to be respected just as working animals deserve to be allowed to eat and individuals who work deserve wages.

It is possible that the quotes in 1 Timothy 5:18 did not communicate the same message to the New Testament church as they do to us. The second quote "the laborer deserves his wages" is also used in Luke 10:7. [125] In Luke 10 this phrase does not mean wages as we currently understand them. The seventy two were commanded to travel with no moneybag. In this passage, this phrase is a guarantee of the provision of food and shelter by God through men of peace; it is not a promise of regular pay. From the point of view of the man of peace providing this hospitality, it is exactly the sort of generosity commanded in Galatians 6:6. This quote is consistent with a culture of generosity towards elders, especially those in financial need or who were unable to work, expressed as individual gifts and acts of hospitality. [126]

The first quote in v. 18 "You shall not muzzle an ox when it treads out the grain," is also quoted in 1 Corinthians 9:9 where Paul uses this quote to justify the financial support of traveling leaders. This quote and the linkage to 1 Corinthians 9 is perhaps the strongest basis in the New Testament supporting the possibility of paying local leaders. However, this very linkage to the support of traveling leaders lends support to the possibility that Paul is not considering what we would call pay in this verse. As noted in Subsection 6.7.3 the difficulties associated with travel in the ancient world resulted in traveling leaders receiving financial support on a sporadic basis. It is unlikely that any human coordinated their support to ensure they received gifts on a predictable schedule and of a predictable amount. I consider it plausible that Paul intended this quote to encourage a culture of generosity towards elders, rather than to encourage payment of a regular salary.

If one considers 1 Timothy 5:17-18 only in the context of 1 Corinthians 9 it is possible to conclude that elders were paid. However, if one considers these verses also in the context of the

---

125. Paul may be paraphrasing Lev. 19:13, Deut. 24:15.

126. Subsection 6.7.3

other passages discussed above it seems more reasonable to me to assume that elders were not paid a regular salary. The New Testament strongly encourages generosity towards elders. I suspect that was mostly expressed through hospitality and gifts especially if the elder had a financial need and no family to help. Some elders who were permanently unable to work and had no family to support them may have received long-term financial assistance from the church.

Frank Viola states, in his book *Pagan Christianity,* that the first reference to paid clergy is in the writings of Cyprian. [127] He also says that the practice of paying clergy did not become common until the time of Constantine, early in the 4th Century.

It is not clear to me how a church which is small enough to meet in a private home could afford to pay a living wage to a plurality of elders, especially as many church members during the New Testament period were slaves. Also, it is possible that a significant portion of the money donated may have been used to provide for widows or traveling leaders.

Another reason to doubt that elders were paid is the impact of paying staff on church dynamics. If some individuals are paid and others not paid, it creates a two tier set up within the church. I believe that the New Testament shows that God does not want this kind of "two-tier" body. Another problem with paying elders is that it can make the church money-centered as it is necessary to raise the money to pay the elders.

An example of the damage paying elders can have on a house church movement is provided in Chapter 32 of *Nexus, The World House Church Movement Reader*. This chapter, which is written by David Garrison, is entitled "A house church explosion in the wake of the Khmer Rouge." After describing the wonderful growth of this movement during the 1990s and the principles underpinning this movement, the author also provides the following explanation for the end of the movement.

> By the year 2000, though, the Cambodia Church Planting Movement had mostly passed. Before the movement began to wane, other denominations and mission agencies such as the Christian and Missionary Alliance, Overseas Missionary Fellowship, Four-Square Gospel, Presbyterians, and Campus Crusade for Christ all reaped a harvest in Cambodia. In the end

---

127. AD 200-258

it suffered, not from lack of missionary attention, but from too many well-intentioned intrusions from the outside. Foreign funds went to subsidize pastors and church planters who had previously done the work without remuneration. Salaries led to a sort of professional minister class that created a gap between church leaders and common laypersons. Funds also accelerated the rate of institutionalization of training, ministry, and leadership. With funds and institutions came internal conflict within denominational hierarchies over who would control these resources.

### 6.7.5 Did house churches have a collection every week?

There is no clear statement in the New Testament about weekly collections. The only passage I know directly addressing this topic is 1 Corinthians 16:1-2 which says:

> Now concerning the collection for the saints: as I directed the churches of Galatia, so you also are to do. On the first day of every week, each of you is to put something aside and store it up, as he may prosper, so that there will be no collecting when I come.

The natural interpretation of the first half of verse 2 is that each one should be responsible for putting aside and storing their own money that they wish to give to the collection. Based on 2 Corinthians 9:5, it appears that some brothers went ahead of Paul and collected the money which each person had been setting aside so it would be ready prior to Paul's arrival. Paul is not instructing the Corinthian church to collect money each week at their meeting.

This passage is specific to a one-time collection to aid the church in Jerusalem. It does not directly address what churches might do to meet ongoing needs such as providing for widows. However if it was the practice of the church to have a weekly collection to provide for widows it is slightly surprising, but not impossible, that Paul would direct a different approach for the collection for the church in Jerusalem.

This interpretation is consistent with other passages that touch on giving. For example, it is likely that individual gifts such as are commanded in Galatians 6:6 were a major focus of New Testament giving.[128] This also seems to have been the pattern in the early chapters of Acts. For example, Acts 2:45 and 4:34-5:4 mention financial needs being met by the sale of property.[129] In Acts 2:45 it

---

128. Subsection 6.7.4

129. Curiously in the first few chapters of Acts there is no mention of donations from earnings.

seems that the individual who sold the property then distributed the money to those in need. In Acts 4:35, 37 and 5:1 the money was laid at the apostles' feet for them to distribute. In Acts 6:1-6 responsibility for distributing the money transitions to a group of seven leaders. It is likely that these men were deacons. There is no hint in any of these passages of collections in meetings.

So in summary, it seems plausible that New Testament assemblies did not have weekly collections. Paul does encourage us to think about giving as we receive income. He and the other New Testament authors do not command a particular pattern for us to follow in implementing our giving.

### 6.7.6 Did the New Testament church teach tithing?

Tithes and tithing are mentioned several times in Hebrews 7 and three times in the Gospels. Hebrews 7 is all about the superiority of Jesus' priesthood, as a priest after the order of Melchizedek, relative to the Levitical priesthood. The author of Hebrews makes this argument based, in part, on Abraham's giving to Melchizedek ten percent of the spoils he captured when releasing Lot. [130] Unlike the tithe taught in the law, this was a onetime gift from the spoils of battle. It was not a continuous giving of ten percent of all income. In fact Abraham kept nothing for himself from the spoils. There is no hint in this passage that the New Testament church should view the giving of ten percent in Genesis 14 as a mandatory example to follow from our normal income.

The other three references to tithing in the New Testament are not entirely positive. Jesus mentions tithing as a source of self-righteousness for the Pharisee in the parable of the Pharisee and the tax collector. [131] In Matthew 23:23 Jesus says "Woe to you, scribes and Pharisees, hypocrites! For you tithe mint and dill and cumin, and have neglected the weightier matters of the law: justice and mercy and faithfulness. These you ought to have done, without neglecting the others." This verse may be a command to all believers to tithe, but to be consistent with the rest of the New Testament, it is more likely that this verse is only relevant to those who choose to be under the law.

In Mark 12:41-44 Jesus comments on the giving at the temple. The clear implication of this passage is that what matters to God is not the

---

130. Gen. 14:8-24
131. Luke 18:9-14

percentage we give but what it costs us. The poor widow "put in all she had to live on" whereas the rich gave out of their abundance. It is distinctly plausible that the rich were tithing. Jesus did not commend them for their generosity. An implication of this passage is that the rich should be giving more than 10 percent.

In Luke 6:38 Jesus teaches "give, and it will be given to you. Good measure, pressed down, shaken together, running over, will be put into your lap. For with the measure you use it will be measured back to you." This teaching also encourages costly generosity rather than compliance with giving a fixed percentage. Incidentally the fulfillment of this promise is not limited to financial blessing during our life on earth. [132]

Acts 2:45 and 4:34-5:4 mention that the financial needs of the Jerusalem church were met by the sale of property. Individuals were giving the full proceeds from the sale of land to the church—not just 10 percent. Peter says in Acts 5:3-4 that Ananias was free to give only a portion of the proceeds of the sale of the land. Ananias' sin was claiming to give all of the money when he did not. These passages do not support tithing. They encourage greater generosity than tithing.

Paul discusses giving in 2 Corinthians 8-9 and touches on this topic in various other places in his letters. [133] Paul does not teach tithing in any of these passages. Paul makes the following key points related to giving:

- Each believer should give generously based on their own financial situation. [134]
- Exercising our free will is an important element of giving. [135] The implication of this principle is that they were not giving to meet an exact percentage target.
- Giving is an act of grace. [136] Again the implication of this principle is that they were not giving to meet an exact percentage target.
- It is fair for those experiencing a season of abundance to give to those in need. [137]

---

132. 2 Cor. 9:10
133. *E.g.*, Rom. 15:25-26, 1 Cor. 16:1-3, Gal. 2:9-10, 6:6
134. 2 Cor. 8:3, 12
135. 2 Cor. 8:3, 9:5, 7
136. 2 Cor. 8:6-7
137. 2 Cor. 8:13-14

- It is important to be very careful to handle donated funds in a manner that is obviously appropriate.[138]
- The principle of sowing and reaping applies to our handling of our finances.[139] Jesus makes the same point in Luke 6:38. In 2 Corinthians 9:10 Paul teaches that the harvest from our generosity is not just financial.
- Our heart attitude is critical. This is expressed in several ways. For example in 2 Corinthians 9:7 Paul says "the Lord loves a cheerful giver." In 2 Corinthians 8:4 he talks of the Macedonians begging earnestly for the favor of taking part in the relief of the saints. 2 Corinthians 8:24 says giving is an evidence of love. Several other verses in these chapters touch on the importance of our heart attitude in giving.
- It is important to complete what we start.[140]

Several of these points appear to be incompatible with tithing.

Of course tithing was commanded in the Old Testament. The purpose of the tithe was to provide for the Levites.[141] The tithe was the Levite's pay for their service in the tent of meeting. Deuteronomy 26:12 commands that the tithe in the third year is also to be used to support those in financial need. The tithe was an important part of the Jewish religious system. This system was centered on paid leaders who performed the religious rituals defined in the law. Jesus' death and resurrection ended this religious system. The command to tithe ended with the need for the temple system.[142]

Frank Viola states, in his book *Pagan Christianity*, that the first reference to believers tithing is in the writings of Cyprian. References to tithing become more common after Constantine. According to Frank Viola, the presumption that the Old Testament teaching on tithing should apply to the church did not become widespread until late in the first millennium.

So in summary, the New Testament does not teach that believers should tithe and the historical record indicates that this teaching did not become widespread until a much later date. The Bible does however teach that believers should be generous. For many believers this

---

138. 2 Cor. 8:20-21
139. 2 Cor. 9:6
140. 2 Cor. 8:11
141. Num. 18:20-32
142. Heb. 6-10

may involve giving around 10 percent of their income, but especially in the rich nations of the world, many believers may be in the place where appropriate generosity involves giving substantially more than 10 percent.

### 6.7.7 To what extent did believers hold all things in common?

In Acts 2:44 it is recorded that "And all who believed were together and had all things in common." Similarly in Acts 4:32 it says "Now the full number of those who believed were of one heart and soul, and no one said that any of the things that belonged to him was his own, but they had everything in common." And in Acts 6:1 it is noted that there was a daily distribution of food for the widows in the community. It is likely that the apostles and then the deacons had a shared moneybag, which was used to buy this food and meet other needs within the community. If this is a correct assumption, it was a continuation of the practice the apostles had when they traveled with Jesus.[143] It is not surprising that the apostles continued this practice, which they had learned from Jesus.

The incident with Ananias and Sapphira shows that this pattern of sharing was a free choice for each individual or couple concerned.[144] Peter says that their property was fully theirs before they sold it and that they were free to do what they wished with the money they received from the sale. Their sin was seeking to look more generous than they really were. They lied to God. The church was not teaching that every member should transfer the ownership of all of their property to the church. However there was a wonderful spirit of generosity about the early Jerusalem church and sufficient individuals chose to sell property for all financial needs to be met. It appears that other New Testament churches handled money differently.[145] It seems that the church became more cautious in its generosity, perhaps because providing for all financial needs has a corrupting effect on many individuals.

It is implicit in the New Testament teaching on giving that each individual (or couple) has discretion over how he chooses to use his money. For example, if the church in Corinth was holding "all things in common" in the sense that all church members pooled their income and assets, then it would make sense for Paul to direct

143. John 12:6, 13:29

144. Acts 5:1-10

145. Subsection 6.7.1

those who administered the common moneybag to set some money aside for the church in Jerusalem. Paul does not do this. Instead he commands individuals to set money aside on a weekly basis for this collection.[146] The implication is that each individual is deciding how he or she spends her own money. Similarly, 2 Timothy 4:13 implies that Paul considered a cloak and some books and parchments to be his personal property.

It is likely that some teams of traveling leaders had a shared moneybag.[147] It seems that the New Testament church concluded that the example Jesus provided by having a shared moneybag during His public ministry was an example for teams of traveling leaders not the whole church. Ultimately everything belongs to God. We are to hold lightly what we consider to be "our" property and be open to share it or give it away.

---

146. 1 Cor. 16:1-2

147. Subsection 6.7.3

# Chapter 7
# Relevance of New Testament Church Practices

## 7.1 Summary of New Testament church practices

The primary elements of the pattern of life of local church assemblies described in the New Testament include:

- New Testament church is a community of believers characterized by their love for God and their love for one another. "One anothering" and mutual submission are core elements of their community life. Each assembly is a community of brothers and sisters in God's family.
- Everyone contributes to the meetings and to ministry outside of meetings. Church assembly meetings are not about spectators watching the paid professionals do the bulk of the work. Church is about every member participating. The goal is for God to be leading each one to contribute in the manner of His choosing. Examples of potential contributions to New Testament church meetings include: leading the group into worship by initiating the singing of a hymn or worship song; praying or sharing a prayer request; reading a passage of scripture; contributing to a Bible discussion; teaching, exhorting and encouraging; sharing a testimony; asking a question; speaking in tongues, providing an interpretation of a tongue, speaking prophetically, sharing a vision, sharing a word of knowledge or of wisdom.[1]

---

1. In order to provide an opportunity for every member to contribute it is likely that most contributions to the meeting will be fairly brief. There may be periods of silence between contributions. These periods of silence may be valuable in multiple ways. Firstly, they give an opportunity to meditate on the contribution which has just happened. Secondly, they give an opportunity for each person present to abide with Jesus and listen to Him. Often this will include asking the question: do You want me to make a contribution to the meeting at this time? I find that having to face this question many times during a meeting helps me keep a healthy focus on God. Thirdly, periods of silence may provide the extra time some individuals need to be sure that this is the right moment to make their contribution.

- Both in meetings and outside of meetings everyone is free to minister as they sense God is leading them to minister. As each one obeys Jesus their contributions fit together to form a beautiful whole that achieves what Jesus wants. There is no need to ask a human leader for permission to minister. Elders and other mature believers help less mature believers to love and minister in a healthy manner. No roles in the life of the local church are exclusively reserved to leaders.
- Many of the contributions to New Testament church meetings and outside of meetings flow from the gifts that the Holy Spirit gives to believers. The church is a community of gifted individuals, who use their gifts, as led by the Holy Spirit, to serve and edify one another and the community around them. All are important and need to flow together in mutual dependence and submission to form a whole, which is much greater than the sum of the parts. Meetings and ministry outside of meetings are not centered around those with the gifts of pastoring or teaching.
- Potential revelatory words (*e.g.*, prophetic words, words of knowledge and visions) are submitted to the individual or group of individuals to whom they apply so that they can evaluate them. These gifts are not to be used to control or manipulate people, but to serve and edify them. The individual who receives the word or vision needs to discern how and when to share it.
- The primary focus of each believer is on Jesus, not a human leader. New Testament believers did not come to meetings thinking "I wonder what the pastor will preach about this week" or "I wonder if I will be given permission to serve in the Sunday school." Instead they came to meetings praying, "Come and meet with us today, Lord Jesus, guide and equip each one of us to contribute" and "What do you want me to contribute to today's meeting?"
- Teaching is a very important part of New Testament church life, taking place both in house church meetings and outside of the main meetings. Everyone is encouraged to contribute to teaching, but it is likely that most teaching was done by those with the gift of teaching.
- Jesus used a wide range of teaching styles. It is likely that a similar wide range of teaching styles were used in New Testament churches. It is likely that extended monologues similar to modern day sermons were rare and that dialog was an important element of New Testament style teaching. Learning by following the example of a mature believer and by personal involvement in ministry is emphasized in the New Testament. New Testament style house churches were a safe place to learn by doing.
- The focus of teaching in the New Testament is on God's truth being written on our hearts. Knowing sound doctrine is also important. Only God can write on our hearts and develop within us the Mind of Christ.

- Church planting and evangelism are high priorities in the New Testament church.
- Decisions impacting a complete house church are made by consensus of the complete house church. This includes church discipline and decisions related to evaluating revelatory words, which apply to the complete house church. Consensus based decision-making can be really hard and can provide opportunities to grow in humility, mutual submission and love for one another.
- Typically each mature house church has several co-equal elders. New house churches comprising new believers may exist for a while with no elders. The only New Testament reference to a church with a predominant elder is negative.[2]
- The essence of New Testament local church leadership (elders) is to watch over the community. It is about helping each believer to abide with Jesus. Elders lead by exercising influence and they facilitate the flow of church life. They provide leadership, but not in the sense of being the key decision-makers and organizers.
- Believers are expected to submit to their leaders and to be open to persuasion by their leaders. These leaders have no authority to direct the activities of others. They should be examples of living out the Christian life including walking in mutual submission.
- New Testament churches are generous. This generosity provides for those in financial need and for the support of traveling leaders. In communities where there are several house churches a group of deacons may coordinate the financial provision to those in need. New Testament local church leaders were not paid.
- The maximum size of a New Testament style house church flows from the commitment to strong bonds of "one anothering," participatory meetings and consensual decision-making. All of these factors combine to place an upper limit on the size of each congregation. This limit is compatible with meeting in homes.
- House churches are complete churches in and of themselves. They engage in the full range of activities mentioned in the Bible concerning church. For example they celebrate the Lord's supper, baptize new believers and when necessary they apply church discipline.
- House churches are autonomous. No other church, nor any traveling leader, can force them to do something.
- All of the churches in a particular community also form the single church of that community and all believers are part of the single, universal church. Part of being the single church in a community includes individual house churches cooperating with one another and encouraging one another. From time to time the house

---

2. 3 John 1:9-10

churches in a community may get together for joint meetings or activities. House churches interact with one another as equals working together by consensus and influence.

- In communities where there are several house churches, members of different house churches may work together in various types of ministry. The same leadership principles apply to these ministry teams as apply to house churches.
- Women are free to contribute to all aspects of the life of the church including teaching and leading.
- New Testament church is "organic." The word "organic" is chosen to emphasize that the church is first and foremost a living being (or organism). All of the parts of the body work together in complementary ways for the common good under the leadership of Jesus.[3]
- New Testament churches are imperfect. They are a community of humans who are being transformed by God's grace. In different ways we all fall short and cause our spiritual community to fall short.

It can be seen from the above summary that the pattern or style of church life provided in the New Testament is not about organization or religious activity; rather it is about every believer directly connecting to God and His life. Each believer's ministry flows out of his connection to God. There is great freedom in the New Testament pattern of church life.

Some of the key elements of New Testament teaching on Christian leadership are as follows:

- The broadest Biblical commands as to how we treat other people (*e.g.*, "love your neighbor as yourself" or "do unto others as you would have them do unto you") are the foundations of Christian leadership.
- Christian leadership is not about lording it over others, it is about being a servant of God and His people. Mutual submission includes leaders submitting to individual believers.

---

3. The church is not an organization. It is a living body or organic community. Organizations are characterized by identified job positions. The essence of leadership in organizations is decision-making and performing specific tasks restricted to the individual who holds that leadership role. In organizations, individuals who do not hold a leadership position, are expected to do what they are told to do or are given permission to do. Individual house churches, networks of house churches within a community and the church universal are all a living, organic body. At none of these levels is New Testament church an organization.

- Christian leadership is not about leading within the context of an organization. It is about being part of a body. Christian leadership is not defined by certain roles and responsibilities that may only be performed by the leader. For example, it is not about organizing meetings and ministry and it is not about deciding who is allowed to participate in certain ministries. Christian leadership is about influencing believers to walk closely with Jesus so that they are available to be used by Him.
- In the Christian community it is not appropriate to grant leaders special positions and titles with special rights. We are all brothers and sisters and Jesus is our only teacher and guide. It is acceptable to acknowledge a pattern of gifting in an individual's life (*e.g.*, teacher or prophet) as long as the focus remains on the Giver of the gift.
- Jesus will deal with the "tares" (or "weeds") in His kingdom at the time of His choosing. Christian leadership is not about pulling up tares and deciding which seeds are good seeds and which are tare seeds. Leaders are expected to protect sound doctrine.
- The New Testament does not teach believers to obey their leaders. It commands believers to be persuaded by their leaders. Being persuaded by someone commonly involves dialog similar to healthy submission. The primary areas where believers are expected to be persuaded by their leaders are sound doctrine and general principles for righteous living. Christians should be looking to Jesus for individual guidance as to the specific ministry contributions He wants them to make.
- Christians should walk in submission to their leaders. This is not an unthinking submission. It will commonly involve dialog, which may result in the leader changing his position. It is a submission that takes place within the broader context of the mutual submission of all believers to one another. This includes the submission of leaders to individuals who are not leaders.
- In the New Testament there are two kinds of Christian leaders: local leaders, who are called elders or overseers; and traveling leaders. Women may serve as local or traveling leaders.
- Traveling leaders start churches in places where there are no churches and support existing churches. In general they stay in a town for a fairly short time, but occasionally stay in one place for a handful of years. In general, full-time traveling leaders interact with a local church assembly like a visitor rather than like a long-term member of the community. Part-time traveling leaders may be a long-term member of one house church and serve that house church as an elder.
- Traveling leaders operate as teams. Within these teams more mature traveling leaders mentor and coach less mature traveling

leaders. New traveling leaders are trained "on the job." This includes watching the experienced traveling leaders and discussing with them how they serve. It also involves stepping into ministry and learning by doing. Membership of these teams of traveling leaders is fairly fluid. As traveling leaders mature they may leave their first team and start a new team where they are the mentor.

- Teams of traveling leaders may have a clearly defined leader or group of leaders. These leaders may be highly influential in deciding where team members minister. Individual traveling leaders remain directly accountable to Jesus and may sometimes not follow the recommendation of the team leader.
- Traveling leaders are expected to be humble and respectful and to use influence as they seek to provide support and encouragement to local churches. They cannot force a local church to do their will.

The New Testament assumes that no individual or group of individuals is immune from spiritual compromise. This may involve any kind of sinful behavior or doctrinal error. In order to minimize the problems that result from individuals or groups becoming compromised, power is carefully balanced in the New Testament church model. Key features of this balance of power are as follows:

- Within each local church assembly there is a group of co-equal elders whose primary role is to help the believers remain focused on Jesus. They are also expected to protect sound doctrine.
- Decisions that impact the local church are made by consensus of the complete local church. Elders, and other mature believers, may be active in facilitating this process: ensuring that everyone gets a chance to speak; helping to maintain a respectful tone to the dialog; and helping everyone approach the question in a spiritual manner.
- Each local church is in fellowship with other local churches and a group of traveling leaders. Relating to a group of traveling leaders is helpful to a local church because each traveling leader is able to bless the local church in a unique way based on his or her personality and gifting. No single human leader is well suited to address the full range of circumstances that can arise in a local church. Relating to a group of traveling leaders also helps to protect both the church and the traveling leaders from slipping into a mindset that a particular traveling leader is the "Bishop" over a particular church or group of churches.
- Each local church is responsible to exercise discernment concerning the traveling leaders to protect themselves from unhealthy traveling leaders. Being in relationship with multiple traveling leaders makes it easier to spot when one gets into sin or

doctrinal error and makes it easier to draw healthy boundaries when that happens.

- Each traveling leader is responsible to interact wisely with individual congregations and individual believers within those congregations. When problems arise one or more traveling leaders may help to resolve the problems. For the most part this is achieved by influencing people. When the issue is sin or the teaching of false doctrine, it may be appropriate for a traveling leader to rebuke the individual(s). They may also encourage a church to initiate the church discipline process. New Testament traveling leaders had no human power (*e.g.*, the authority to replace local leaders) to force change on congregations that do not want to receive it.
- These features represent the ideal presented in the New Testament. Not all New Testament house churches would have had the benefit of all of these features at all times.

The above points describe the "wineskin" of New Testament church practices. It should never be forgotten that the wineskin only exists to be a container for the wine. What matters most is the wine. Is the local spiritual community (church assembly) full of the love and life of our living and loving God? This is the new wine Jesus came to bring. This wine flows from the place of intimate abiding with Jesus. The wineskin of church life described in the New Testament creates an environment that is particularly well suited to welcoming the love and life of our God. It is well suited to keeping our spiritual lives both as individuals and as a spiritual community fresh and dynamic. It also helps individuals to grow into spiritual maturity and godly character.[4]

One of the reasons I like to use the word wineskin in the context of church practices is that wineskins are flexible. Wine bottles are rigid and inflexible and wine bottles may shatter into many dangerous pieces of glass. The pattern of church life described in the New Testament is flexible like a wineskin. It is not a rigid organizational structure. It includes several important checks and balances that help to protect both individuals and the complete community.

The model of community and leadership presented in Scripture and discussed in this section is extremely hard to implement in groups larger than a house church. This gives each church a choice as it grows. Either it can divide to remain small enough so that it can continue to implement this Biblical model or it can grow and adopt a new model.

---

4. See section 7.3

## 7.2 Relevance of house church model in times of persecution

Meeting in homes instead of church buildings provides a measure of protection during times of persecution. Church buildings and meetings in church buildings are attractive targets to persecutors. Meetings in homes typically draw less attention. Obviously, determined persecutors, like Saul in Acts 8:3, can and do persecute believers who participate in these meetings.

There is a second and more significant way that the New Testament church model helps in times of persecution. In Matthew 26:31, Jesus quotes Zechariah 13:7 which says, "Strike the shepherd, and the sheep will be scattered." Matthew 26:31 shows that the primary application of this prophecy is to the death of Jesus. However there is a broader spiritual principle underlying this verse that applies to churches experiencing persecution. If the people are taught to look to a trained pastor (shepherd) to initiate and lead meetings, it is quite likely that the church will be scattered if the pastor is arrested or killed. If instead the church is not centered on a pastor and the people are taught that meetings are about participation by every member as led by the Holy Spirit, it is much more likely that the church will continue if the elders are arrested or killed.

The survival and growth of the church in the face of Roman persecution is an example of the resiliency that results from the relative lack of dependence on leaders. As Rodney Stark observes:

> Ramsey MacMullen recognized that the failure of Roman authorities to understand this fact accounts for the strange aspects of the persecutions: that only leaders were seized, while crowds of obvious Christians went unpunished. That is, when the Romans decided to destroy Christianity, "they did so from the top down evidently taking it for granted that only the church leaders counted." This mistaken judgment was according to MacMullen, based on the fact that paganism was utterly dependent on the elite and could easily have been destroyed from the top. [5]

In some countries where churches are required to register with the government the term "house church" is used to describe any church that is not registered. Such churches often meet in homes, but in some cases meet in a larger building or outdoors. In some

---

5. Stark, Rodney, *The Rise of Christianity*, Harper Collins, 1997, pg. 208, copyright permission courtesy Princeton University Press and MacMullen, Ramsey, *Paganism in the Roman Empire*, New Haven: Yale University Press, 1981 pg. 129.

cases these churches follow the New Testament pattern for church as described in this book. In other cases, like many churches that meet in homes in countries with no persecution, they are centered around a pastor.

## 7.3 Impact of the pattern of church life on spiritual development

If one agrees that church in New Testament times was as I have described it in this book, it begs the question: was the transition from the New Testament style of church with every member participation in ministry and decision-making, to the leader-centric model, which has dominated the church scene for the last seventeen centuries, a good development that God always wanted to bring forth as the church matured, or a divergence from His preferred plan for the church? In this section I discuss the impact of these two ways of being church on the spiritual development of believers. In the next section I will discuss risks associated with these two ways of being church.

### *Leader-centric pattern of church life*

Belonging to a church led by a paid religious professional can be a positive experience for almost everyone involved. Most believers agree that only the paid professionals are qualified to do certain important types of ministry. The paid professionals like this because it justifies their salary and their status. Much of the rest of the church likes this as it gives them an excuse to avoid certain responsibilities. Some church members like this arrangement as it allows them to be passive and/or spiritually lazy. Passivity and spiritual laziness result in continuing spiritual immaturity among the church members. The challenges of church leadership help many clergy to grow to spiritual maturity. These dynamics help maintain a spiritual maturity gap between the clergy and most of the laity, which justifies the laity continuing to depend on the clergy for most meaningful ministry. It is a stable and comfortable system for most of the individuals involved, which may be one reason that it has been the dominant church model for seventeen centuries.

In traditional leader-centric church services the congregation follows the lead of the pastor(s) with limited opportunities to contribute to the meeting. Obviously they are supposed to join in the worship and prayers selected by the leaders and they are supposed to listen carefully to the Bible reading(s) and sermon. They are also expected to give generously to pay for the buildings, staff and programs. In many cases the believers will genuinely worship, pray and learn as they follow along.

For believers who are not involved in leading a church service, their participation in the service is somewhat analogous to spectators at some sporting events. For many sports, some spectators become highly engaged in the game, regularly shouting words of encouragement and cheering good plays. In a similar manner, some believers become actively engaged in conventional church services, which is excellent. Even so the members of the sports team have the opportunity to be much more fully engaged in the game than the spectators. Similarly, meetings based on every member participation give believers the opportunity to be more fully engaged than is possible in conventional leader-centric church services.

An unspoken message associated with conventional leader-centric church services is that ordinary believers are not qualified to contribute to the focal point of church life. They are only qualified to follow the leadership of the paid religious professionals. In many churches the spoken message from the pulpit encourages believers to be active contributors to various forms of ministry. In many of these churches however, believers require the permission and oversight of a paid professional if they wish to follow this encouragement and become active contributors to a particular ministry (*e.g.*, teaching a Sunday School class). This requirement to receive permission and ongoing oversight reinforces the unspoken message that it is risky for ordinary believers to be active in ministry. Given the lack of spiritual initiative shown by many church attendees it seems that many of them pick up on the unspoken message that they are unqualified to be anything other than passive followers or spectators. Only a few pick up on the spoken message calling them to active engagement.

In most conventional leader-centric churches the clergy are both trained and paid to love and care for their congregation. The intent underlying this is excellent. Unfortunately the law of unintended consequences distorts this good intent in a most pernicious manner. In many churches a significant proportion of the congregation interprets the presence of paid clergy as implying that they are not equipped or needed to be active in loving and caring for other members of the congregation.

Typical Sunday morning services are the antithesis of healthy body life. A few individuals are very active but most are spectators. The structure of most church meetings prevents the majority of the congregation from being, during the service, the part of the body God intends them to be. In many cases these church services provide limited opportunities for "one anothering."

Many churches realize the importance of the church being a body with multiple diverse gifts and they realize the importance of "one anothering." So they seek to provide other settings for these important elements of healthy body life. Unfortunately many believers treat these opportunities for healthy body life as an optional extra and do not participate in them. Some of this is because people are busy and some of it may be because people have picked up on the unspoken message of the leader-centric meetings that they are not qualified to be active participants in church life. Another factor in some cases is that paid clergy justify their position by making participation in the clergy-centric Sunday service the most important part of the life of the community. This is very unfortunate, as participation in meetings where the church operates as a body and where individuals can "one another" is particularly valuable for our growth into spiritual maturity.

I once heard a sermon at a conventional leader-centric church where the pastor expounded on John 5:19-20, which states that Jesus only did what He saw the Father doing. The pastor taught the congregation that this is an example for all of us to follow. He illustrated this point with various photographs of life situations we all commonly encounter. He taught that we should all be looking to see what the Father was doing in each of these circumstances and then following the Father's lead. This is a great teaching, which I fully endorse. However, it most likely did not occur to the pastor or any of the congregation that an important photograph was missing: there was no photograph of a church meeting. Jesus wants us to observe the Father and follow His lead in church meetings and in all other settings. Traditional leader-centric church services are structured in a manner that prevents the vast majority of attendees from following the Father's lead during the service. This is a huge loss to the church as the main weekly meeting is a wonderful place to learn how to observe the Father and then follow His lead. I believe that the Father wants to use this safe setting to teach believers this way of living.

Good teaching content is one of the best things provided by many leader-centric churches. Good teaching is very important, especially when it reaches our hearts instead of getting stuck in our heads. Unfortunately, this good teaching is sometimes put on a pedestal and the inscription on the pedestal says: "It is so important for you to be well taught before you attempt ministry that you should delay stepping out into ministry until you have received more teaching." This message is implicit in services where only the trained religious professionals are allowed to teach. Clearly we are not qualified until we have received as much teaching as is included in a seminary degree. Based on this logic many believers hold back from ministry. But active participation in ministry is part of the path to growth, so they remain stuck in their immaturity. Another pernicious result of placing teaching on a pedestal is that it can be used by some teachers to keep their followers dependent on them—instead of on God.

An unfortunate outworking of the heavy emphasis on the need for teaching by a paid professional is that many believers do not attempt to learn how to feed themselves. If it is essential to have a seminary-trained professional provide the teaching on Sunday mornings then some believers conclude that they are not qualified to study the Bible for themselves. Other believers cannot be bothered to take the time and make the effort to meaningfully study the Bible for themselves when they are spoon fed every week. [6] This is a huge impediment to becoming spiritually mature. It is the spiritually immature who need to be fed. The spiritually mature feed themselves and also look to receive from others. Part of the journey to spiritual maturity is the transition from depending on others to feed us to learning to feed ourselves by our own study of Scripture. It seems that as we learn to feed ourselves we become better positioned to allow God to write His truth on our hearts.

Another problem with over emphasizing the importance of being taught by a paid professional is that some ordinary believers develop a "feed me" mentality. The desire to learn is good, but often there can be an inappropriate thread of self-centeredness mixed in. It is easy to get into the mindset of only attending church in order to receive the blessing of being fed. The next step on this journey is to blame the pastor when we realize we are not growing. A major reason for not growing may be that we are depending on being bottle-fed milk by the pastor, instead of learning to feed ourselves and receive truth directly from God and His word. Shepherds lead sheep to food, they do not feed them. [7]

---

6. Heb. 5:12-13
7. Ps. 23:1-2. Not all "feeding" of believers by a teacher is bad (1 Cor. 3:2, John 21:17).

I mentioned previously that a strength of many conventional churches is that the content of the teaching they provide is excellent. Most of this teaching is provided in sermons or other "lecture style" presentations. Unfortunately, these teaching methods are not very effective. Research performed by George Barna's polling organization shows that by mid-Sunday afternoon most church attendees have forgotten the topic of the sermon they heard that morning. The sermon content that is remembered may be added to our head knowledge with very little reaching our hearts. Certainly God can and sometimes does write his truth on our hearts through sermons but it seems that other teaching methods may be better suited to achieving this goal. [8]

Another positive associated with many conventional churches, especially larger churches, is that they offer many specialized ministries, such as youth groups, singles groups, divorce recovery groups, campus ministry, etc. Each of these ministries may only be relevant or of interest to a small percentage of the congregation, but in a large church, this still results in enough people being involved to have a viable program. An individual house church, owing to its small size, cannot support these kinds of specialized ministries. A network of house churches can however provide the context for specialized ministries.

In a healthy church influence will flow from the individual's character, wisdom and understanding of Biblical truth. In some situations healthy influence may also flow from relevant giftedness (*e.g.*, revelatory words, evangelism, pastoral care and teaching). The beauty of leading by influence is that it requires no formal organization and it does not require leaders to have particular titles and roles.

Having a formal organization that includes paid leaders can be a severe impediment to the healthy flowing of influence and giftedness within a church. Individuals assume that they need to turn to the paid pastor to get the best help when they face a challenge. Given the huge range of issues that come up, it is not reasonable to expect a pastor to be the ideal person to address every issue. Also it is not reasonable to expect a single pastor to have the time and emotional energy to address all issues. So having a paid leader(s) often results in four bad outcomes:

- The paid leader bears a load God never intended him to carry. This problem is a contributor to many failed marriages.

---

8. See also Chapter 5 of *To Preach Or Not To Preach* by David Norrington.

- Issues are not always addressed by the individual with the most appropriate combination of personality, wisdom and giftedness.
- Other individuals in the church are excluded from opportunities to serve that would have been excellent opportunities for them to grow and mature.
- It encourages an attitude of dependency on the paid leader rather than on God.

It is incredibly sad that many fine Christian leaders burn themselves out and harm their families because they think they are supposed to do the majority of leading in their congregation. In many cases they are carrying a burden that God never intended them to carry. If they would trust God to play the part He wants to play and allow others to receive leadership directly from Him, their life would become much more pleasant. Others who are frustrated because they have limited freedom to contribute as God intends them to contribute would have the satisfaction of doing so.

An excellent summary of how clergy become an impediment to spiritual growth for many members of the laity is provided by Christian Smith:

> The clergy profession is fundamentally self-defeating. Its stated purpose is to nurture spiritual maturity in the church—a valuable goal. In actuality, however, it accomplishes the opposite by nurturing a permanent dependence of the laity on the clergy. Clergy become to their congregations like parents whose children never grow up, like therapists whose clients never become healed, like teachers whose students never graduate.
>
> The existence of a full-time, professional minister makes it too easy for church members not to take responsibility for the on-going life of the church. And why should they? That's the job of the pastor (so the thinking goes). But the result is that the laity remain in a state of passive dependence. Imagine, however a church whose pastor resigned and that could not find a replacement.
>
> Ideally, eventually, the members of that church would have to get off of their pews, come together, and figure out who would teach, who would counsel, who would settle disputes, who would visit the sick, who would lead worship, and so on. With a bit of insight, they would realize that the Bible calls the body as a whole to do these things together, prompting each to consider what gift they have to contribute, what role they could play to build up the body.[9]

---

9. "Church Without Clergy," *Voices in the Wilderness*, Nov/Dec 1988, quoted in Frank Viola, *Reimagining Church*, 2008 pg. 163.

### *New Testament house church pattern of church life*

There are several aspects of New Testament church life that challenge individuals to be spiritually active and not to be lazy. Each member is encouraged to contribute every week to the meeting. Regularly seeking God's leading concerning contributions to the weekly meeting is a valuable form of spiritual exercise. Similarly being involved in joint decision-making when the church needs to address a tricky question is an excellent growth opportunity both for individuals and for the community. In particular, making decisions concerning church discipline in a healthy manner provides an opportunity to grow in wisdom, godly character and dependence on God. Reserving all church discipline to the full congregation is also an exceptionally wise protection of believers from misguided or domineering elders. It is difficult to put this in to practice in a church that is larger than a house church.

Spiritual growth happens as we step out and attempt to actively love God and enter into ministry. The most important things we need to know we learn by doing, often by making mistakes. This means that church meetings that encourage participation by all believers, especially immature believers, are particularly helpful for spiritual growth. This is especially true if the meetings are safe places to experiment with observing and following the lead of the Father.

Regular physical exercise develops strength and helps to maintain good health. Similarly spiritual gifts need to be regularly exercised to develop and strengthen them. For some spiritual gifts the main weekly meeting is a very good setting to develop and exercise these gifts. Many individuals will not discover and grow in their spiritual gifts unless they regularly participate in meetings where there is freedom to use these gifts. [10]

---

10. It seems that the development of spiritual gifts is also similar to the growth of a plant. The branches of plants (*e.g.*, vines) are sometimes attached to a support structure to help them grow in a particular direction. For spiritual gifts that are exercised within a church community, the pattern of church we choose to embrace acts as a structure for the development of those gifts. If that structure is a conventional leader-centric church the gifting is likely to grow to fit the model of conventional church. I believe that this explains why so many pastors feel that there is a wonderful match between their gifting and their experience of leader-centric church. It is easy to conclude that this fit is so good it must be God and thus it is evidence that this is the way God wants us to do church. I think that this is only evidence of God's grace allowing His gifting to grow to fit the model of church we embrace. An individual who had been an associate pastor in a conventional church and who then moved to a New Testament style house church told me

The New Testament church model of teaching has several advantages over the sermon format. Firstly, a wide range of teaching methods were used including learning by observing and doing instead of only learning by listening. Also the format of brief presentations followed by dialog helps ensure relevance. If the topic is not of interest to anyone there will be no dialog and the meeting will move on. If the topic is of interest, individuals can ask their specific questions and receive teaching that is focused on their particular concerns. Attempting to teach others is one of the best ways to learn, because it gives the teacher an opportunity to consider carefully what he will say. So the New Testament church practice of encouraging everyone to participate in teaching is another helpful way of ensuring that everyone learns.

Another aspect of house church assemblies is that God brings diverse people together in a manner that causes our rough edges to rub on each other. Often these rough edges get exposed as individuals make contributions to the meeting. This gives great, if sometimes painful, opportunities for character development. Obviously this can also happen in various kinds of small groups associated with conventional churches, but it is less likely if the meetings are centered on a leader. The more individuals are free to contribute the more likely it is that their rough edges will be exposed.

Owing to their small size, it is possible to protect people in New Testament style house churches from well-meaning but hurtful attempts at ministry. For example, if in a house church meeting someone prays aloud for some else in a hurtful manner, it will be obvious to several people and they can graciously handle the situation. It is possible to protect people without leaders controlling who may minister.

Some enlightened employers are discovering that expecting everyone to contribute based on their gifting, and making decisions based on consensus is much more effective in dealing with certain issues than typical centralized leadership models. Not only do better ideas surface, but also individual contributors feel valued—energizing them. Is it possible that the companies which do this have stumbled onto a godly principle?

---

that he needed two years to "detox" from the conventional church way of doing things. I suspect that part of this was his gifting growing into the new structure of church leadership which he had chosen to embrace.

There are some strong parallels between multi-disciplinary work teams in some corporations and house church assemblies. For example in both settings it is expected that everyone will come to meetings with something to contribute for the common good. It is also understood that the team represents a diverse range of specialized skills/gifts and experience so it is critical to get every contribution. Good leadership is about building teams that work well together and which effectively draw out each person's unique contribution. In some cases, the team members are drawn from several organizations and the team leader may have limited authority to direct the work of the team members. This kind of environment is very stimulating and far more effective than traditional leadership-centered ways of doing business, which is of course why it is being embraced. It also sends a powerful message of respect to each team member.

A potential weakness for house church assemblies is that their small size makes it hard to support specialized ministries. As the house church movement grows and clusters or networks of house churches develop, it is possible to support these ministries at the house church network level. Individuals from several house churches with a shared calling to a specific form of ministry can work together. The development of relationships between nearby house churches also provides opportunities for mutual encouragement and support. It can be a lonely journey being the only house church in a community.

## 7.4 Risks associated with various patterns of church life

### *Risk that the church will not embrace sound doctrine*

Supporters of conventional churches often cite the lack of a seminary-trained pastor or priest as a major risk associated with house churches. They are concerned that these churches will embrace false doctrine or some other unhealthy practices. It is reasonable to expect that house churches will represent the full range of theological understanding and misunderstanding that is also present within conventional leader-centric churches. It is likely that some house churches will embrace doctrines that are considered to be false doctrines by almost all of the portion of the church that is committed to the truth and authority of the Bible. This is no different from what happens amongst conventional churches. Every Sunday many seminary-trained clergy teach things that are clearly contrary to the Bible. Requiring seminary training as a qualification for teaching in church provides no protection from false doctrine. In fact it seems that seminary training has been a major entry point for unbiblical doctrine into the church.

Those who believe that seminary training is essential to church leadership counter this point by saying that leaders need to attend not just any seminary, but a "good" seminary in order to protect their church from false doctrine. The in-depth Bible teaching and theological teaching provided by "good" seminaries is very valuable. However, most people fairly quickly forget much of what they learned in formal education if they are not regularly using the material. So it is likely that in many areas of doctrine many pastors who attended good seminaries only remember enough to spot false doctrine. In some cases they may have forgotten the detail required for a complete refutation. This is not a problem as they can easily access teaching materials that will refresh their memory.

In many countries, all believers have easy access to accurate translations of the Bible and to excellent Bible and theological teaching and reference material. Given a reasonable level of diligence and time, it is not that hard for believers who have not attended seminary to reach a good level of understanding of orthodox doctrine and to be able to detect false doctrine. In some cases they may not know the detail required for a complete refutation, but they have access to resources that can provide this information. This is all that is needed to protect a church from false doctrine.

The open participation style of New Testament house churches does result in some strange ideas getting aired. In general this is good because it is possible for another member of the group to graciously present appropriate truth and for the whole group to learn. A further benefit with the New Testament house church approach is the reliance on a team of mature believers to detect and refute false doctrine. Only one member of the team needs to notice an issue and then an appropriate individual may refute the error, possibly after doing some research. New Testament style house churches are small enough for every regular attendee to have regular contact with one or more of these mature believers who are able to recognize false doctrine.

Conventional churches led by seminary-trained pastors typically provide relatively few opportunities for individuals to discuss their beliefs in front of the pastor. So it is possible for believers to believe all sorts of false doctrines for a long time without the pastor being aware of it. If the pastor is unaware of the problem he cannot address it. The best seminary training in the world does not address this issue.

Some major missionary societies do not require their missionaries to have any formal Bible school or seminary training. They do require their missionaries to have a good understanding of orthodox doctrine and an ability to spot false doctrine. As I have previously noted believers who have studied the Bible diligently can meet this requirement fairly easily. Many doctrinally healthy churches have been successfully planted and nurtured by missionaries with no formal Bible school or seminary training.

In summary the claim that seminary training is required to protect sound doctrine does not seem to fit the facts. The key to being able to protect sound doctrine is to be committed to the truth and authority of Scripture and to be committed to the ongoing in-depth study of the Bible. Plenty of pastors trained in excellent seminaries drift into error later in life either because they lose their commitment to the truth and authority of Scripture or because they forget what they learned. Having a pastor with a seminary degree does not magically protect a church from error. [11]

### *Risk of developing an inappropriate inward focus*

Another risk all churches face is the risk of becoming an inward looking "bless me club." Healthy churches are characterized by strong bonds of friendship, love and "one anothering." This is absolutely wonderful and just what God intends. Unfortunately a risk associated with this kind of community is that we pour all of our time and emotional energy into relating with other members of the community and forget about the need to love and reach out to those outside the community. To protect against this we need to remain strongly connected to Jesus always looking to follow His lead. He will not forget the needs of others outside the community. Remaining

---

11. My point in this subsection is that seminary training is not required for someone to be a leader in a local church assembly. Diligent leaders who have not been to seminary can effectively protect local assemblies from false doctrine. It is great that there are many Bible Colleges and that many universities and colleges have theology departments where individuals can learn in depth about the Bible. Individuals with the benefit of this education are well placed to provide in depth Bible teaching to bless the body of Christ. Among the community of those who take the authority of Scripture seriously there are differences of understanding on several important topics. This diversity of understanding is present both in conventional churches and in house churches.

strongly connected to Scripture will also provide substantial protection as it is full of reminders of the importance of being outward looking.

In larger churches with many programs, an inappropriate inward focus sometimes results from dedicated believers spending so much time attending good meetings that they have no time left to love and reach out to others. Ironically some of these good meetings may be teaching people the importance of outreach! It is very easy to slip into the dangerous lie "I will start reaching out (or ministering in some other way) when I am fully taught." That day will never come because the most important learning occurs when we attempt to do ministry.

### *Risk of inappropriate focus on a gifted leader*

A risk for all churches that are led by a particularly gifted individual is that appropriate respect for this individual may gradually become corrupted into inappropriate focus on the leader and in extreme cases something close to a personality cult. Usually this only shows itself in small ways, but occasionally it can become totally pervasive to the life of the community. Personality cults are a form of idolatry. Glory that is due to God is given to a part of His creation—in this case the leader. Unfortunately, churches with particularly gifted leaders may ignore any checks and balances that exist in their pattern of church life and they may give the gifted leader a great deal of power, which sometimes has a corrupting effect.

The pattern of house church life described in the New Testament is structured to protect against the risk of inappropriate focus on a gifted leader. New Testament style house church is not centered on human leaders. It is centered on participation by every member, mutual submission and shared decision-making. There are some hints in the New Testament of inappropriate focus on highly gifted traveling leaders. [12] By limiting the time any of these leaders spent in one place the New Testament church mitigated the risks associated with the human tendency of idolizing great leaders.

### *Problems that can arise when leaders are given power over a church*

One problem with concentrating power in leaders is that they become a ministry choke point. If everything has to be approved by a powerful leader much good ministry does not happen. Sometimes this is because individuals assume that all ministry initiatives should

---

12. *E.g.*, 1 Cor. 1:12-15

come from the leadership, so they choose not to submit ministry ideas that God may have laid on their heart. In other cases the leader may reject a good ministry idea that is submitted for his consideration. In yet other cases the delay associated with gaining approval for an idea may result in the ministry opportunity passing. Regrettably many individuals in churches that concentrate power in a small leadership group conclude that they are not qualified to do meaningful ministry. This results in much wonderful ministry never happening.

Many churches that give substantial power to leaders ignore the warning of the parable of the tares. [13] With the best of intentions these leaders pull up tares. This limits the fruitfulness of God's kingdom as described in this parable. Another justification for giving power to leaders is to empower someone to deal with sin in the church. Giving this authority to leaders removes an important "check and balance" from the Biblical process of church discipline and may lead to pastoral abuse as discussed in the following subsection.

These problems associated with giving too much power to leaders can occur in churches of any size, including churches that meet in homes. New Testament style house churches protect against these risks by limiting the power given to leaders. This open environment may allow "tares" to remain longer than many of us would like. Jesus has chosen this path for His body. In time, some individuals who seem at first to be like "tares" mature into great fruitfulness. Extending grace to those who seem like "tares" is a wonderful opportunity for the development of godly character.

### *Risk of pastoral abuse*

Pastoral abuse is a risk for all churches. The key factor driving this risk is not the size of the church but the relationship between the leader and the congregation. The risk of pastoral abuse is particularly high in churches that concentrate power in a single leader or in a small group of leaders. The classic quote says "power tends to corrupt, absolute power tends to corrupt absolutely." Unfortunately, this principle applies to churches. The more power is concentrated in a single leader or a small group of leaders the greater the tendency for corruption. I am not saying that all Christian leaders with substantial power are corrupted by power; many are not corrupted. Pastoral abuse however is common among churches where the leadership has become corrupted by power.

---

13. Matt. 13:24-30

Unfortunately most pastoral abusers—and most of their congregations—are completely blind to their pastoral abuse. Typically, they and their congregation believe that Christian leadership includes directing the activities of others. The leaders act as permission givers and permission withholders. They may also assume that they have the right to implement church discipline without involving the full congregation. They cross the line into pastoral abuse when they use this power to crush other believers. The leader may think he is moving in wonderful leadership doing a tough thing for some greater good, when in reality he has forgotten the basics of mutual submission and treating others as he would wish to be treated. Some cases of pastoral abuse flow out of the insecurities of the leader. The leader thinks he is hearing God, but in reality his soul is demanding that he protect himself from an individual who has triggered his insecurities.

The pattern of house church life described in the New Testament provides substantial protection from pastoral abuse, by distributing power and decision-making. In particular, church discipline decisions are made by the full congregation.

## 7.5 Does the New Testament teach that the New Testament pattern of church is to be universally embraced?

Section 7.3 discussed several ways in which New Testament style house churches create an environment favorable for spiritual growth among ordinary believers. This section addresses whether or not the Bible teaches that all churches should follow this pattern.

### *New Testament commands related to traditions and practices*

In several passages Paul commands his readers to be imitators of him and of what he has taught them.[14] For example 1 Corinthians 11:1-2 says:

> Be imitators of me, as I am of Christ. Now I commend you because you remember me in everything and maintain the traditions even as I delivered them to you.

This command to imitate Paul includes imitating Paul's example and teaching concerning righteous living and doctrine. These verses however are the introduction to a multi-chapter discussion of church assembly meetings. So the context of these verses links the command to imitate Paul to imitating his participation in church meetings. The

---

14. 1 Cor. 4:16-17, 11:1-2, 16, Phil. 4:9, 2 Thess. 2:15

use of the word "everything" in this passage also makes it hard to exclude the application of this verse to church meetings. It is highly likely that in other passages where Paul is commanding his readers to imitate him he is intending them to imitate the pattern of church life that he demonstrated to them by example—as well as imitating him in righteous living and sound doctrine. The pattern of church life Paul demonstrated and taught was a pattern or style that gave freedom to each believer to live out his priesthood in direct relationship with God. It was not a pattern that defined an organization.

1 Corinthians 11:2 is one of three verses where Paul urges his readers to follow the *paradosis* he gave them.[15] The literal meaning of this Greek word is something delivered or handed over. In the New Testament it commonly refers to traditions or teachings. As noted in the discussion of the command to imitate Paul, the context of Paul's commending of the Corinthians for maintaining the traditions he gave them is directly linked to church meetings. So, the natural interpretation of this verse is that we should follow Paul's teachings concerning church meetings and concerning righteous living and sound doctrine. In both 2 Thessalonians 2:15 and 3:6 Paul commands the Thessalonians to follow the traditions he taught them. In 2 Thessalonians 2:15 Paul mentions traditions taught in person and by letter. It is highly plausible that the letter Paul is referring to is what we now call 1 Thessalonians. So at least some of the material Paul considered to be "traditions" has been recorded as Scripture and thus has the authority of Scripture. The references to Jewish traditions in Matthew 15:2-6 and Mark 7:3-13 also indicate that in this time period traditions were for all practical purposes commands.

In 1 Corinthians 11:16 Paul closes a discussion on the appropriate role of women in the church by saying "If anyone is inclined to be contentious, we have no such practice, nor do the churches of God." This shows that there were established practices within all of the New Testament churches and that individual church assemblies were not free to deviate from these practices. The pattern of church life and leadership described in the New Testament is radically different from the previous religious experiences of Jewish and pagan converts to Christianity. These religions placed a heavy emphasis on the role of human leaders and on structured religious services in religious buildings. The New Testament pattern of church life is completely different than this. The only way the uniformity of church practices

---

15. The other two verses are 2 Thess. 2:15, 3:6.

implied in 1 Corinthians 11:16 could have arisen was by church planters teaching, demonstrating and commanding the expected pattern of New Testament church life. [16]

The passage that Paul is concluding in 1 Corinthians 11:16, relates to head coverings and hair length. Christians vary in their understanding of how to apply this passage. It seems that most believers, based on other related New Testament passages, take the view that the specific commands in 1 Corinthians 11:3-15 are an application of unchanging spiritual principles to a specific culture. [17] Based on this understanding most churches do not expect women to cover their heads to pray or prophesy. Similarly most churches are relaxed about hair length for both men and women.

Some believers are quick to extend this approach to teaching and commands about church life in the New Testament. They jump to the conclusion that these commands and teachings are specific to a particular historical setting and are optional in other settings. This is a risky approach to the interpretation and application of Scripture. In contrast to the discussion of head coverings and hair length in 1 Corinthians 11, there is no hint elsewhere in the New Testament of underlying spiritual principles that may be consistent with alternative implementations of church. In fact, as discussed in Section 7.3, the principles underlying the New Testament house church model have a direct link to the spiritual development of believers. These principles are not culturally specific, they are universal. [18] Similarly the other Scriptures that will be discussed in the rest of this section are universal.

### *God's desire for variety and freedom to move through whomever he pleases*

Most leaders of conventional churches assume that recognized leaders will plan and lead the weekly service(s) and various other ministries. In John 3:8 Jesus says:

---

16. See also 2 Cor. 12:18 and Titus 1:5.
17. See Section 6.4 for a further discussion of this passage.
18. Obviously some details about the pattern of church life mentioned in the New Testament are specific to the culture. For example in 1 Cor. 16.2 Paul commands individuals to set aside money for giving on a weekly basis. Some individuals now receive their income on a bi-weekly or monthly basis. I am sure that Paul would be comfortable with these individuals setting aside money for giving on a bi-weekly or monthly basis.

> The wind blows where it wishes, and you hear its sound, but you do not know where it comes from or where it goes. So it is with everyone who is born of the Spirit.

This is true of everyone born of the Holy Spirit because it is true of the Holy Spirit. He blows where He wishes when He wishes. We see this working out in the diverse and creative ways that He achieves His purposes in our lives. Given that this is the nature of our God, it strikes me that it is very unlikely that He wants only to move through the same small group of leaders every week. He delights in interacting with every one of His children and He delights in using the weakest and least suitable (in the world's eyes) to achieve his purposes. Similarly it also strikes me as implausible that God wants every service to follow the same pattern. I very much doubt that He wants to blow through the same people in the same way every week. God wants flexibility in church life like a new wineskin.

### *Priesthood of all believers*

1 Peter 2:5, 9 teach that all believers are a royal priesthood. Similarly Revelation 1:6 and 5:10 say that God has made us priests. Priests have the right to perform religious ministries that ordinary people are not allowed to perform. For example, the book of Leviticus contains many commands concerning religious rituals that could only be performed by priests. Even princes and kings had to respect the priest's monopoly on certain religious rituals.[19] For example, King Uzziah was instantly punished with leprosy for being angry when the priests told him to stop offering incense in the sanctuary. This leprosy remained with him until his death and forced him to live in a separate house. This was not a light punishment.

Priests also have special access to God.[20] Only priests could go into the inner portion of the Israelite tabernacle/temple and only the high priest could go into the Holy of Holies.[21] The Israelites believed that God's name and glory were in some sense especially present within His temple.[22] So the priests, in some sense, were in the par-

---

19. Ezek. 46:2, 2 Chron. 26:18-21
20. Num. 16:40
21. Heb. 9:6-7, Exod. 29:30, 35:19, 39:41, Ezek. 40:45-46, 42:13-14, 44:13-16, 45:4
22. Deut. 12:11, 14:23, 16:2-6, 26:2, 2 Chron. 5:11 - 6:11, 7:1-3, Ps. 27:4, Ezek. 8:6. In a few places the Old Testament says that God is in the temple (Hab. 2.20, 1 Kings 8:10-13, *cf.* Acts 7:48).

ticular presence of God when they performed their rituals in the temple. [23]

Some churches call their clergy "priests" and other churches use other titles such as "pastor." In many denominations, regardless of the title given to the clergy, they are priests in the sense that there are ministries that only the officially ordained clergy may perform. Also many people behave as if they believe that clergy, like the priests in the Old Testament, have special access to God. These are some of the reasons why some believers seek to approach God through a priest, rather than approaching Him directly.

Conventional leader-centric churches make it hard for ordinary believers to move in the fullness of what God intends for us as a Royal Priesthood. In significant ways, these churches restrict the role of priesthood to the ordained clergy. In New Testament style churches it is possible for every believer to be part of the Royal Priesthood God wants us to be. He wants each one of us to be in direct relationship with Him, the only High Priest. [24] He does not want us depending on a priest or anyone else as an intermediary. He also wants the freedom to move through whomever He chooses not just through a small group of ordained clergy.

### *Matthew 23:8-12*

In this passage Jesus commands us not to use the title "rabbi" because we only have one teacher and we are all brothers and sisters. He also commands us not to use the title instructor/leader because we have only one instructor/leader: Jesus. Most churches do not use the title rabbi, instructor or leader for their clergyman. So in a very narrow sense they are not violating this command. However if Jesus was speaking today, it is possible that He might restate these commands using the words "pastor" or "priest." It seems to me that the role of most clergymen in conventional leader-centric churches is similar to the role of the leaders Jesus mentions in these verses.

The critical questions we have to ask based on this passage are: does the leader see himself as more than just one believer among many? Do members of the congregation see the leader as more than just one brother among many? Does the leader in any way place himself between other believers and God? Do members of the

---

23. 2 Chron. 29:4-6, 11, Exod. 25:8. David (Psalm 63:2) and Isaiah (Isa. 6:1) had visions of God in the temple.
24. Heb. 2:17, 3:1, 4:14-15, 5:5, 10, 6:20, 7:26, 8:1, 9:11, 10:21

congregation in any way place the leader between themselves and God? If the answer to any of these questions is yes, I believe there is a violation of the principles Jesus teaches in Matthew 23:8-10.

In some churches the clergyman, or a small group of leaders, regularly make decisions that God does not wish to delegate to human leaders. These leader(s) may also regularly make decisions on behalf of individual believers, which God wishes to be made by the individual believers themselves. Such patterns of decision-making are an example of a human leader becoming the type of leader Jesus forbids in this passage. Section 1.4 provides a more complete discussion of this passage.

The author of an article, in a secular news magazine, about churches in East Africa described a number of these churches as being "owner-operator churches." [25] From the context, it seems that the author is using this phrase to describe churches where the senior pastor behaves like the owner of a business who is actively engaged in the day-to-day operation of his business. This leadership style is not God's plan for His church. He wants to be the Owner-Operator of His church. He does not want to share this role with a human leader. But just as with the Israelite kings, He is still willing to bless in some measure even though He has been displaced from His desired role. [26]

Some people are so used to the central role of the pastor in the life of a conventional church, that they have become convinced that churches need leaders who make key decisions concerning the life of the assembly. After one has spent a while in a church that is not centered on a decision-making leader, one discovers that the Holy Spirit is remarkably competent at leading. He delights in moving through all of the members of the community to provide this leadership.

If a conventional church is built around a highly gifted leader, it is likely that members of the congregation, and sometimes even the senior pastor himself, will give the human leader, or sometimes the church, honor that is due to God alone. This is a form of idolatry. Also the stronger the human leadership the more likely it is that members will look to and depend on their human leader(s) rather than God.

---

25. *The Economist* (US edition) July 3-9, 2010, pg. 44
26. Section 1.6

### *Old Testament Patterns of Religious Leadership and Activity*

Some defend leader-centric churches and leader-centric services that follow the same pattern every week by pointing to the Old Testament. The Israelite religious system revolved around priests and religious rituals, which followed an annual pattern with very limited change from year to year. In many respects it was very similar to leader-centric churches today. The Israelite religious system described in the Old Testament was put in place by God and must therefore be good. But is it good for all circumstances or only in specific circumstances?

There are three huge changes for the people of God between the Old and New Testaments. Firstly, during the time of the Old Testament only a few of God's people were continuously indwelt by the Holy Spirit. Examples of this include Joseph, Moses, Bezalel, Joshua, Othniel, David, Elijah and Elisha. [27] The Spirit was with Saul for an extended period but then left. [28] Saul did have one more, most unusual and brief encounter with the Holy Spirit! [29] David was aware of the risk that his sin could cause the Spirit to leave him. [30] It seems that larger numbers of individuals in the Old Testament were touched by the Holy Spirit at specific times for specific reasons. Examples of this include Balaam, Sampson and the messengers sent by Saul to arrest David. [31] The vast majority of the Israelites had limited or no interaction with the Holy Spirit. I am only aware of one reference that directly implies this. [32] But many of the Old Testament references to individuals who were indwelt by the Holy Spirit are written in a way that implies that this indwelling was rare during that time period. Also many of the prophecies concerning the release of the Spirit upon the church and Israel in the End Times indicate that this is a new thing. [33] Many references in the New Testament teach that every believer is indwelt by the Holy Spirit. [34] This universal outpouring of the Holy Spirit

27. Gen. 41:38, Exod. 31:2-5, 35:30-34, Num. 11:17, 25, 27:18, Jud. 3:9-10, 1 Sam. 16:13, 2 Sam. 23:2, 2 Kings 2:9, 15
28. 1 Sam. 10:6-13, 1 Sam. 16:14
29. 1 Sam. 19:22-24
30. Psalm 51:11
31. Num. 24:2, 13, Judges 14:6, 19, 15:14, 1 Sam. 19:20-21
32. Num. 11:29
33. Isa. 32:15, 44:3, Ezek. 11:19, 36:26, 37:14, 39:29, Joel 2:28-29, Zech. 12:10
34. John 3:8, 20:22, Acts 2:16-18, 33, 38, Rom. 8:9-11, 1 Cor. 3:16

onto the people of God after the resurrection is a complete change from the experience of the people of God in the Old Testament.

The second major change for the people of God from the Old Testament to the New Testament concerns the priesthood. During the Old Testament period after the exodus, the priesthood was restricted to Aaron and his sons. [35] As I have already discussed, a key feature of the church is the priesthood of all believers.

The third major change concerns the temple. The Old Testament religious system was centered on the tabernacle and then on the temple where God's name and glory were understood to dwell. The tabernacle and temple were also the place where the priests led the spiritual life of the nation and performed most of the rituals that only the priests could perform. In the Epistles, it is the people of God, both individually and corporately, who are the temple of God. [36] So individually and corporately we are both the dwelling place of God and the place where He wishes ministry to happen. God did away with the Old Testament system of a physical temple building and a restricted priesthood and replaced it with a new system based on a universal priesthood where His body, the Christian community, is the temple. [37] No physical building is an appropriate dwelling or resting place for our God. But, incredibly, He wishes to dwell and rest with "he who is humble and contrite in spirit and trembles at my word." [38]

Based on these three major changes I think that anyone who wishes to argue for organizing the church in a manner similar to the Old Testament religious system has a major challenge on his hands. In Galatians 4:1-9 Paul contrasts the situation of his readers before and after they were redeemed and received the indwelling by the Holy Spirit who cries "Abba, Father." We are now sons who have come of age and have direct and intimate access to the Father. We are no longer under the control of religious stewards. For some of

---

35. Exod. 28:1-4, 41, 30:30, 40:15, Josh. 21:19, 2 Chron. 29:21
36. 1 Cor. 3:16-17, 6:19, 2 Cor. 6:16, Eph. 2:21
37. Jesus also referred to his physical body as a temple (John 2:19-22). In Revelation 21 and 22, which provides us with a prophetic preview of the new heaven and the new earth, God is the temple. Revelation 21:22 says: "And I saw no temple in the city, for its temple is the Lord God the Almighty and the Lamb." Is it possible that our unity with God will be so complete that there is no contradiction between God being the temple in the new heaven and the new earth and God's people being the temple prior to this (John 17:21, Eph. 5:31-32)?
38. Isaiah 66:1-2

Paul's readers it was the Old Testament religious system that had acted as a tutor/guardian and steward/trustee/manager and which had controlled them prior to their coming to faith and freedom. The Old Testament religious system was intended for the time period when the Holy Spirit was not fully released on all believers. The New Testament pattern of church assembly life is intended for a community of priests who are all indwelt by the Holy Spirit. There are also several scriptures that reveal that God was less than delighted with the Old Testament religious system. [39] He is looking for obedience and relationship, not religious activity.

In Matthew 11:7-15 Jesus discusses the significance of the ministry of John the Baptist. Jesus says that John is more than a prophet. He is according to v. 10 the one about whom it is written "I will send my messenger ahead of you, who will prepare your way before you" (NIV). John had the privilege of preparing the way for the Messiah and being the individual who baptized Jesus. [40] John heralded the turning point in God's dealing with men. Not only did Jesus come to earth as a man to teach and heal and then die for us. But Jesus also came to bring forth His bride; a bride who is also a community of priests each indwelt by the Holy Spirit.

Recent discoveries of papyri have shed new light on Matthew 11:12. The KJV translates this verse, "And from the days of John the Baptist until now the kingdom of heaven suffereth violence, and the violent take it by force." This translation is hard to understand and its relevance within a passage where Jesus is discussing the significance of John's role is not clear. The key Greek word in this verse is *bia*, which has traditionally been translated "force," "impetus" or "violence." However, recent discoveries of papyri indicate that:

> The Greek word *bia* refers to illegal "forcible acquisition," and is a technical legal term referring to the act of hindering an owner or lawful possessor from the enjoyment of their property. The use of actual physical force is not required under the term. From the papyri, there is now actually firm evidence to show that the words used in this verse were legal terms used with reference to unlawful acquisition. This has revealed that the verse has nothing to do with heaven suffering violence or forcefully advancing but to people hindering Christians from enjoying their rights. [41]

---

39. 1 Sam. 15:22, Isa. 1:11, 66:3, Jer. 7:22-23, Hos. 6:6, Matt. 9:13, 12:7
40. Matt 3:13-17
41. Ann Nyland, "Papyri, Women and Word Meaning in the New Testament," *Priscilla Papers*, Volume 17, Number 4, Fall 2003, pp. 3-9, published by Christians for Biblical Equality (www.cbeinternational.org).

In this same article, Ann Nyland offers the following translation for Matthew 11:12 based on this understanding of the meaning of *bia*:

> From the time of John the Baptizer until now, heaven's realm is being used or even robbed by people who have no legal right to it. This stops those who do have a legal right to it from enjoying their own property.

So what has been stolen from God's people and why did Jesus date this theft to the time of the coming of John the Baptist? Is it possible that Jesus is saying that the Old Testament pattern of a two-tier religious system has ended? In particular has the division of God's people into a priestly caste that has special religious rights and ordinary believers who are expected to be religious spectators ended? Is it possible that those who seek to continue the Old Testament religious pattern are robbing the Kingdom of Heaven and that they are stopping other believers from moving in their full rights and privileges as Spirit filled priests? If this is the correct interpretation, what is being robbed from the kingdom of heaven? Might it be the lost fruitfulness of the disenfranchised priests? Is it because of this potential fruitfulness of Spirit filled priests that Jesus said "yet he who is least in the kingdom of heaven is greater than he?"[42]

### *Continuity of the Role of Elders*

Some argue for a leader-centric church pattern based on the continuity of the role of elders as leaders within the Old and New Testaments. The primary role of elders in the Old Testament and in the non-Christian Jewish community in the New Testament is similar to the role of elders in the New Testament Christian community as discussed in this book.[43] In general Israelite and Jewish elders were not decision-making leaders and organizers comparable to many modern-day pastors. In most situations they were advisers and facilitators.

### *Summary*

The New Testament shows that Jesus, the apostles and the early church rejected the Old Testament model of leader-centric religious organization. Given that this would have been the natural model for them to embrace and that they had the opportunity to embrace it, it is reasonable to assume that they had very good reasons for making this choice. The primary reason for this change is that every believer

---

42. Matt. 11:11 NIV

43. Subsection 2.1.1, Appendix 3.1.6, 3.1.7

is now indwelt with the Holy Spirit and God wants to relate directly to every believer as a priest. He wants to move through each believer as He sees fit without being restricted to moving through a small group of religious professionals. He wants to pour His love and life into each one of us as individuals and as a part of His complete Bride, who is a living body not a religious organization. New Testament style church is a wineskin particularly well suited to the free flow of the wine of God's love and life.

Also, as I have discussed in Section 7.3, in general, the New Testament church assembly model is more conducive to healthy "body-life," spiritual growth and ministry than conventional leader-centric churches. Of course I am not saying that the free flow of God's love and life and spiritual growth and ministry cannot happen in conventional churches. They clearly do. Over the centuries God has brought huge blessing through conventional churches. Similarly I am not saying that all New Testament style house churches will be healthy. Several key sections of the New Testament were written in response to the problems of unhealthy house churches.

I believe that the most reasonable interpretation of the verses where Paul commands church assemblies to follow his traditions and practices is that they are commands to all churches in all time periods and cultures to follow the New Testament pattern for church. Similarly I believe that the most reasonable interpretation of Matthew 23:8-10 forbids leader-centric expressions of church.

### *What Next?*

I anticipate that time will show that God is drawing His people back to New Testament style house church assemblies as one part of His restoration of His church in preparation for the return of Jesus. This restoration process has been ongoing over the last several centuries. A couple of examples of other elements within this restoration process include the rediscovery of the doctrine of salvation by grace through faith and the reacceptance of the supernatural gifts of the Holy Spirit.

It seems that God chooses to achieve the changes He wants as part of this restoration process very gradually. Each area of restoration is controversial. Not everyone who loves Jesus and accepts the authority of His word embraces the change. There is extended debate while God brings about the change He wants. While this debate is going on, it is important for each believer to consider the topic carefully and prayerfully from a Biblical perspective. However it is even more important to maintain an appropriate heart attitude towards those with whom we disagree. There are so many controversial topics in the life of the church that we will all eventually discover, perhaps only after death, that we were wrong in at least a few areas. We need to remain open to God and the possibility that He is bringing change and we need to treat others with respect. God will choose which of His children he wants to be early adopters of a particular change He is bringing to his body. He extends His grace both to those who are early adopters and to those who are open to change but are not early adopters.

The number of believers embracing the supernatural working of the Holy Spirit may have grown from less than a million in 1900 to more than 600 million in 2010.[44] With the benefit of hindsight it now seems fair to say that this scale of change, and all of the associated good fruit, is only possible if God is the one bringing the change. Several decades ago this was far less clear and there was a great deal of debate, some of which continues, about this topic. While the debate goes on, God achieves His purposes by touching and changing individuals. He teaches by directly writing His truth on our hearts.

I expect a similar process to play out concerning New Testament style church. It is important to study and debate respectfully what the Bible teaches concerning appropriate expressions of church. It is even more important to keep our hearts open to God, so that He can write on them the message of His choosing at the time of His choosing. There are many messages He wants to write on each of our hearts. The most important messages are His personal love letters to each one of us. Maybe He will also write a message about house church on your heart. I believe He is the one who has written this message on my heart.

---

44. Christianity 2010: *A View from the New Atlas of Global Christianity*, Todd M. Johnson, David B. Barrett, and Peter F. Crossing, Center for the Study of Global Christianity at Gordon-Conwell Theological Seminary, South Hamilton, Ma.

# Appendix 1
# Roles and Responsibilities in Church

This appendix discusses roles and responsibilities associated with New Testament Christian assemblies. The focus is on understanding who may be involved in each role or activity. This appendix complements Table 1.[1] The first six topics listed in this table were discussed in Chapter 1. The remaining 21 topics are discussed in this appendix.

## 1.1 Teaching

Colossians 3:16 and 2 Timothy 2:24 teach that all believers are expected to teach one another. Hebrews 5:12 makes it clear that this expectation assumes believers have learned the basics. NRSV, ESV and NIV all translate Romans 15:14 "able/competent to instruct one another." This verse is addressed to all believers. The Greek verb used in this verse is also translated admonish and warn.[2] Teaching took place both during and outside of house church assembly meetings.[3]

These verses should be held in balance with James 3:1 that warns against rushing into becoming a teacher, as teachers will be judged more strictly. Similarly, Paul instructs Timothy in 2 Timothy 2:2 to focus on "faithful men" for training as teachers. Teaching is listed as a spiritual gift in Romans 12:7, 1 Corinthians 12:28-29 and Ephesians 4:11, which implies that in most local assemblies there are some people who are particularly equipped by God to be teachers. In summary, it seems that in New Testament churches all reasonably mature believers were expected to contribute at least occasionally to teaching and some had a teaching gift. Presumably these gifted individuals did a lot of the teaching in each church.

---

1. Pages 22, 23
2. Appendix 1.2
3. 1 Cor. 14:26, Acts 18:24-26

Acts 15:35 describes Paul and Barnabas' ministry in Antioch between the first and second missionary journeys. This verse says that they were active in "teaching and preaching the word of the Lord, with many others also." The implication of this verse is that even when two apostles were in town there was plenty of opportunity for other believers to be active in teaching and preaching. Teaching and preaching were not restricted to significant leaders.

Teaching is an important part of the qualifications to be an elder given in 1 Timothy 3:2 and Titus 1:9. Teaching is also mentioned in the context of elders in 1 Timothy 5:17. There is no hint that only elders may serve as teachers. Teaching is of course also a responsibility of traveling leaders. Teaching in the New Testament church is further discussed in Section 6.1.

### 1.2 Admonishing

The Greek word for admonish is *noutheteo*, which may be translated: to put in mind, to admonish, to warn. Colossians 3:16, 1 Thessalonians 5:14 and 2 Thessalonians 3:15 all teach that all believers are expected to admonish or warn other believers. Colossians 3:16 commands believers both to teach and to admonish other believers. Sometimes *noutheteo* is translated instruct. [4]

Acts 20:31 says that Paul admonished everyone night and day with tears. Similarly in 1 Corinthians 4:14 Paul says that he is writing to the Corinthians to admonish them as beloved children. This confirms that traveling leaders were also involved in admonishing. In Ephesians 6:4 Paul teaches that fathers are expected to admonish/instruct their children.

### 1.3 Challenging an individual about his sin

Galatians 6:1, which deals with correcting a brother caught in sin, only mentions one qualification for helping to restore this individual: to have the Spirit, which usually in Scripture is tied to salvation. [5] However, the same Greek word is used in 1 Corinthians 14:37 where the NIV translates this word as "spiritually gifted." Galatians 6:1 may be talking about a group of individuals receiving a specific anointing

---

4. *E.g.*, Rom. 15:14 in NRSV, ESV and NIV
5. Gal. 6:1, "Brothers, if someone is caught in a sin, you who are spiritual should restore him gently. But watch yourself, or you also may be tempted (NIV)." The broader context of this verse (Gal. 5:16, 25) is those who "walk by the Spirit" which may include recent converts as well as mature believers.

of the Holy Spirit to help in a particular case. Sometimes God gives spiritual gifts to brand new believers. So even if this verse is talking about a particular anointing it would be hard to exclude the possibility that God's chosen instruments in some cases may include a new believer. Similarly, mature believers who are not elders commonly move in spiritual anointing. So any believer, who has been selected and equipped by the Holy Spirit, may be involved in challenging someone about their sin. This is consistent with James 5:19-20, which says, "My brothers, if anyone among you wanders from the truth and someone brings him back, let him know that whoever brings back a sinner from his wandering will save his soul from death and will cover a multitude of sins." 1 John 5:16 teaches that any believer who sees a brother commit a sin that does not lead to death should pray for him.

### 1.4 Rebuking an individual about his sin

Rebuking is discussed in detail in Section 4.3 and in Appendix 6. In the New Testament the rebuking of humans is almost always associated with sin and is occasionally associated with false doctrine or convincing individuals of the truth about Jesus. In the New Testament, appropriate rebukes are not associated with correcting the approaches other people take to ministry. [6]

We should seek to correct others gently first and only move to a rebuke if gentle correction is rejected. Everything we say should be to build others up and to benefit the listener.[7] We should never rebuke someone to hurt them or as an outflow of our anger towards them. In Luke 17:3-4 Jesus commands us to both rebuke and forgive a brother who sins against us. The context provided by verse 4 implies that rebuking is most appropriate in cases of repeated sin where the sinner is fully aware that he is sinning.

The only verse explicitly linking elders to rebuking is Titus 1:9. The focus in this verse is on responding to false teaching and it appears that the emphasis of this verse is on refuting false teaching rather than rebuking a false teacher. [8] Part of good teaching is to refute false teaching. So non-elders may also refute false teaching. There is no Biblical basis for suggesting that elders may rebuke in a different

---

6. Situations may arise where an individual's approach to ministry is rooted in false doctrine. In this circumstance, I recommend focusing on the underlying doctrinal issue.
7. Gal. 6.1, Eph. 4:29
8. Section 4.3

manner or in different circumstances to any other believer, who is not a leader. It seems that traveling leaders may have been expected on occasion to rebuke more severely than other believers. [9]

### 1.5 Hearing a confession of sin

James 5:16 is a command to all believers. Hearing a confession of sin is not restricted to elders.

### 1.6 Assisting with conflict resolution and lawsuits among believers

Matthew 18:15-17 and 1 Corinthians 6:1-6 teach that any believer or group of believers may assist in conflict resolution and lawsuits among believers. Matthew 18:15-17 also teaches that the whole church assembly is the final arbiter in a conflict between brothers. My interpretation of Matthew 18 is that when you reach the last stage of the process with the whole church involved, the church is serving like a jury. They get to hear the facts of the case and prayerfully decide who is right and who is wrong. Sometimes attempts at conflict resolution fail. In this circumstance the conflict resolution process may morph into the church discipline process and the full congregation acts both as jury and judge. [10]

### 1.7 Protecting church unity

John 17 makes it clear that unity among believers is very important to Jesus. Four times in this chapter Jesus prays for the unity of the church. Ephesians 4:1-3 commands all believers "to maintain the unity of the Spirit in the bond of peace." Romans 14:1-15:2 and 1 Corinthians 10:15–11:1 teach that all believers are expected to be sensitive to the perspectives of other believers and do their best to avoid offending them. Romans 14:4 says that a believer should not judge another believer as that is passing judgment on the servant of another. Romans 14:19 commands believers to "pursue what makes for peace and for mutual upbuilding."

God likes having a variety of personalities and perspectives and backgrounds in a church. As we pursue God together, our rough edges rub against each other and we have an opportunity to learn how to love. He appears to be much more interested in developing love, humility, mutual respect and mutual submission within His children than in developing uniformity (except concerning key doctrines). In

---

9. Section 4.3, Appendix 6
10. Subsection 1.1.4

my experience the dynamics of assembly meetings, where everyone is expected to contribute, bring these issues to the fore in a manner that happens less often in conventional leader-centric meetings.

### 1.8 Reaching out with the Gospel

As discussed in Section 6.2 and Appendices 4.3 and 4.4, evangelism was a very important activity within the New Testament church. However, I am only aware of one verse directed to all believers commanding us to be involved in evangelism.[11] Most of Matthew 28:18-20 applies to all believers, but these verses are directed to the remaining eleven disciples/apostles.[12] So we need to establish the role of believers, who are not apostles, in outreach from other scriptures to avoid a circular argument. Similarly, Paul commands Timothy in 2 Timothy 4:5 to "do the work of an evangelist." The Greek for "do" in this verse is in the second person singular. So this command applies to Timothy as an individual traveling leader. This verse does not tell us about Paul's expectations for believers who are not traveling leaders.

1 Peter 3:15 commands all believers to be ready to reply to questions about their faith. Matthew 5:14-16 tell us that we are the light of the world and that this light should be obvious to all "so that they may see your good works and give glory to your Father who is in heaven." As we are obedient to this command it is likely to result in the kinds of questions that 1 Peter 3:15 commands us to be ready to answer.[13] Acts 8:1-4, 11:19-21 record that many believers were involved in evangelism.

In Matthew 9:37-38 we are commanded to pray for laborers to be sent out into the harvest. In the following verses, Jesus calls the initial twelve apostles and sends them out on a preaching tour with authority to do deliverance ministry and to heal. Praying for laborers includes praying for God to raise up apostles and evangelists to act as laborers in His harvest. Both of these roles are at core spiritual gifts, so we are praying for God to release giftedness to the individuals He selects.[14]

---

11. Jude 1:23a "Save others by snatching them out of the fire"
12. Section 3.5
13. John 1:7 and 5:35 link John the Baptist's ministry as a light to drawing individuals to belief in Jesus as the supreme light of the world. Similarly when we act as the light of the world there is an explicitly evangelistic dimension to it.
14. Eph. 4:8-12

## 1.9 Preaching

The key Greek words translated "preach" in English Bibles mainly apply to evangelistic preaching and the proclaiming of Jesus. [15] The modern Christian usage of the word preaching to describe a sermon aimed at believers is not consistent with the meaning of these words in the New Testament. The vast majority of what we call sermons would be called teaching by the authors of New Testament. [16]

In the Bible, preaching is closely linked to the work of Jesus, the apostles and other traveling leaders. However Acts 8:1-4, 11:19-21 note that, after the Jerusalem church, was scattered by persecution, many ordinary believers were active in preaching Jesus. Also Acts 15:35 records that "many others" preached with Paul and Barnabas in Antioch. Preaching was not restricted to apostles even when there were apostles in town.

The Gospels record three examples of individuals who were so excited by the healing/deliverance that Jesus had done for them, that they went around proclaiming (preaching) it. [17] Many individuals responded positively to these testimonies. In Acts 9:20 it is recorded that Paul started preaching Christ immediately after his conversion—i.e., before he was recognized as a Christian leader. In summary, it seems that all believers were free to preach. The content of New Testament preaching is discussed in Section 6.2.

The key Greek words translated "preach" in English Bibles are not used in the New Testament in the context of elders. However it is likely that some elders preached regularly. Some modern translations use the word "preach" in 1 Timothy 5:17 to describe an activity of elders. [18] The KJV provides a literal translation ("they who labor in the word") of the Greek phrase in this verse.

## 1.10 Baptizing

Many passages, especially in Acts, record the baptisms of new believers. As will be seen from the summary of these passages in the following paragraphs, in some cases baptisms are associated with traveling leaders planting new churches. But in several other

---

15. Appendix 4.3, 4.4
16. It is unlikely that the sermon format was used in New Testament meetings (Section 6.1).
17. Mark 1:45, 5:20, 7:36
18. *E.g.*, NIV, ESV

cases it seems that the traveling leaders held back to allow others to perform baptisms. There is no hint in scripture that performing baptisms is restricted to recognized local or traveling leaders. In a few cases it is plausible that non-leaders performed baptisms. We need to be careful with such arguments from silence, but on balance it seems reasonable to conclude that any believer could baptize a convert. This is consistent with the very broad freedom believers, who were not leaders, clearly had during the New Testament period to participate in almost all forms of local church ministry.

In Matthew 28:19 Jesus commands the apostles to baptize people as part of the great commission. Most of Matthew 28:18-20 applies to all believers, but these verses are directed to the apostles. So we need to establish the freedom of believers who are not apostles to baptize from other scriptures to avoid a circular argument.

Acts 2:41 records that 3,000 individuals came to faith on the day of Pentecost and implies that they were all baptized that day. No mention is made of who performed these baptisms. If they were all performed by the 12 apostles it would have been very time consuming.

Acts 8:12 records baptisms in Samaria. It is likely that Phillip was involved but other believers may have also been involved. Acts 8:38 records Phillip baptizing the Ethiopian eunuch. Phillip was an evangelist and one of the seven men selected to distribute food to widows. [19] There is no hint that he was an elder or an apostle.

Acts 9:18 strongly implies that Paul was baptized by Ananias. He is described as a disciple and as a devout man. [20] There is no hint that he was an elder or other leader.

Acts 10:48 records the baptism of the household of Cornelius. The verse implies that Peter did not personally do the baptisms. So it seems reasonable to assume that they were done by "the circumcised believers" who were with Peter. [21] The implication is that these individuals were not elders or other leaders.

Acts 16:33 implies the Philippian jailer and his family were baptized by Paul or Silas. Acts 16:15 and 18:8 record the first baptisms in Philippi and Corinth. In both cases it is reasonable to assume that these baptisms were done by the traveling church planting team.

---

19. Acts 6:5, 21:8
20. Acts 9:10, 22:12
21. Acts 10:23, 45

Both Jesus and Paul did very few baptisms. [22] From the context of 1 Corinthians 1:10-17 it appears that one reason Paul baptized relatively few people was to reduce the risk of inappropriate dependence on him. In at least one case Peter allowed other believers to baptize when we might have assumed that he would do it. [23] These passages are all consistent with the freedom of any believer to baptize another believer. In particular, it is likely that some new churches would have individuals coming to faith during the time period between the departure of the traveling leaders, who planted the church, and the appointment of the first elders in the new church assembly. Anyone baptized during this period would have been baptized by someone who was not a recognized leader.

### 1.11 Serving the Lord's supper (communion)

1 Corinthians 11:17-34 provides teaching on the Lord's supper. The Lord's supper was part of a joint meal not just a small piece of bread (or a wafer) and a sip of wine (or juice). Verses 21-22 indicate that individuals were doing their own thing in a sinful manner. This shows that the Lord's supper was not a structured ritual led by an elder. In verse 30 Paul says that the problems with the handling of the Lord's supper by the Corinthian church assembly were causing weakness, illness and death. Paul did not deal with these problems by having an elder take charge and organize the Lord's supper in a God-honoring manner. His specific commands are for the church members to wait for one another and for them to eat at home if they are hungry. Paul did not limit each believer's freedom to serve one another and pray during this shared meal focused on the death of Christ.

### 1.12 Praying publicly

In many places the New Testament commands all believers to pray. Some of these Scriptures relate to private prayers. [24] 1 Corinthians 11:1-16 is a tough passage to understand and I discuss its implications to the role of women in house church in Section, 6.4. For the purposes of this Section, it is sufficient to say that this passage makes no sense if it is not addressing spoken prayers and prophecies in assembly meetings and other settings where believers

---

22. John 4:1-2, 1 Cor. 1:14-17
23. Acts 10:48
24. Matt. 6:6

have gathered together. It is clear from this passage that any believer could contribute to a meeting with a spoken prayer.

Similarly, 1 Corinthians 14:6-20 shows that praying aloud in tongues was normal in house church assembly meetings. This passage emphasizes the importance of interpretation so that everyone present may understand the prayer. As the gift of tongues was not restricted to elders it also follows that praying aloud was not restricted to elders.

It is likely that 1 Timothy 2:8-9 and James 5:16 are also describing prayers in house church meetings and other situations where believers are gathered together. Again, praying aloud is not restricted to elders. James 5:14 and 1 Timothy 4:14 are examples of elders praying for individuals.

### 1.13 Praying for healing

Healing [25] was a major part of Jesus' public ministry and it was also an important part of the ministry of the 12 and the 72. [26] After Pentecost, healing continued to be an important part of the ministry of the apostles and other traveling leaders, who were careful to ensure that Jesus received the glory for this ministry. [27] Mark 16:18, 1 Corinthians 12:9, 28 and James 5:14-16 show that healing is a ministry associated both with believers who are not recognized leaders and with believers who are leaders. Healing is a spiritual gift that God gives to some but not all of His children. [28]

### 1.14 Praying for deliverance

Delivering people from demons was a major part of Jesus' public ministry. Deliverance ministry was also an important part of the ministry of the 12 and the 72. [29] Jesus gave these traveling leaders the authority and training they needed for this ministry. After Pentecost, deliverance ministry continued to be an important part of the ministry of the apostles and other traveling leaders. [30] Mark 16:17

---

25. In the New Testament healing is closely associated with deliverance. Many verses mention both healing and deliverance (Matt. 4:24, 8:16, 10:1, 8, Mark 1:32, 34, 6:13, 16:17-18, Luke 6:18, 7:21, 8:2, Acts 5:16, 8:7, 19:12) and in some cases it is explicitly stated that a particular healing was the result of a deliverance (Matt. 12:22, 17:14-20, Luke 8:36, 9:42, Acts 10:38).
26. Matt. 10:1, 8, 17:16, Mark 6:13, Luke 9:2, 6, 10:9
27. Acts 3:1-8, 3:12-16, 4:10, 30, 5:12-16, 8:6-7, 9:34, 14:8-10, 19:12, 28:8
28. 1 Cor. 12:30. The gift of healing, like other gifts, may be given to meet a one-time need, or it may be given for regular use.
29. Matt. 10:1-8, 17:14-21, Mark 3:14-15, 6:7-13, 9:17-29, Luke 9:1, 10:17-20
30. Acts 5:16, 8:7

and 1 Corinthians 12:10 teach that casting out demons is a ministry associated with believers who are not recognized leaders as well as with believers who are leaders. [31]

### 1.15 Prophesying and speaking in tongues

In 1 Corinthians 12:7-11 Paul teaches that each believer receives one or more spiritual gifts for the common good. [32] The Holy Spirit decides, which gift or gifts to give to each individual. Acts 19:5-6 is an example of believers receiving the gifts of prophecy and tongues after being baptized and Acts 10:44-48 is an example of individuals receiving the gift of tongues after hearing the Gospel but before being baptized. The gifts of prophecy and tongues are extensively discussed in 1 Corinthians 12 and 14. These gifts and other gifts mentioned in these chapters (*e.g.*, message of wisdom, message of knowledge, faith, healing, miracles, discernment of spirits, interpretation of tongues) were used both in assembly meetings and outside of these meetings.

### 1.16 Living as an example

Hebrews 6:12 encourages believers to be "imitators of those who through faith and patience inherit the promises." This verse is challenging all believers to live so as to inherit the promises. This means that all believers should be living in a manner such that other believers may imitate them. Obviously some believers (including some Christian leaders) fall short of this. We all need to be discerning as to whose example we choose to follow.

Similarly, Matthew 5:16 and 1 Peter 2:12 command all believers to lead good lives that will be observed by others. In both of these verses the focus is on the observers giving glory to God rather than on the observers following their example.

---

31. Mark 16:9-20 is not included in some early manuscripts. Even if this passage was not included in the original edition of the gospel, it is strong evidence that individuals who were not elders or traveling leaders were actively engaged in deliverance ministry in the New Testament church. 1 Cor. 12:10 includes the gift of discerning between spirits in a list of gifts distributed to all members of the Christian community. Some believers who are not elders or traveling leaders receive the gift of discerning spirits, which is a key spiritual gift associated with deliverance ministry. Other passages consistent with God using individuals who are not leaders in deliverance ministry include Mark 9:38-40, Luke 9:49-50 and Rom. 16:20.
32. This message is repeated in Rom. 12:4-8, 1 Cor. 12:28-30.

1 Peter 5:3 says that elders should be examples. Most of the qualifications for being an elder relate to character.[33] Part of the reason for this is that elders are supposed to be an example. Traveling leaders are also expected to be an example. 1 Timothy 4:12 and Titus 2:7 are commands, in the singular, to Timothy and Titus to be an example to other believers. Paul talks about his life being an example.[34] In several of these verses Paul says that living his life as an example is part of the way he teaches.

### 1.17 Overseeing

In Hebrews 12:15 all believers are commanded to "see to it that no one fails to obtain the grace of God." All believers are to be actively watching out for their brothers and sisters. This is a key dimension of pastoral care. The Greek verb used in this verse is *episkopeo*, which means to oversee. This verb is also used in 1 Peter 5:2 to describe a key activity of elders in local church leadership: looking out for members of the community. This verb is related to the Greek noun *episkopos* (overseer), which is one of the two primary words used in the New Testament for leaders within local Christian assemblies. These links, between an activity all believers are commanded to perform and the nature of leadership within a local Christian assembly, show that leadership within New Testament house churches consisted of activities that were open to all believers.

### 1.18 Building the church

In Matthew 16:16 Peter says "You are the Christ, the Son of the living God" to which Jesus replies in v. 18 "on this rock I will build my church." Jesus is the one who is building His church or to translate the Greek literally His "assembly."[35] This verse is not talking about Jesus building a building or an organization. It is talking about Him building a community of believers. Ephesians 4:15-16 says that Jesus is the head of the body and He causes it to grow under His direction. Ephesians 5:23-32 teaches that Jesus is preparing a glorious church and bride for Himself. Similarly Psalm 127:1 says "Unless the LORD builds the house, those who build it labor in vain." Obviously humans

---

33. 1 Tim. 3:1-7, Titus 1
34. 1 Cor. 4:16-17, 11:1-2, 2 Thess. 3:7, Phil. 3:17, 4:9
35. The Protestant interpretation of verse 17 is that the foundation (rock) on which Jesus builds His church is the revelation from God the Father that Jesus is the Christ the Son of the living God. This interpretation is consistent with one of the primary conclusions of this book: New Testament churches were centered on Jesus not human leaders.

need to labor with Jesus in the building of His church. But we need to avoid the subtle trap of thinking that ultimately we are responsible for building the church.

## 1.19 Deciding who is a local or traveling leader

Section 2.2 discusses the appointing of elders and Section 3.2 discusses the appointment of traveling leaders. Apart from emphasizing the primacy of the Holy Spirit, the New Testament provides limited information concerning the appointment of leaders. [36] There are hints that in at least some cases the whole congregation nominated new elders. In at least some cases it seems that prophetic words played a part in identifying new elders. In these cases, to be consistent with other Scripture, it is reasonable to expect that the words were tested by the whole congregation. This implies that in these cases the whole congregation had a role in confirming new elders. It is very likely that this decision-making process would have been consensual, but it is possible that a vote was held. It is very likely that prayer with laying on of hands was a standard way of publicly confirming the new elders. It appears that in some cases a traveling leader may have helped facilitate the process of identifying and publicly confirming elders. It is possible that this assistance was most needed by relatively young churches.

Prophetic words are particularly emphasized in the verses that address the appointment of traveling leaders. The recommendation of their local church assembly and prayer with laying on of hands are also mentioned.

## 1.20 Shepherding/Pastoring

Acts 20:28 and 1 Peter 5:2 both mention that elders are expected to shepherd or pastor. In both cases a verb is used to indicate that this is an activity that the elders perform. It is not a job title. As discussed in Subsection 2.1.3 the Biblical concept of pastoring has four primary dimensions: protection, leadership/direction setting, care and teaching. [37] Only Jesus as the Chief Shepherd can fully fill all four dimensions. [38] Elders are often Jesus' agent to care for and teach other believers. Elders also have a role in protection (protecting sound doctrine [39]) and leadership by example and influence.

---

36. Acts 13:4, 20:28
37. Subsection 2.1.3
38. 1 Pet. 5:4
39. Titus 1:9

I am unaware of any Scripture reference explicitly linking pastoring to believers who are not elders or traveling leaders.[40] However, all believers are expected to teach and to care for other believers. These are two of the four dimensions of pastoring. Also, all believers were expected to participate in the leadership of meetings and other ministry by making contributions as led by the Holy Spirit. Protecting sound doctrine is also a dimension of pastoring. In the New Testament this role is linked to elders and traveling leaders.[41] As will be discussed in the next section, believers who were not elders were also free to contribute in this area. So it seems that believers who are not elders were free to be involved in all aspects of pastoring and shepherding. In many cases individuals function as elders for a while before they are formally acknowledged as elders. It is desirable that they demonstrate an aptitude for pastoring and shepherding before this formal acknowledgment as an elder. New Testament style church provided individuals the opportunity to demonstrate their aptitude for pastoring prior to becoming elders.

In linking elders to pastoring we need to be very careful that we do not read into the meaning of this word more than the original readers of the New Testament would have understood by it. The New Testament role of an elder is much narrower than the role of a pastor in the vast majority of churches today. In certain circles care is also needed with the use of the word "shepherd." Some groups of Christians have used this term to describe accountability relationships that became inappropriately controlling.

## 1.21 Protecting sound doctrine

Elders had an important role in ensuring sound doctrine was taught in the local church assembly and in uncovering the teaching of false doctrine.[42] The ability to serve in this manner is a requirement to be an elder. Given the culture of ministry freedom associated with New Testament style house churches, it is extremely plausible that non-

---

40. Heb. 12:15 comes very close. This verse commands all believers to *episkopeo*. This is the Greek verb related to the Greek noun *episkopos* which is commonly translated "overseer" and is used as a title equivalent to elder. The primary meaning of this verb is to oversee. In Hebrews 12:15 all believers are being commanded to watch out for other believers. In this verse all believers are being commanded to serve in the same manner as elders. Subsection 2.1.2 and Appendix 1.17, 3.2 provide further information about this family of words.
41. Section 3.5
42. Titus 1:9

elders were free to be involved in the protection of sound doctrine—especially as this role is closely related to teaching, which was an activity expected of all believers. Allowing individuals, who were not elders, to be involved in protecting sound doctrine gives them an opportunity to show their competence in this area. This helps show which individuals are qualified to become elders.

# Appendix 2
# Authority

This appendix summarizes New Testament teaching concerning authority. The first section of this appendix summarizes the authority held by God, traveling Christian leaders, local Christian leaders, individual believers, leaders in civil government and demons. The next section addresses the authority of Paul to direct the travels of his co-workers. Is this an example of a New Testament leader having the authority to direct the ministry of another believer? The third section addresses 1 Corinthians 4:14-21 where Paul says that he is the father of the Corinthian church assembly and that he can come "with a whip, or in love and with a gentle spirit" (NIV). How does this fit with everything else the New Testament says about authority and leadership? The final section of this appendix discusses the various Greek words translated "authority." The primary Greek word translated "authority" is *exousia*. This word may also be translated "right."

## 2.1 Overview of who held various types of authority in the New Testament

### *Divine authority*

During his earthly ministry Jesus had authority to teach, heal, drive out demons and forgive sins. He had authority to give eternal life to all whom the Father had given to him. He also had authority to execute judgment and to lay down his life and take it up again. Jesus had authority to impart authority to his disciples.[1]

---

1. Matt. 7:29, Mark 1:22, 27, Luke 4:32; Matt. 8:5-13, 9:6-8, Mark 2:10-12, Luke 7:3-10; Mark 1:27, Luke 4:36; Matt. 9:6-8, Mark 2:10-12, Luke 5:24; John 17:2; John 5:27-30; John 10:18; Matt. 10:1, Mark 3:14-15, 6:7, Luke 9:1, 10:19.

After his death and resurrection Jesus told his apostles that, "All authority in heaven and on earth has been given to me."[2] This truth is celebrated in several other passages.[3] Jesus' authority is held in a delicate balance with the authority of the Father as a part of the unity of the Holy Trinity.[4] God has authority to do as He wills with each of our lives and to appoint governing authorities.[5]

### *Traveling leaders*

In John 17:18 and 20:21 Jesus tells his apostles that he is sending them into the world in just the same way as the Father sent Him into the world. The implication of these verses is that this includes most, but not all, of the authority that Jesus had during his earthly ministry. During his earthly ministry Jesus gave his disciples authority to preach, to cast out demons and to heal.[6] These are some of the key elements of authority that Jesus had during his earthly ministry. John 20:21-22 links Jesus' commission to his apostles to go into the world to their receipt of the Holy Spirit. Since Pentecost, apostles and many other believers have had God's authority to preach, teach, cast out demons and heal.

Jesus also had the authority during His earthly ministry to forgive sins. In John 20:23 He says to His apostles, "If you forgive the sins of anyone, they are forgiven." In this verse Jesus gives His apostles a role in people coming to forgiveness of their sins. This truth has to be held in balance with passages that affirm the unique role of Jesus in the forgiveness of sins.[7] The role of the apostles, and other believers, in individuals receiving forgiveness of sins includes presenting the Gospel so that they have the opportunity to respond in faith.[8] It also includes declaring the forgiveness of specific sins that a believer has confessed. The authority to declare the forgiveness of sins based on the death of Jesus and the promises in Scripture is a priestly role and all believers have this authority because they are all priests.[9]

---

2. Matt. 28:18
3. Eph. 1:20-22, Col. 2:10, 15, Jude 1:25, Rev. 12:10
4. John 17:2, Acts 1:7
5. Rom. 9:20-21, 13:1-3
6. Matt. 10:1, Mark 3:14-15, 6:7, Luke 9:1, 10:17-19
7. Matt. 26:28, Acts 5:31, 10:43, Eph. 1:7, Col. 1:14, Heb. 9:22, 1 John 1:7-2:2
8. Luke 24:47, Acts 2:38, 13:38, 26:15-18, Rom. 10:9-14
9. James 5:15-16, *cf.*, Lev. 4-6, 13-14

In John 20:23 Jesus says to His apostles, "if you withhold forgiveness from anyone, it is withheld." Many passages command us to forgive those who sin against us, so this verse is not giving permission to the apostles, or any other believer, to withhold forgiveness from an individual who sins against them. [10] The first half of John 20:23, "if you forgive the sins of anyone, they are forgiven," states the positive side of preaching the gospel: some individuals respond in faith and receive forgiveness. The second half of John 20:23, "if you withhold forgiveness from anyone, it is withheld," states the other side of preaching the gospel: some individuals reject the gospel and do not receive forgiveness. [11] It is probable that the second half of John 20:23 also applies to the role of all believers in church discipline, in settling disputes between believers and in the final judgment. [12]

Traveling leaders have the authority to build up local believers. They are not to use this authority to tear down or destroy. [13] All believers are expected to be active in building one another up. [14]

Part of the authority to build up believers is the authority of the apostles to pray for individuals to receive the Holy Spirit. [15] It is very unlikely that the apostles were the only individuals used by God in this manner. It is likely that Ananias praying for Paul to be filled with the Holy Spirit is an example of God using an individual who was not an apostle in this way. Also the Holy Spirit was sometimes released upon individuals with no human praying over them. [16]

Matthew 20:25-28, Luke 22:25-26 and Mark 10:42-45 teach that Christian leaders do not receive delegated authority to "lord it over" other believers. Christian leaders, both local leaders and traveling leaders, are to act as servants. They do not have the authority to direct the ministry of believers or of Christian assemblies. They do not have the authority to discipline believers, but they may participate in the church discipline process with the full assembly. [17]

---

10. Matt. 6:12-15, 18:21-35, Mark 11:25, Luke 6:36-37, 17:3-4, Col. 3:13
11. Matt. 11:20-24, John 3:19-21, 9:39, 2 Cor. 2:15-16
12. Matt. 18:15-18, 1 Cor. 5:11-6:5. Matt. 19:28 and Luke 22:29-30 seem to teach that the initial 12 disciples will judge Israel. Possibly Jesus' words in these passages apply to all believers.
13. 2 Cor. 10:8, 13:10
14. Rom. 15:2, 1 Thess. 5:11
15. Acts 8:19, 19:6
16. Acts 10:44
17. Subsection 1.1.4

### *All Believers*

The foundational authority given to all who receive Jesus is the right to become children of God. We also receive the right to the tree of life and the right to enter the heavenly city. Believers who conquer and keep Jesus' works to the end will receive authority over the nations. [18] Many passages mention different aspects of the right, or authority, of God's children to be free. [19]

All believers were expected to participate in the process of evaluating potential prophetic words. [20] 1 Corinthians 5:1-6:3 teaches the authority of believers to participate in the church discipline process, to settle disputes between believers and it also says that believers will judge the world and angels. Similarly in Matthew 18:15-17 Jesus teaches the process for conflict resolution within the church. The final step in this process is for the complete church to hear the case and if necessary expel the sinner from the community. So this verse is affirming the authority of all believers to participate in the church discipline process. This authority is conditional on the believers meeting in the name of Jesus. [21] If we enter into the church discipline process in a carnal manner we may make decisions that horrify heaven.

In Matthew 18:18 Jesus says, in a passage directed to all believers, "Truly, I say to you, whatever you bind on earth shall be bound in heaven, and whatever you loose on earth shall be loosed in heaven." The terms loosing and binding had a technical meaning in Jewish culture describing things forbidden or permitted by decisions of the scribes. So it is likely that Jesus is teaching that the authority, which was once held by the scribes, to decide appropriate behavior in various circumstances has now been given to the complete community of faith as opposed to a group of leaders. Unlike the Jewish community, which had detailed rules applying to a wide range of circumstances, the Christian community is characterized

---

18. John 1:12; Rev. 22:14; Rev. 2:26.
19. Matt. 17:26 temple tax; John 8:32, 36 freedom resulting from encountering Jesus, the truth; Acts 5:4 money; Rom. 14 meat offered to idols, special days; 1 Cor. 7:35-37 marriage; 1 Cor. 14:26 contributing to leading meetings; Gal. 5:1 circumcision and law; 1 Pet. 2:15-16 freedom to do good. We are not to allow this freedom to become a stumbling block to the weak (1 Cor. 8:9).
20. Subsection 1.1.5
21. Matt. 18:20

by freedom.[22] The New Testament Christian community did not legislate the details of individual's lives. It was open to diversity and emphasized respecting the perspectives of others concerning contentious topics.[23] So it is likely that the authority to loose and bind in the sense of determining appropriate behavior was rarely used by New Testament congregations.

In Matthew 16:19 Jesus says to Peter, "I will give you the keys of the kingdom of heaven, and whatever you bind on earth shall be bound in heaven, and whatever you loose on earth shall be loosed in heaven." The second part of this verse is identical to Matthew 18:18, which applies to all believers. The first portion of this verse, "I will give you the keys of the kingdom of heaven" refers to the authority Peter had to preach the gospel, thus making it possible for individuals to enter the kingdom. Obviously this authority is not unique to Peter. Any believer, to whom the Father has revealed that Jesus is the Christ, the Son of the living God, has the authority to preach the gospel. This truth is the rock on which Jesus builds his church.[24]

It is very likely that the passages where Jesus gives the apostles authority to go into the world just as the Father sent Him into the world apply to all believers.[25] Certainly all believers receive the Holy Spirit and all believers have a role in proclaiming the Gospel, so that individuals can come to forgiveness and be baptized and discipled. The only aspect of these passages that does not apply to all believers, is the command to travel to all nations. Most believers are sent to the people who live near where they live. When God grants authority to a believer to minister in a particular way (*e.g.*, to teach, preach or heal) he is granting authority to bless others. He is not granting that individual authority to become a decision-making leader. This applies to recognized leaders (*i.e.*, elders and traveling leaders) and to individuals who are ministering (and perhaps leading) in a particular circumstance.

### *Local Leaders*

I am not aware of any references in the New Testament to local leaders having particular authority that was not available to ordinary believers. Possible exceptions to this are protecting sound doctrine

---

22. Matt. 17:26, John 8:32, 36, Gal. 5:1, 1 Pet. 2:16
23. Rom. 14, 1 Cor. 8
24. Matt. 16:16-18
25. Matt. 28:18-20, Mark 16:15-18, John 17:18, John 20:21, Acts 1:8

and pastoring. These roles are mentioned only in the context of elders. [26] But it is very hard to make the case that individuals who were not elders were excluded from these roles.

Some interpret Matthew 16:19 as giving Peter and other Christian leaders, such as pastors and bishops, authority to rule over a local congregation or over many congregations. As discussed above, this interpretation is inconsistent with Matthew 18:18 and many other passages in the New Testament.

### *Civil Government*

Many verses in the New Testament mention the authority of the civil government. [27] Even though in many cases members of the civil government abuse their authority by persecuting Jesus' followers, the New Testament teaches that they have received their authority from God. [28] We are to submit to the authority of the civil government unless submission would result in us disobeying God. [29] The New Testament is clear that the authority of Jesus is far greater than the authority of any human leader. At the end, all human authority, except for authority appropriately delegated within the kingdom of God, will be destroyed. [30]

Some references to the authority of governmental leaders are positive. For example, Jesus commends the Roman centurion for his faith when he compares Jesus' authority with his authority over the soldiers and servants under him. [31] Jesus is not suggesting that this is an example of the type of authority He is giving to Christian leaders. Jesus teaches that the authority exercised by governmental leaders is not a pattern for Christian leaders to follow. [32]

### *Authority of Satan, demons, the anti-Christ and of the beast*

Several verses in the New Testament mention the authority of Satan, demons, the anti-Christ and the beast. [33] This authority will be

---

26. Appendix 1.20, 1.21
27. Luke 12:11, 20:20, 23:7, Acts 9:14, 26:10, 12, Rom. 13:1-3, 1 Cor. 15:24, Col. 1:16, Rev. 17:12-13
28. John 19:10, Luke 12:11, Acts 9:4-5; John 19:11, Rom. 13:1-5, Col. 1:16
29. Rom. 13:5, Titus 3:1, 1 Pet. 2:13-15; Acts 4:19-20, 5:29
30. Eph. 1:20-22, 1 Cor. 15:24-25
31. Matt. 8:5-10, Luke 7:1-9
32. Matt. 20:25-26, Mark 10:42-43, Luke 22:25-26
33. Luke 4:5-7, 22:53, Acts 26:18, Eph. 2:2

particularly evident during the End Times.[34] These spiritual powers were created through Jesus and for Jesus.[35] Jesus' victory over demonic authority is complete and will be enforced at the appropriate time.[36] God's goal, with our cooperation, is to set people free from the kingdom of darkness so that they may enter the kingdom of the beloved Son.[37] This transfer takes place at our salvation. Some individuals also need deliverance ministry. Our role in setting people free may include wrestling against demonic authorities in the heavenly places.[38] As individuals come to salvation and freedom, the wisdom of God is revealed to the rulers and authorities in the heavenly places through the church.[39]

## 2.2 Did Paul have the authority to direct the ministry travels of his coworkers?

In several places the Scriptures record that Paul sent a team member or pair of team members to minister in a particular city or region. Examples of this include:

- Timothy and Erastus sent to Macedonia (Acts 19:22).
- Timothy sent to Corinth "to remind you of my ways in Christ, as I teach them everywhere in every church" (1 Corinthians 4:17).
- An unnamed brother sent to Corinth with Titus (2 Corinthians 12:17-18).
- Tychicus sent to Ephesus so "that you may know how we are, and that he may encourage your hearts" (Ephesians 6:21-22). It is plausible that Tychicus was hand delivering the letter to the Ephesians. 2 Timothy 4:12 also mentions Paul sending Tychicus to Ephesus. Given the generally accepted dating of these epistles it likely that these are two different visits.
- Paul hopes to send Timothy to Philippi soon so "that I too may be cheered by news of you" (Philippians 2:19).
- Tychicus sent to Colosse. "I have sent him to you for this very purpose, that you may know how we are and that he may encourage your hearts" (Colossians 4:7-9).
- Timothy sent to Thessalonica "we sent Timothy, our brother and God's coworker in the gospel of Christ, to establish and exhort you in your faith,...when I could bear it no longer, I sent to learn about

34. Rev. 9:3, 10, 19, 13:2-12, 17:12-13
35. Col. 1:16
36. 1 Cor. 15:24-25, Eph. 1:20-22, Col. 2:15, 1 Pet. 3:22, Rev. 13:5, 17:12
37. Acts 26:18, Col. 1:13
38. Mark 16:17, Eph. 6:12
39. Eph. 3:10

your faith, for fear that somehow the tempter had tempted you and our labor would be in vain" (1 Thessalonians 3:2,5). In verse 5 Paul uses the singular (I sent). This is consistent with all of the other references listed above which record Paul sending various traveling leaders to various cities. However, in verse 2, Paul uses the plural (we sent). This implies two things: firstly that the decision to send Timothy to Thessalonica was a group decision; and secondly that Paul is comfortable in describing this group decision using a singular ("I sent").

In several places the Scriptures record that Paul urged a team member or team members to minister in a particular city. Examples of this include:

- 2 Corinthians 8:6 records that Paul urged Titus to go to Corinth as part of a collection for the saints in Jerusalem. Verses 16-17 of this chapter show the delicate balance between Paul urging Titus and his own desire to go: "But thanks be to God, who put into the heart of Titus the same earnest care I have for you. For he not only accepted our appeal, but being himself very earnest he is going to you of his own accord."
- 2 Corinthians 9:3, 5 appear to be discussing a follow up visit by a group of brothers to Corinth concerning the collection mentioned in 2 Corinthians 8. In verse 5 it is recorded that Paul had thought it necessary to urge the brothers to make the trip and in verse 3 it is recorded that he is sending them. This pair of verses seems to indicate that the words "send" and "urge" can both be applied to a single trip. If leaders of teams of traveling leaders have the authority to send traveling leaders on trips then there is no need to urge anyone. So this pair of verses supports the case that the use of the word sent does not indicate authority to order individuals to various cities.
- 2 Corinthians 12:17-18 seem to be discussing the same trip to Corinth by Titus that was discussed in 2 Corinthians 8. It is again recorded that Paul urged Titus to make the trip. Verse 18 also records that a brother was also sent with him. Is it possible that Paul is using different verbs to describe his different interactions with these two individuals prior to the trip? Is it possible that the brother immediately sensed it was right to go and so there was almost no dialog when Paul suggested the trip? Is it possible that Titus took a little longer to become sure that he should go on this trip? Is it possible that while he was considering Paul started urging?
- In 1 Timothy 1:3 Paul urged Timothy to "remain at Ephesus that you may charge certain persons not to teach any different doctrine."
- 1 Corinthians 16:12 Paul strongly urged Apollos to go to Corinth: "I strongly urged him to visit you with the other brothers, but it was not

at all his will to come now. He will come when he has opportunity." Paul could urge Apollos to make a certain trip, but ultimately it is up to Apollos to decide where he should go and when he should go there. There is no hint in this passage or any other passage that Apollos' disagreement with Paul about this trip was sin.

- In Acts 21:12 the traveling leaders traveling with Paul and some believers in Caesarea urged Paul to avoid Jerusalem because Agabus had prophesied his arrest. This verse again makes clear that urging is not a command. It also shows that "urging" may be a two way street. Traveling leaders and other believers may "urge" the leader of a team of traveling leaders.

It is certainly possible to interpret all of the references to Paul sending traveling workers to various cities as indicating that Paul had authority to direct the activities of his co-workers. However, if Paul could order his teammates to other cities why are there so many references to him urging them to go? Is it possible that the verses that say Paul sent individuals on ministry trips apply to situations where Paul proposed a trip and the individuals immediately agreed? Is it possible that the verses that say Paul urged individuals to go on trips apply to situations where Paul proposed a trip and the individuals did not immediately agree? Acts 16:9 records a situation where Paul saw a vision of a man urging him to come to Macedonia. The next verse uses a plural form of the verb "concluding," which shows that Paul did not make the decision to go to Macedonia alone. The wording of this verse implies that the whole team jointly evaluated the vision and concluded that God was calling them to Macedonia.

In summary, it is not possible to make a compelling Biblical case that Paul had the authority to direct his teammates to visit specific cities. This is consistent with the assumption that Luke 22:25-26 is a general command to all Christian leaders (*i.e.*, elders and traveling leaders) not to lord it over other believers. This command applies to teams of traveling leaders as well as to local church assemblies.

## 2.3 Does 1 Corinthians 4:14-21 teach that traveling leaders have power over churches they have planted?

1 Corinthians 4:14-21 says:

> I am not writing this to shame you, but to warn you, as my dear children. Even though you have ten thousand guardians in Christ, you do not have many fathers, for in Christ Jesus I became your father through the gospel. Therefore I urge you to imitate me. For this reason I am sending to you Timothy, my son whom I love, who is faithful in the Lord. He will remind you of my way of life in Christ Jesus, which agrees with what I teach everywhere in every church.

> Some of you have become arrogant, as if I were not coming to you. But I will come to you very soon, if the Lord is willing, and then I will find out not only how these arrogant people are talking, but what power they have. For the kingdom of God is not a matter of talk but of power. What do you prefer? Shall I come to you with a whip, or in love and with a gentle spirit? (NIV).

What is the nature of the power that Paul is discussing in this passage? What is the "rod" (KJV, ESV) or "whip" (NIV) that he mentions in verse 21? Is Paul claiming the authority to direct certain activities within the Corinthian church assembly?

Many denominations have the organizational infrastructure required to implement "rods" based on human power or authority. For example some denominations punish clergy, and their congregations, by forcing clergy to move to another congregation or, more rarely, out of ministry. The root of this power is commonly in the centralized control of the ordination of priests and of the licensing of priests to serve particular congregations. Another element of this power may be financial control, for example over pay, pensions and building ownership. In some cases denominational authorities are able to stop the pay of a priest who defies them; in other cases they can limit a priest's pension; and in yet other cases they can go through the civil courts to gain control of the buildings used by a congregation that defies them. The organizational infrastructure necessary for these kinds of "rods" was totally absent in the New Testament church. If a local congregation chose to ignore a traveling leader there was nothing a traveling leader could do to force them to change their mind. It is extremely implausible that Paul had in mind any such use of human power or authority when he next visited Corinth.

If the "rod" of 1 Corinthians 4:21 is not organizational power, what might it be? In 1 Corinthians 4:20 Paul says that the Kingdom of God is not a matter of talk but of power. Many scriptures teach that this is not human or organizational power but supernatural power. For example 2 Corinthians 12:12 shows that Paul considers signs and wonders to be part of the way God authenticates true apostles. It seems plausible that the "rod" is some kind of supernatural power demonstration authenticating a rebuke combined with a call to repentance.

What might a supernatural "rod" look like? Maybe Paul has in mind a power demonstration such as 1 Samuel 12:17-20 where Samuel prays for a storm to destroy the harvest to show the people that they were wrong in asking for a king; or 1 Kings 13:1-6 where Jeroboam's arm was shriveled up and the altar split to show that he was wrong to set up worship centers in the northern kingdom of Israel; or Acts 5:1-10 where Ananias and Sapphira were struck dead for lying about their gift; or Acts 13:11 where Elymas the magician was struck blind for opposing Paul's presentation of the Gospel. Is it possible that in Acts 13:11 a demon of spiritual blindness was forced to show itself in the natural? Is it possible that in writing 1 Corinthians 4:18-21 Paul was contemplating commanding the demonic in the arrogant to show itself?

1 Corinthians 2:4, 2 Corinthians 10:1-11 and 13:2-3 all seem to support some spiritual power demonstration authenticating Paul's message. We need to be cautious concerning spiritual power demonstrations. On the one hand, Paul can speak of "the authority the Lord gave us," but on the other hand God is the one who decides when a power demonstration happens and what the demonstration will be. [40] The New Testament, records many power demonstrations. But there are also many examples of God allowing hard things to happen to His children, when they may have much preferred a power demonstration to deliver them. Paul cannot control God and tell Him when to perform a power demonstration.

Perhaps one reason why power demonstrations are relatively rare is that very few believers have the depth of humility and obedience required for God to safely use them in this manner on a regular basis. [41] God may decide against performing a power demonstration because of the risk that His human instrument for the demonstration may become proud and controlling. Another reason may be the shallowness of our faith. In some cases, God may choose against doing a power demonstration, because He already knows that the individuals are so hardened in their sin that they would ignore the power demonstration.

If after a power demonstration, the majority of a local church rejects a traveling leader's rebuke and call to repentance there is

---

40. 2 Cor. 10:8

41. 1 Kings 13:7-32 is a warning concerning the high expectation of obedience that God has for individuals He uses in power demonstrations. This passage describes the death of the man of God mentioned in 1 Kings 13:1-6 for what may seem to us a fairly minor act of disobedience in a situation with strong mitigating circumstances. 1 Kings 13:33-34 records that these power demonstrations did not cause Jeroboam to repent.

precious little he can do but wipe the dust off his feet to them and leave them to Jesus. [42]

In summary, it seems that 1 Corinthians 4:14-21 teaches that there may sometimes be a place for a supernatural power demonstration by a traveling leader as part of his attempt to persuade a troubled church to return to a healthy place. The Biblical and historical context show that it is not appropriate to use this passage as a justification for traveling leaders having organizational authority to direct the affairs of a local assembly.

### 2.4 Greek words translated authority

The word studies in the appendices are based on the Strong's number system and the associated edition of the Greek New Testament. In a few cases new manuscript evidence has resulted in scholars concluding that alternative readings are more likely to be accurate. [43] Unless otherwise stated, the translations for each Greek word studied in these appendices are taken from the *Analytical Greek Lexicon* revised by H. K. Moulton and D. Holly and published by Bagster in 1977.

**2.4.1 *Exousia* (Strong's # 1849)** – power, ability, faculty, efficiency, energy, liberty, license, authority, rule, dominion, jurisdiction, privilege, prerogative, right

Strong gives the following translations: power of choice, liberty of doing as one pleases, physical and mental power, power of authority (influence) and of right (privilege), the power of rule or government. Ninety-three [44] verses in the New Testament contain the Greek noun *exousia*, which is typically translated authority, power, jurisdiction or right. This is the predominant word for these topics in the New Testament. The range of meanings associated with this Greek word is broader than the range of meanings associated with the English word authority. In English this word can be strongly associated with leaders of organizations and typically has no connotation of working by influence.

---

42. Luke 10:11, Rev. 2:16, 3:3, 16
43. *E.g.*, Matt. 23:8 (*cf.* Appendix 4.5.7), John 8:9 (*cf.* Appendix 6.1)
44. Some passages in the synoptic gospels (Matthew, Mark, Luke) are word for word identical. However, for simplicity, this verse count total and all similar verse or word count totals in this book includes all references, even if they are part of parallel passages with identical wording.

**2.4.2 *Exousiazo* (1850)** – have or exercise authority, be brought under power or enslaved

Three verses in the New Testament contain the Greek verb *exousiazo*, which is related to the noun *exousia*. This verb is used twice in 1 Corinthians 7:4 where Paul discusses the mutual authority husbands and wives have over their partner's bodies. It is also used in 1 Corinthians 6:12 where Paul says that all things are lawful to him but that he will not allow anything to enslave him.

**2.4.3 *Katexousiazo* (2715)** – exercise lordship over, domineer

Two verses in the New Testament contain the Greek verb *katexousiazo*. It is derived from *exousiazo* by combining it with the preposition *kata*, which means "down from." This verb seems to have a very similar meaning to *exousiazo*. It is used in Matthew 20:25 and Mark 10:42 to describe the authority of Gentile kings. The parallel passage in Luke uses *exousiazo* in place of *katexousiazo*. [45]

**2.4.4 *Kurieuo* (2961)** – be lord over, be possessed of mastery over, to exercise sway over

Seven verses in the New Testament contain the Greek verb *kurieuo*. It is related to the noun *kurios*, which means lord or master. This word is used in Luke 22:25 and 2 Corinthians 1:24 to describe a leadership style that Christian leaders should avoid. This verb is also used of death, sin, the law and Jesus.

**2.4.5 *Katakurieuo* (2634)** – to get into one's power, to bring under, master, overcome, domineer over

Four verses in the New Testament contain the Greek verb *katakurieuo*, which is derived from *kurieuo* by combining it with the preposition *kata*, which means "down from." It seems that the meanings of *kurieuo* and *katakurieuo* are very similar. *Katakurieuo* is used in Matthew 20:25, Mark 10:42 and 1 Peter 5:3 to describe a leadership style that Christian leaders should avoid. Luke 22:25 is the parallel passage to Matthew 20:25 and Mark 10:42. Luke uses *kurieuo* where Mathew and Mark use *katakurieuo*. In Acts 19:16 *katakurieuo* is used of a demon possessed man overcoming the seven sons of the Jewish high priest Sceva while they were attempting to deliver him of his demon.

---

45. Luke 22:25

**2.4.6 *Kuriotes* (2963)** – lordship, constituted authority, (pl.) authorities, potentates

Four verses in the New Testament contain the Greek noun *kuriotes*, which is also derived from *kurios*.

**2.4.7 *Epitage* (2003)** – injunction, decree, authoritativeness, strictness

Seven verses in the New Testament contain the Greek noun *epitage*. In Titus 2:15 KJV, ESV and NIV translate this word "authority." In this verse Paul commands Titus to, "Declare these things; exhort and rebuke with all authority." In the Greek there is an "and" between "declare these things" and "exhort." So the phrase, "with all authority" appears to apply to all three activities (teaching, exhorting and rebuking) mentioned in this verse.

**2.4.8 *Authenteo* (831)** – act by one's own authority or power, have authority over, domineer

The only place this verb is used in the New Testament is 1 Timothy 2:12 where it is translated usurp, exercise or have authority. The meaning of this word and this verse is discussed in Section 6.4.

**2.4.9 *Archon* (758)** – one invested with power or dignity, chief, ruler, prince, magistrate

Thirty seven verses in the New Testament contain the Greek noun *archon*, which is usually translated ruler or prince. Occasionally it is translated authorities or magistrate. This word is never used concerning Christian leaders.

**2.4.10 *Politarches* (4173)** – a ruler or prefect of a city, a magistrate

This noun is used twice in the New Testament. Some translations render it as city authorities.

**2.4.11 *Dunatos* (1415)** – having power, powerful, mighty

Thirty five verses in the New Testament contain the Greek adjective *dunatos*, which is typically translated possible, able, mighty or strong and occasionally translated authorities.

# Appendix 3
# Local Church Leaders

This appendix complements Chapter 2 by providing additional information concerning the Greek words used for local church assembly leaders in the New Testament. In some cases, I also address the use of these Greek words for leaders in the Septuagint Greek translation of the Old Testament, as it sheds additional light on the New Testament use of these words.

The New Testament includes a brief introduction to the leadership title "apostle" the first time that it is used.[1] Presumably, this is because this leadership title was not used in Israel nor was it used in the New Testament Jewish community. In contrast with this, there is no introduction to the use of the term "elder" within the New Testament Christian community. Also, there are many references to elders in the Old Testament and to elders in the New Testament Jewish community. Based on this, it is reasonable to assume that there is a measure of continuity between the role of Israelite/Jewish elders and Christian elders. So, in the case of elders, I also summarize the available Biblical information on the role of elders in the Old and New Testament Israelite and Jewish communities and compare this to the role of elders in the New Testament church.

The final section of this appendix discusses if there was ever a senior elder within a New Testament local Christian assembly.

**3.1 *Presbuteros* - *Presbutis* - *Presbutes* - *Presbuterion* - *Sunpresbuteros*** — Elder - Old woman - Old man - Assembly of elders - Fellow elder

---

1. Matt. 10. It is likely that Acts 6:1-6 is an introduction to the role of deacons, but this word is not used in this passage.

This family of words is used 75 times in the New Testament. On 34 occasions it is used to refer to Jewish leaders, 17 times to elders within the Christian community, 12 times to elders in heaven, six times to old people and in six cases the translation could be elder or old man. This is the most common word in the New Testament for local church assembly leaders. I believe that the early church chose to use this word as its primary word for leaders, because of its emphasis on leaders as influencers and not decision-makers.

The existence of several verses where the meaning of the word is ambiguous may mean that it was not critical to the New Testament authors to carefully distinguish between old men and elders. This is consistent with an emphasis on elders providing wisdom and life experience rather than being religious decision-makers.

Elders are almost always referred to in the plural in the Old and New Testaments and there is no hint of a hierarchy amongst the group of elders. This is consistent with other indicators that each house church typically has a team of co-equal elders. The few references to elder in the singular are for obvious reasons based on the context. [2]

As will be seen in the detailed discussion below, points of continuity between the roles of elders in the Old Testament Israelite community and in the New Testament Jewish community with the roles of elders in the New Testament Christian community include: providing advice and wisdom; protecting sound doctrine; co-equal group of leaders working by influence and with no hierarchy. Points of difference include: Christian elders have no legal or judicial role—church discipline and certain aspects of the final judgment are handled by all believers; also Christian elders are not communications intermediaries—God wants to interact directly with each of His children.

**3.1.1 *Presbuteros* (Strong's # 4245)** – elder, senior, older, more advanced in years, dignitary, member of the Jewish Sanhedrin, (in plural) ancients, ancestors, fathers.

This word is used 67 times in the New Testament. 32 times this word is used to refer to Jewish leaders, 15 times to elders within the Christian community, 12 times to elders in heaven, four times to old people and in four cases the translation could be either elder or old man. [3]

---

2. 1 Tim. 5:19, 1 Pet. 5:1, 2 John 1, 3 John 1
3. 2 John 1, 3 John 1, 1 Tim. 5:1, 1 Pet. 5:5. In the first two references John is referring to himself in his old age. So either translation may be appropriate.

### 3.1.2 *Presbutis* (4247) – an aged woman

This word is used once in the New Testament and it appears that this is a generic reference to older women within a congregation.[4] It is possible that it is a reference to female elders. The women mentioned in this verse are commanded to teach and train the younger women. Teaching is open to all believers so the fact that old women are expected to teach does not prove that they were elders.

### 3.1.3 *Presbutes* (4246) – an old man, aged person

This word is used three times in the New Testament. One reference is obviously a reference to an old man.[5] The other two references are most likely to old men but may possibly refer to local church leaders.[6] In Philemon, Paul is referring to himself. He could be describing himself as an elder or as an old man or as both.

### 3.1.4 *Presbuterion* (4244) – a body of old men, an assembly of elders, the Jewish Sanhedrin

This word is used three times in the New Testament.[7] Two of these references are to Jewish leaders and one applies to Christian leaders.

### 3.1.5 *Sunpresbuteros* (4850) – fellow elder

This word is used once in the New Testament.[8] The context relates to local church assembly leaders. This verse shows that Peter designated himself as an elder as well as an apostle.[9]

### 3.1.6 Elders in the Old Testament

Elders are mentioned more than 120 times in the Old Testament. The definition of the word elder is somewhat fluid. It can apply at several different levels within the life of the Israelite nation. Sometimes the word elder applies to a group of individuals who interact with Israel's overall leader. In other cases the word elder applies to a group of individuals within a town or tribe and in some cases the

---

It is possible that he had both meanings in mind. The latter two references also mention younger men so I tend to the view that these passages are discussing older men.

4. Titus 2:3
5. Luke 1:18
6. Titus 2:2, Phm. 1:9
7. Luke 22:66, Acts 22:5, 1 Tim. 4:14
8. 1 Pet. 5:1
9. 1 Pet. 1:1, 2 Pet. 1:1

word applies to elders within a household.[10] In Isaiah 24:23, the word is used in an End Times prophecy.[11]

The following paragraphs discuss the roles and responsibilities of elders as described in the Old Testament. I have ordered these paragraphs based on the frequency of mentions in the Old Testament of each role. I discuss roles mentioned most frequently first and roles mentioned less frequently later.

### *Elders as representatives of the people*

The role of elders most frequently mentioned in the Old Testament is acting as representatives of the people of Israel to the national leader. This role included communicating messages and orders from the national leader to the people. This role is particularly prominent under the leadership of Moses and continues under Joshua into the period of the Judges and Kings.[12] In some cases the role of elders as representatives of the people included the elders telling the national leader the concerns and opinions of the people.[13]

### *Elders' role in legal processes*

Deuteronomy mentions that elders had certain specific roles in administering the law.[14] Mentions throughout the rest of the Old Testament show that elders undertook these legal responsibilities.[15] Elders are also mentioned as being involved in cases of murder, marriage and the sale of land.[16]

There was a balance between the role of elders and the role of the complete assembly of the community in certain legal processes. For example in Joshua 20:1-6 elders would interview individuals wishing to enter a city of refuge to gain protection from the avenger of blood. However, the murder trial for these individuals would be held in the presence of the assembly as is also commanded in Numbers 35:24. Similarly, in the case of a stubborn and rebellious son the parents

---

10. Gen. 50:7, 2 Sam. 12:17
11. *Cf.*, Rev. 4:4, 10, 5:5, 6, 8, 11, 14, 7:11, 13, 11:16, 14:3, 19:4
12. Exod. 3:16, 18, 4:29, 12:21, 17:5-6, 18:12, 19:7, 24:1, 9, 14, Lev. 4:15, 9:1, Deut. 5:23, 31:9, 28; Josh. 23:2, 24:1; 1 Sam. 8:4; 1 Sam. 15:30, 16:4, 1 Kings 8:1, 3
13. 1 Sam. 8:4-10
14. Deut. 19:12, 21:2-6, 18-21, 22:15-18, 25:7-10
15. Josh. 20:1-6, 1 Kings 21:7-11, Ruth 4:1-11, Ezra 10:8, 14
16. Deut. 19:12, 21:2-6; Deut. 22:15-18, 25:7-10; Ruth 4:1-11

are to bring the child to the elders and they are to report his sin to the elders. However, if the situation warrants it, it is all the men of the town who are expected to stone him to death. [17]

There are numerous mentions of judges in the Old Testament. [18] It seems that judges handled the majority of legal issues and that elders only handled certain specific situations. Several passages list judges and elders separately. [19] This implies that many elders were not judges and many judges were not elders. It is highly plausible that some elders were also judges.

### *Elders' role in appointing a king or leader*

In Judges 11:4-11 the elders of Gilead invited Jephthah to lead the Gileadites against the Ammonites. They promised him that he could be the leader of Gilead if he succeeded. It is not absolutely certain in this passage if the elders made the decision to extend this invitation to Jephthah or if they were acting as the spokesmen for the town. The Spirit of the Lord came on Jephthah and after he defeated the Ammonites and Ephraimites he became the leader not only of Gilead but of all Israel. [20]

In 2 Samuel 3:17 Abner consults the elders about making David the king of Israel and in 2 Samuel 5:3 David makes a pact with the elders as part of his coronation. 1 Chronicles 11:3 also mentions this pact and the elders anointing David as king. In 2 Samuel 19:11-12 after the rebellion of Absalom, David wanted the elders to show they supported his reinstatement as king. 2 Kings 10:1-7 records another instance where the elders were expected to select a king following the death of the previous king. In this case the elders did not make an independent decision, but instead submitted to the evil will of Jehu and did not select a son of Ahab to replace Ahab as king.

As with the role of elders in legal processes, so with their role in appointing leaders, there is an element of balance between the elders and the complete assembly in the appointment of kings and leaders. 2 Samuel 15:13, 19:10 and 1 Kings 12:1 indicate some role for the full nation in selecting kings. Similarly, Judges 11:11 indicates

---

17. Deut. 21:18-21
18. Exod. 18:13-26, 21:22, Num. 25:5, Deut. 1:16, 16:18, 17:9, 12, 19:17-8, 21:2, 25:1-2, Josh. 8:33, 23:2, 24:1, 2 Chron. 19:5, Ezra 7:25, Isa. 3:2, Micah 7:3
19. Deut. 21:2, Josh. 8:33, 23:2, 24:1, Ezra 10:14
20. Jud. 11:29, 12:7

that both the people and the elders had a role in appointing Jephthah as the leader of the Gileadites. Elders and the full nation occasionally had a role in selecting kings during the early period of the monarchy. It seems that this practice ended after this period.

### *Elders provide advice to kings and leaders*

2 Samuel 15:31, 16:20 and 17:4-15 record the high regard that David and Absalom had for the advice they received from elders. Elders had substantial opportunity to influence the king, but the king was free to ignore their advice. For example, shortly after his appointment as king, Rehoboam, following the advice of the young men rather than the advice of the elders, chose to be harsh towards the people, which resulted in the secession of the northern tribes.[21] In 1 Kings 20:7-8 King Ahab requested advice from the elders and he received advice both from the elders and the people. This passage hints at the overlap between elders acting as advisers to the king and elders acting as spokesmen for the people, which is part of their role as the representatives of the people.

### *Elders provide advice, guidance and teaching to the people*

In several passages elders are associated with providing advice and guidance to the people.[22] In Deuteronomy 32:7, elders are available to help parents teach their children the history of Israel. Joshua 24:31 and Judges 2:7 imply that it was the elders, who had seen all that God did during the period of Joshua's leadership, who helped to keep the Israelites in a good place during their lifetime. It is likely that this positive influence was achieved by their advice, guidance and teaching of the people.

### *Elders' formal leadership role*

As can be seen from the preceding paragraphs the primary roles of elders included: acting as representatives of the people to their leaders; certain specific roles associated with legal procedures; an occasional role in selecting kings and leaders; being advisers to the king; and providing advice, guidance and teaching to the people. Both in their legal role and in their role selecting leaders there is a balance between the authority of the elders and the authority of the people. So the vast majority of the role of elders was to act as representatives

---

21. 1 Kings 12:6-13, 2 Chron. 10:6-14
22. Job 10:20, Isa. 9:14-16, Jer. 26:17, Ezek. 7:26

and advisers. In some specific circumstances they had the authority to make decisions.

Several passages list elders and officials (NIV) or officers (ESV in selected verses) separately.[23] Some of these passages also list judges as yet another category of leader. As with judges, the separate listing of elders and officials implies that many elders were not officials and many officials were not elders. Numbers 11:16 indicates that some individuals were both elders and officials.

Presumably these officials or officers were decision-making leaders supporting the national leader or making decisions for their town.[24] In Judges 8:5-16 Gideon asks the men of Succoth for bread. It seems that the decision not to give Gideon's men bread was made by the town officials. It is possible that the whole town had some say in this decision. Gideon punished the elders of Succoth for this decision. Even though the elders did not make this decision, as respected members of the community, they were an ideal group to punish in order to humiliate the whole town. It is possible that verse 14 implies that the town officials were also punished.

A few passages may imply that in some cases elders had a leadership role with broader decision-making authority. For example, 1 Samuel 11:3 may imply that the elders of Jabesh Gilead made the decision as to how to respond to Nahash the Ammonite's offer of a treaty to end his siege of their city. However, verses 1, 9 and 10 of this chapter record the active involvement of the men of Jabesh Gilead. So it is likely that in verse 3 the elders were acting as spokesmen for the town not decision-makers.

There is a similar ambiguity in Judges 21. This passage deals with the provision of wives for the surviving Benjamite men. All of the Benjamite women had been killed as part of the punishment of the tribe of Benjamin for protecting the men of Gibeah, who had murdered the concubine of a traveling Levite as he passed through the town.[25]

Judges 21 describes an extended assembly of the Israelites addressing the question of how to provide wives for the remaining

---

23. Deut. 29:10, 31:28, Josh. 8:33, 23:2, 24:1, Jud. 8:14, 2 Kings 10:1, Ezra 10:8, 14

24. Exod. 18:13-26, which also indicates that part of their role initially included acting as judges; Jud. 8:5-7.

25. Jud. 19, 20

600 Benjamite men. [26] In Judges 21:1-15 there are about 12 references to the complete assembly being engaged with this question and jointly deciding on a course of action. This resulted in 400 women being provided as wives at the cost of the lives of their parents and siblings! In verse 16 the elders are mentioned for the only time in this chapter. They ask what should be done for the remaining men. In verses 17-22 a plan is created to kidnap 200 women to become wives for the remaining Benjamite men! It is not clear in these verses, who had the decision-making authority for this plan. If verses 16-22 are considered in isolation it is possible to conclude that the elders made this decision. However, from the context of the complete chapter, including verse 25, it is more plausible that the complete assembly made this decision.

Another possible example of elders acting as decision-making leaders is found in Ezra, chapters 5 and 6. These chapters record elders having a role leading the construction of the new temple. In Ezra 5:5, 9-11 and 6:14 only the elders are mentioned as building the temple. Based on Haggai 1:12, 14 we know that the "we" in Ezra 5:11 included the complete remnant of Israel living in the land at that time. Ezra 5:10 indicates that the elders were among the leaders of the effort. Similarly the focus in Ezra 6:14 on the role of the elders in building the temple most likely means that they provided most of the leadership for the effort. However, in Ezra 5:1-5 Zerubbabel the son of Shealtiel and Jeshua the son of Jozadak are recorded as initiating the rebuilding of the temple in response to the message of the prophets Haggai and Zechariah. Similarly, in Ezra 6:7 Cyrus gave permission for the governor of the Jews and the elders to rebuild the temple.

We know from Haggai 1:1, 14, 2:2, and 21 that Zerubbabel was the governor of Judah. It is widely believed that Jeshua the son of Jozadak was the same person as Joshua son of Jehozadak who was the high priest at this time. [27] It is very likely based on Ezra 4:3 that both Zerubbabel and Jeshua were also considered to be elders. From the context of Ezra 5:5, 9 it seems that the elders mentioned in these verses include Zerubbabel and Jeshua. It is possible that these two individuals are the only individuals being referred to in these verses. This fits with Haggai 1:12-14, 2:2-4 which emphasizes the role of these two individuals working with the complete remnant

---

26. Jud. 20:47, 21:13
27. Hag. 1:1, 12, 14, 2:2, 4

of the people. Zechariah 4:6-10 focuses on the role of Zerubbabel alone as both the starter and finisher of the rebuilding work. It is also possible that the elders mentioned in Ezra 5 and 6 not only include Zerubbabel and Jeshua but also include other elders who advised them and assisted them in the work. It is possible that Haggai and Zechariah were also considered to be elders and were included in the references to elders in these chapters.[28]

In summary, it seems that the references to elders as decision-making leaders in Ezra 5 and 6 are an example of elders who also happen to have a decision-making leadership role. Numbers 11:16-30 is another example of some elders also being decision-making leaders.

#### *Summary of Role of Elders in the Old Testament*

Elders were very important leaders mainly acting as advisers and representatives, not decision-makers. They also had a role in certain legal procedures and sometimes had a role in the appointment of kings and leaders. In these last two roles they had some limited decision-making authority. This decision-making authority was partially shared with the assembly of the people. There is no hint of any hierarchy existing within groups of elders.

It is not possible to make a compelling case from the Old Testament that part of being an elder was to be a decision-making leader. The passages that can be used to support this position are either talking about individuals who held a decision-making leadership position and who happened to also be elders; or they contain substantial hints that the decision-making process included the complete assembly. In several passages elders are listed as a group of leaders within the Israelite community existing in parallel with other groups of leaders who did have decision-making authority (*e.g.*, officials, officers, judges). In general these are distinct groups but some individuals were both elders and officials.

### 3.1.7 Jewish Elders in the New Testament

For simplicity in this subsection I refer to elders in the non-Christian Jewish community as "Jewish elders" and I refer to elders within the Christian community as "Christian elders." I realize that many of the Christian elders during the period of the New Testament were ethnically Jewish.

---

28. Ezra 5:2, 6:14

There are many references to Jewish elders in the Gospels and in Acts. In the Gospels most of these references relate to the chief priests and elders investigating what Jesus was teaching, opposing Him, arresting Him, trying Him and pushing Pilate to execute Him. [29] Similarly, in Acts rulers, elders, scribes and chief priests investigate Peter and John's teaching and preaching and jail them. [30] In Acts 6: 12 elders are mentioned in the context of Stephen's arrest. Acts 23:14, 24:1, 25:15 record the role of elders in Paul's trials.

The focus of many of these references is on the protection of sound doctrine—as the Jews understood it. This role was also performed by elders in New Testament churches. [31] So in this respect there is complete continuity between the role of Jewish elders and Christian elders during the period of the New Testament. This is not to say that the way the Jewish elders undertook the role of protecting sound doctrine was always correct. In fact, their behavior as they attempted to perform this role often falls into the "example to avoid" category of Scripture. It is possible that Old Testament elders were involved in protecting sound doctrine but this role is not explicit.

Matthew 15:12 and Mark 7:3, 5 refer to the traditions of the elders. This phrase indicates that Jewish elders had a role in teaching and interpreting the Scriptures. This is another role performed both by Jewish and Christian elders. However, in both communities much teaching was done by individuals who were not elders. [32]

One area of difference between Jewish elders and Christian elders concerns judicial processes. It is highly plausible that some Jewish elders served as members of either the main Jerusalem court or of local town courts. These courts were called Sanhedrin. They had between 7 and 23 members who acted as a jury. Decisions were made by voting. There is uncertainty as to the range of responsibilities of the Jewish courts during this time period. Whatever the exact judicial role of Jewish elders, this is an area of difference with Christian elders. As discussed in Subsection 1.1.4, the full congregation had the final say in matters of church discipline.

---

29. Matt. 16:21, 21:23, 26:3, 47, 57, 27:1, 3, 12, 20, 41, Mark 8:31, 11:27, 14:43, 53, 15:1, Luke 9:22, 20:1, 22:52, 66
30. Acts 4:5, 8, 23, 5:21
31. Titus 1:9
32. Matt. 23:2-3, Acts 5:21, Heb. 5:12

The extent to which Jewish elders in the New Testament period continued other roles of elders from the Old Testament period is uncertain. It is likely that Jewish elders continued to act as advisers and as representatives of the people.

### 3.2 *Episkopos - Episkope - Episkopeo* — Overseer - Inspection - Oversee

This family of words is used 11 times in the New Testament. Six references are to local church assembly leaders, three are to Jesus, one is to apostolic leadership and the final reference is to believers in general.

The use of this verb in a command to all believers shows that all believers are expected to be contributing to the role described by this family of words.[33] This is an indicator that this family of words is not describing a group of decision-making leaders. The emphasis associated with this family of words appears to be on seeing that things are done properly, rather than having the authority to decide what should be being done and who should do it. This is consistent with broader New Testament teaching on the limited role local church leaders have in decision-making. The use of singular and plural forms of this family of words is consistent with each local church having a team of elders.

In two places a form of this word is used of a visitation. In the first case, which is discussing Jesus' incarnation, the word refers to a visit by Jesus to see what is happening and to give individuals an opportunity to repent.[34] If this opportunity is ignored judgment will come. This verse is consistent with the general meaning of this family of words in the New Testament: it is about watching over the community and inviting individuals to respond appropriately to God. The meaning of the word visitation in 1 Peter 2:12 is not clearly defined by the context. In this case, the visitation of God causes unbelievers to change from speaking negatively about believers to giving glory to God. So is it possible that this verse is talking about a visitation of God to each unbeliever giving him a chance to come to faith? This interpretation makes this verse consistent with Luke 19:44.

The use of this family of words in the Septuagint shows that it had a wide range of meanings. These words can be used to describe

---

33. Heb. 12:15
34. Luke 19:44

decision-making leaders. However, in more than 70 percent of the verses where these words are used the meaning does not relate to decision-making leaders. In many places in the Septuagint this word is used to describe visiting and relationship which result in well-informed caring. The early church may have selected this word to describe local leaders because of this connotation.

### 3.2.1 *Episkopos* (1985) – an inspector, overseer, a watcher, guardian

Strong's translation of this word is "a man charged with the duty of seeing that things to be done by others are done rightly, any curator, guardian or superintendent." This noun is used five times in the New Testament. In four instances it is used of local church leaders. This word is also used in 1 Peter 2:25 to describe Jesus' oversight of our souls.

### 3.2.2 *Episkope* (1984) – inspection, oversight, visitation

This noun is used four times in the New Testament. It is used twice of a visitation of God.[35] In 1 Timothy 3:1 it is used in the singular to refer to the role of a local church leader. In one case *episkope* is used interchangeably with apostle,[36] which shows that part of the role of an apostle is to visit or oversee. This is consistent with other passages, which indicate that apostles do not have decision-making authority over local assemblies.

### 3.2.3 *Episkopeo* (1983) – to oversee

This verb, which is related to the noun *episkopos*, is used twice in the New Testament. In both cases it is a plural present participle. In 1 Peter 5:2 it is used of the activity of elders in local church leadership, and in Hebrews 12:15 it is used to command all believers to "see to it that no one fails to obtain the grace of God." All believers are commanded to watch over other believers to assist them in obtaining God's grace in their lives.

### 3.2.4 Use of *Episkopos - Episkope - Episkopeo* in the Septuagint

This family of words is used in 43 verses in the Septuagint Greek translation of the Old Testament. This subsection reviews the ESV translation of these 43 verses to see what light they shed on the

---

35. Luke 19:44, 1 Pet. 2:12
36. Acts 1:20, 25

meaning of this word. Obviously the ESV is primarily translating the Hebrew original of the Old Testament not the Septuagint. Also, because the Septuagint translation was undertaken during the second and third centuries BC, it is possible that the meaning of this family of words may have changed prior to its use in the New Testament. So some caution is appropriate in handling the results of this study.

In eight of these verses the ESV translation is "visit." In three other verses English words with a similar meaning are used. In seven of these verses God is the one visiting and twice a human is visiting. [37] In five cases God is visiting to rescue or bless; and in two cases He is visiting to punish. [38] In two of these verses this word is used for a visitation of harm or death. [39]

In four of the verses where the Septuagint uses one of this family of Greek words the ESV translation relates to punishment and in four other verses these words are used concerning a census. [40]

In 12 of the verses where the Septuagint uses one of this family of Greek words the ESV translation relates to leaders. [41] In these verses the most common ESV translation is overseer or oversight. In a few cases ESV uses "one set over" or officer. It is likely that the leaders mentioned in these verses had some level of decision-making authority.

In the remaining 12 verses, where the Septuagint uses one of this family of Greek words, the ESV offers a range of translations including: friend/friendship; care; watchman; make an inquiry; and make a distinction. [42] In Ezekiel 7:22 this word is used to describe God's sanctuary as his "treasured place." Perhaps this is another way of saying that it is the place God especially visits and watches over. In Job 34:9 this word is used twice as indicated in italics: For he has said, 'It *profits* a man nothing that he should take *delight* in God.'

In summary, at the time that the Septuagint translation was undertaken, this family of Greek words had a wide range of meanings. In

---

37. Num. 7:2, Prov. 29:13
38. Gen. 50:24, 25, Exod. 3:16, 13:19, Job 7:18; Isa. 23:17, 29:6
39. Prov. 19:23; Num. 16:29
40. Isa. 10:3, 24:22, Jer. 6:15, 10:15; Exod. 30:12, Num. 14:29, 26:22, 43
41. Num. 4:16, 31:14, Jud. 9:28, 2 Kings 11:15, 12:11, 2 Chron. 34:12, 17, Neh. 11:9, 14, 22, Ps. 109:8, Isa. 60:17
42. Job 6:14, 29:4; Deut. 11:12, Job 10:12; 2 Kings 11:18; Job 31:14, *cf.*, Esth. 2:11; Lev. 19:20

many cases, the meaning is relational (*e.g.* visit, friend, care); in some cases the meaning relates to the outcome of a visit (*e.g.* punishment or blessing); in other cases the meaning is associated with collecting information (*e.g.*, counting in a census, making inquiry, watchman); in yet other cases, the meaning is associated with leadership (*e.g.* overseer, officer). It seems that the primary meaning of this word family relates to visiting and being in relationship, which together result in well informed caring. This emphasis fits very well with the New Testament description of the role of local Christian leaders.

### 3.3 *Poimaino - Poimen - Poimne - Poimnion* — To pasture - Shepherd - Flock

Of the 30 uses of *poimaino* (to feed or to tend to a flock) and *poimen* (shepherd) in the New Testament, 19 references are to Jesus, seven references are generic, three references are to church assembly leaders and one reference is to the spiritual gift of being a shepherd. The three references to church leaders are verbs describing what they do. These references apply to traveling and local leaders. One of the two references applying to local leaders is in the plural and the other reference is an infinitive associated with a plural noun for the overseers. [43] This is consistent with usually having multiple elders in each local Christian assembly.

Of the ten uses of *poimne/poimnion* (flock), seven are specific to the believing community and all of these seven references emphasize Jesus' ownership of His flock. The other three references are generic. Jesus as owner of the flock has a unique authority to lead and direct each member of the flock. The implication of these verses is that Jesus wishes to directly interact with each of his children.

#### 3.3.1 *Poimaino* (4165) — to feed, pasture, tend a flock, to pamper, to tend, direct, superintend, to rule

This verb is used 11 times in the New Testament. Five of these references are to Jesus, one is to a traveling leader and two are to local leaders. The remaining three references are generic. In John 21:16 Jesus commands Peter to care for His sheep and in 1 Peter 5:2 Peter commands elders to shepherd the flock. Acts 20:28 mentions shepherding as an activity of elders. [44]

---

43. 1 Pet. 5:2; Acts 20:28

44. 1 Cor. 9:7 mentions shepherding along with serving as a soldier or a vinedresser as an activity for which one expects to get paid. This verse is contained in a passage where Paul is justifying his receiving financial

As can be seen from the list of possible translations given above a wide range of meanings are associated with this verb. The contexts of the three verses, which use *poimaino* to describe an activity of Christian leaders, provide no insight as to which meaning of the word is appropriate. In the broader context of Biblical teaching about elders it seems plausible that translations such as "feed" or "care for" are appropriate and this is the sense of most translations. In some of the verses where this verb is used of Jesus the context shows that a translation indicating direction-giving leadership is appropriate. [45]

**3.3.2 *Poimen* (4166)** – one who tends flocks or herds, a shepherd, herdsman

This noun is used 18 times in the New Testament. Of these references, 13 relate to Jesus and four relate to the shepherds at the nativity. The eighteenth reference is to the spiritual gift of being a shepherd. The related noun *archipoimenos* (chief shepherd) is used once (of Jesus) in 1 Peter 5:4.

The New Testament does not use *poimen* as a title for a Christian leader, nor does it use this noun to describe a position of organizational or decision-making leadership within the church. This noun is used in Ephesians 4:11 to refer to individuals with the spiritual gift of shepherd or pastor. The individuals with the gifts listed in this verse are given as gifts to the church "to equip the saints for the work of ministry, for building up the body of Christ." [46] This is consistent with the New Testament teaching that all believers are equipped by the gifting of the Holy Spirit to minister and that all believers are expected to build up the body of Christ. [47] It appears from the New Testament (and the on-going experience of the church) that the gifts of prophecy, evangelism and teaching were widely distributed. [48] Many individuals who were not elders or traveling leaders received these gifts. It is reasonable to assume that the gift of shepherding was similarly widely distributed—especially as the use of the definite

support. This verse is not necessarily describing the activities of traveling leaders.

45. Rev. 2:27, 12:5, 19:15 "he will rule them with a rod of iron."
46. Eph. 4:12
47. 1 Cor. 12:7
48. Appendix 1 and Section 3.1. It appears that the gift of apostleship is the only gift mentioned in Eph. 4:11 which is only associated with leaders (in particular traveling leaders). The other gifts are associated both with leaders (elders or traveling leaders) and with individuals who are not elders or traveling leaders.

article in this verse strongly links the gift of shepherding with the gift of teaching. [49] Spiritual gifts equip believers to minister. They are not a basis for creating decision-making hierarchies.

### 3.3.3 *Poimne* (4167) - *Poimnion* (4168) — a flock, metaphorically of disciples

*Poimne* occurs five times in the New Testament. One reference is to the flocks of the shepherds in the nativity story. Two references refer to the community of believers and contain direct references to Jesus as the shepherd. [50] *Poimne* also occurs twice in 1 Corinthians 9:7 where Paul is discussing his rights as an apostle, in particular his right to receive financial support. He asks "who tends a flock without getting some of the milk?" Paul's primary point in this verse concerns the financial support of traveling leaders.

*Poimnion* also occurs five times in the New Testament, in all cases referring to the community of believers and also in all cases emphasizing the connection of the flock to God.

### 3.3.4 Use of *Poimaino* - *Poimen* - *Poimne* - *Poimnion* in the Septuagint

This family of words is used in one hundred and sixty verses in the Septuagint translation of the Old Testament. The vast majority of these references are to shepherds, flocks and pasturing. Several verses refer to God as the Shepherd of Israel. [51] Other passages prophesy the coming of a single true shepherd of God's people. [52] Joshua, David and the judges are also called shepherds of God's people. [53] In David's case, he is called both a shepherd and a prince and in Joshua's case the title shepherd is being used to describe decision-making leadership as well as caring for the people. This is consistent with the New Testament use of the term shepherd for Jesus, whose leadership includes both decision-making and caring for His people.

The use of the word shepherd in the Old Testament to describe decision-making leadership does not prove that New Testament believers with the spiritual gift of being a shepherd have authority

---

49. Appendix 1.20
50. Matt. 26:31, John 10:16
51. Ps. 23:1, 28:9, 78:52, 80:1, Isa. 40:11, Jer. 31:10, Ezek. 34:12, 31
52. Ezek. 34:23, 37:24, Micah 5:2-5, Zech. 13:7
53. Num. 27:15-23, 2 Sam. 5:2-3, 7:7, 1 Chron. 11:2, 17:6-7, Ps. 78:70-71

to be decision-making leaders. These Old Testament leaders are commonly understood to be "types" of Christ.[54] This means that various aspects of their lives are included in Scripture to help us understand Jesus' life and ministry. In particular describing their decision-making leadership with the title shepherd shows that Jesus has authority to direct what His people do.

In Jeremiah, Ezekiel and Zechariah there are many references to the leaders of Israel as shepherds.[55] Almost all of these references are negative. They are a reminder to Christian leaders that their treatment of those they lead is of great concern to God. In two passages, God promises to raise up good shepherds for his people.[56] These verses, which seem to relate to humans with the spiritual gift of shepherd, do not mention direction-giving leadership. They emphasize feeding/teaching and pastoral care.

**3.4 *Hegeomai* (2233)** – to lead the way, to take the lead, to be chief, to preside, to govern, to rule, to think, to consider, to count, to esteem or regard

This verb is used 28 times in the New Testament. On 20 occasions the translation is: to think, consider, count, esteem or regard. All eight occasions where the translation is related to leading, the verb is used as a participle to indicate an individual or group of people who are leading. As with pastoring the emphasis is not on an office of leader but on the people who are doing the leading.[57]

One leadership reference of *hegeomai* is to Jesus and one is to Joseph.[58] Acts 14:12 refers to Paul as the principal speaker, relative to Barnabas, when they visited Lystra. The other five references are to individuals providing leadership within the church. Of these references only Luke 22:26 and Acts 14:12 are in the singular. It appears that the term can be used both for local and traveling church leaders. In Acts 15:22 this term is applied to Silas who is known in Scripture as a traveling leader.[59] The references in Hebrews appear from the

---

54. *Cf.*, Exod. 7:1
55. Jer. 10:21, 12:10, 23:1-2, 25:34-36, 50:6, Ezek. 34:2-10, Zech. 10:3, 11:3-17
56. Jer. 3:15, 23:4
57. Unfortunately, some translations sometimes use nouns instead of participles. This can make some verses read as if the author is referring to a leadership position.
58. Matt. 2:6, Acts 7:10
59. Acts 15-18

context to apply to local leaders.[60] The related noun (*hegemon*, 2232) is used 22 times in the New Testament. It is typically translated governor and describes a leader with decision-making authority. This noun is almost always used to refer to Roman governors. It is never used of Christian leaders.

In a gift based, shared leadership setting such as a New Testament church assembly, anyone may be chosen by God to lead at a particular time or in response to a particular situation. God is not restricted to only working through individuals who have particular titles. Various portions of each meeting (*e.g.*, a teaching) may be led by an individual who is not an elder. Similarly God expects believers to be involved in ministry outside of meetings. In many cases, He will choose to lead specific ministries through individuals who are not elders. It is likely that the authors of the New Testament use *hegeomai* to refer to all individuals providing leadership, not just the elders of a local congregation.

As can be seen from the start of this section, a wide range of meanings are associated with *hegeomai*. The point Jesus is making in Luke 22:26 is that Christian leaders should not lord it over other believers, but that they should be like servants. This implies a softer leadership style. Hebrews 13:17 is interpreted by some as a mandate for Christian leaders to expect obedience from believers. This verse is discussed in Section 4.1, where I conclude that this command applies to matters of doctrine and moral behavior. This command does not apply to ministry. The context of the other three references gives limited insight into what part of the spectrum of meanings of this word the author had in mind.

**3.5 *Proistemi* (4291)** — to set before, (metaphorically) to set over, appoint with authority, to preside, govern, superintend, to undertake resolutely, to practice diligently, to maintain the practice of

This verb is used eight times in the New Testament. At least two of these references apply to all believers, instructing them to diligently practice good works.[61] In 1 Timothy 3:4, 5, 12 this verb is used of leading a household. These verses are part of the lists of requirements to be an elder or deacon. In 1 Timothy 5:17 this verb is used of elders. In Romans 12:8 and 1 Thessalonians 5:12 it appears that this word is

60. Heb. 13:7, 17, 24

61. Titus 3:8, 14

being used of any believer, not just an elder or traveling leader, who is being used by God to provide leadership in a particular situation.

The related noun *prostatis* (4368) is used in Romans 16:2 of Phoebe. This is a feminine noun, which can be translated one who stands in front or before, a leader, a protectress, a champion, a patroness.

### 3.6 *Kubernesis* - *Kubernetes* — Government - Pilot

This family of words is derived from the verb *kubernao*, which means to steer or direct.

#### 3.6.1 *Kubernesis* (2941) — government, office of a governor or director

The only use of this word in the New Testament is in 1 Corinthians 12:28, which is part of a list of the gifts of the Holy Spirit. Of the translations I have checked only the KJV translates this word "governments." ESV translates this word "administrating," NIV "administration," NASV "administrations," RSV "administrators," NRSV "forms of leadership" and NEB "power to guide."

This word is used four times in the Septuagint Greek translation of the Old Testament.[62] In three of these verses both the NIV and ESV translate the associated Hebrew word as "guidance." In Proverbs 12:5 the NIV translation is "advice" and the ESV translation is "counsels." In light of this Old Testament usage, it seems that the NEB provides the best translation ("power to guide") of this word in 1 Corinthians 12:28. This translation is also an excellent fit with the essence of what it means to be an elder.

The spiritual gift of the "power to guide" is a gift given by God to any individual He chooses within the whole church.[63] Just like the gift of teaching it is not restricted to elders. In some situations God chooses to guide through an individual who is not an elder.

#### 3.6.2 *Kubernetes* (2942) — pilot, helmsman

This word is used twice in the New Testament: Acts 27:11 and Revelation 18:17. It is also used four times in the Septuagint version of the Old Testament. The word "pilot" applies to maritime pilots. Each pilot knows the approaches to one particular harbor or river. Pilots focus on guiding ships through these potentially dangerous

62. Prov. 1:5, 11:14, 12:5, 24:6
63. 1 Cor. 12:28

areas. Typically they do not remain with the ship for the entire voyage. Navigating through open seas is a different skill and a local pilot will know the safe way to approach the harbor at the other end of the voyage.

In Acts 20:28 elders are commanded to "keep watch over yourselves and all the flock of which the Holy Spirit has made you overseers (NIV)." In this verse the Greek word *prosecho* is translated "keep watch" in the NIV and "pay careful attention" in the ESV. This word may also be translated "to bring a ship to land." This alternate meaning suggests that the role of a New Testament elder is analogous to the role of a maritime pilot or helmsman. In both cases, the primary role is to provide guidance thus enabling a safe journey.

### 3.7 *Diakonos* - *Diakonia* - *Diakoneo* – Servant - Service - Serve

This family of words is used 95 times in the New Testament. About 30 percent of these references are explicit to material service including serving food or providing financial aid. About 40 percent of these references are explicitly linked to spiritual service and the other 30 percent may refer to material service and/or spiritual service.

More than 30 percent of all uses of this family of words in the New Testament are explicitly linked to various forms of Christian leadership. It is clearly taught that the essence of Christian leadership is servant leadership. This includes citing Jesus' servant leadership style as an example to Christian leaders and it includes commands to Christian leaders to be servant leaders. [64] It is also clearly taught that all believers should be servants.

There are only five uses of this family of words that are explicitly linked to a formal position of deacon within a church assembly. Four of these references occur in the passage, which provides the qualifications for deacons. [65]

#### 3.7.1 *Diakonos* (1249) – one who renders service to another, an attendant, a servant, one who executes a commission, a deputy, a minister, a deacon, a devoted follower

*Diakonos* is used eight times in the gospels. Four references are to Christian leaders as servants. [66] In each of these references there

---

64. Matt. 20:28, Mark 10:45; Matt. 20:26, 23:11, Mark 9:35, 10:43, Luke 22:26-27

65. 1 Tim. 3:8-13

66. Matt. 20:26, 23:11, Mark 9:35, 10:43

is an emphasis on the greatest being the servant. Three references are generic references to servants and the final reference is to all believers as servants of Jesus.[67]

*Diakonos* is used 21 times in the Pauline epistles. Only three of these references appear to apply definitely to a formal leadership role within the local church.[68] An additional four references may apply to individuals who served as deacons in local churches.[69] The reference to Phoebe in Romans 16:1, where her church is mentioned, likely refers to a formal leadership role within a church. In the next verse, Phoebe is called a *prostates*, which describes a leadership role.[70] In nine passages, Paul refers to traveling leaders as *diakonos* of God, of the gospel, of a new covenant and of the church.[71] The other five uses of the word *diakonos* are generic references to servants. The word *diakonos* is not used in the books of Acts and Revelation and it is not used in the non-Pauline epistles.

**3.7.2 *Diakonia* (1248)** – serving, service, waiting, attendance, the act of rendering friendly services, relief, aid, a commission or ministry, service (in the gospel), a function, ministry or office, a ministering

This word is used 34 times in the New Testament. Nine references relate to the provision of material assistance including financial assistance and serving food. As many as 15 references relate to various forms of explicitly spiritual ministry and nine of these references have an explicit link to apostolic ministry. The remaining nine references are generic and may either relate to material service and/or spiritual service. Several references relate to specific believers, some relate to all believers and one reference relates to angels.[72] Service is also included as a spiritual gift in Romans 12:7.

**3.7.3 *Diakoneo* (1247)** – to wait, attend upon, serve, to be an attendant or assistant, to minister to, relieve, assist or supply with the necessities of life, provide the means of living, to perform the office of a deacon, to administer

---

67. Matt. 22:13, John 2:5,9, 12:26
68. Phil. 1:1, 1 Tim. 3:8,12
69. Phoebe in Rom. 16:1, Epaphras in Col. 1:7, Tychicus in Eph. 6:21, Col. 4:7.
70. Section 2.5
71. 1 Cor. 3:5, 2 Cor. 6:4, 11:23, 1 Tim. 4:6; Eph. 3:7, Col. 1:23, 1 Thess. 3:2; 2 Cor. 3:6; Col. 1:24-25
72. 1 Cor. 16:15, Col. 4:17, 2 Tim. 4:5,11; Eph. 4:12, Rev. 2:19; Heb. 1:14

This word is used 37 times in the New Testament. 17 references relate to the provision of material assistance including financial assistance and serving food. Nine references relate to various forms of explicitly spiritual ministry. Two of these references cite Jesus' servant leadership style as an example to Christian leaders and three of these references command Christian leaders to have a servant leadership style.[73] The remaining six references are generic and may either relate to material service and/or spiritual service. Serving is also included as a spiritual gift in 1 Peter 4:11.

## 3.8 Possible examples of senior elders in local Christian assemblies

This section looks at five situations where the New Testament records individuals providing significant leadership within a local Christian assembly. The intent is to see if these situations support the possibility that some assemblies had a senior elder.

### *Leaders in Jerusalem*

Acts 15 uses the phrase "the apostles and the elders" in verses 2, 4, 6, 22, 23 to describe the leadership of the Jerusalem church. Galatians 2:9 implies that James, Peter and John had a special role in the Jerusalem church. The ESV translation uses the phrase "seemed to be pillars," the NIV "reputed to be pillars" and the NRSV "acknowledged pillars." The key word is *dokountes*, which is the present participle of *dokeo*: to think, imagine, suppose, presume, seem or appear. A literal translation of *dokountes* is "the seeming ones." This word is also used in Galatians 2:2, 6 (twice) where it is translated "those who seemed influential," (ESV). The word "influential" is not in the Greek. The text says, "the seeming ones" using *dokeo* as in v. 9. This phrase may refer to James, Peter and John and/or some others. My take on this is that James, Peter and John may have been particularly influential leaders within the wider group of apostles and elders. The text, especially verse 6, shows that this leadership role was informal, not some kind of official office or management position. So, I conclude, that Jerusalem did not, at the time of Acts 15, (~ AD 50) have a senior elder/leader. Leadership was exercised by the apostles, when they were in Jerusalem, and elders with James, Peter and John being particularly influential.[74]

---

73. Matt. 20:28, Mark 10:45; Luke 22:26-27

74. Gal. 2:8 notes Peter's role as an apostle to the Jews. It is likely that this role involved extensive travel.

By AD 50 the Jerusalem church was about 20 years old and it seems there was an established group of elders there. There would have been plenty of time for a senior elder or a small group of senior elders with organizational leadership authority to arise. But it seems that this did not happen in Jerusalem.

### *Diotrephes*

3 John 1:9 refers to Diotrophes "who loves to be first." This may be an example of an individual wanting to be a senior elder of a church. It seems from verse 10 that he had great influence and authority in church discipline. John says that Diotrophes' love of being first is part of the pattern of sin in his life. He may even be hinting that this love of being first is the root sin, which underlies the other sins listed in verse 10. This passage not only condemns the specific sins listed in verse 10, but it also is a rejection of a leadership style based on loving to be first.

### *Titus*

Paul asked Titus to remain in Crete to "put in order what remained to be done" and to appoint elders in every town, to teach and to be a good example.[75] He was also expected to "silence" and "rebuke sharply" deceivers and false teachers who are upsetting whole families.[76] Certainly, Paul was expecting Titus to provide significant leadership to the churches in Crete. To perform this role Titus would have needed to travel throughout Crete. Titus 3:12 records that this assignment in Crete was temporary. This, in conjunction with other Biblical data on his travels, shows that he was a traveling leader.[77] Titus is not an example of a single "senior" elder.

### *Timothy*

Some believe that Timothy was the senior elder of the church in Ephesus at the time of the writing of the epistles addressed to him. As discussed in Appendix 7, Timothy was a traveling leader. He was in Ephesus at Paul's request to deal with a specific problem.[78] So this appears to be an example of a traveling leader helping a church at a difficult time.[79] Even if Timothy was acting as an elder during his time

---

75. Titus 1:5, 2:1, 7
76. Titus 1:10, 13
77. Appendix 7
78. 1 Tim. 1:3-4
79. Section 5.2. It is possible that Timothy was dealing with the problem Paul prophesied in Acts 20:30.

in Ephesus, it is pure speculation to suggest that he was the single senior elder of the Ephesian church.

### *John*

In 2 John 1 and 3 John 1, John refers to himself as "the old man" or as "the elder." It is speculation to suggestion that this reference implies that John was the senior elder of his church. This possibility seems particularly implausible in an epistle where John is criticizing another leader for "liking to put himself first." [80]

80. 3 John 1:9

# Appendix 4
# Apostleship and Other Types of Ministry

This appendix provides additional detail concerning the use in the New Testament of five key-word families associated with ministry: apostle, prophet, evangelist, proclaimer (or evangelistic preacher) and teacher. As noted in Chapter 3 all of these ministries are associated in the New Testament with traveling leaders. However, as discussed in Section 3.1 and Appendix 1, any believer or local leader may minister in prophecy, evangelism, proclaiming or teaching. These ministry areas are not restricted to traveling leaders. In contrast to this, as discussed in Section 3.1 and further discussed below, apostleship is intrinsically associated with traveling leadership.

A sixth New Testament ministry area is pastoring. In many Christian communities this word has become synonymous with local church leadership, so it is discussed in Appendix 3 along with other New Testament words associated with local leadership. In the New Testament pastoring is associated with traveling leaders, local leaders and individual believers. [1] Given the prominence of pastoring in the church today, it is striking that pastoring and the gift of being a pastor are only mentioned four times in the New Testament. The five ministry areas discussed in this appendix are each mentioned at least 80 times in the New Testament. The word families associated with prophecy and teaching are mentioned about 200 times each in the New Testament. These numerous references indicate the importance of these ministry areas within the New Testament church.

**4.1 *Apostolos* - *Apostole*** — Messenger or agent or apostle - Apostleship

**4.1.1 *Apostolos* (Strong's # 652)** — one sent as a messenger or agent, the bearer of a commission, messenger, apostle

---

1. Section 3.1, Appendix 1.20

The word apostle means an individual who is sent to deliver a message. Jesus' commands to His initial group of apostles make clear that the message is the Gospel and that the destination is the whole earth.[2] In many verses the word apostle is linked to the related verb *apostello* (649) to send forth, to put forth into action, to dismiss, send away.[3]

*Apostolos* is used 80 times in the New Testament. Very few of these references are to generic messengers.[4] The vast majority of uses of this word refer to apostles as leaders within the church. In the gospels and the first half of the book of Acts the focus is on the apostles who were trained by Jesus during His earthly ministry. In the second half of Acts and in the epistles, the focus is on Paul and Barnabas and a handful of other individuals. Reference is also made to false apostles. In Hebrews 3:1 Jesus is called "the apostle and high priest of our confession."

**4.1.2 *Apostole* (651)** – a sending, expedition, office or duty of one sent as a messenger or agent; office of an apostle, apostleship

This word is used four times in the New Testament. In all four cases it refers to church leadership: twice to Paul, once to Peter and once to Judas Iscariot. In Acts 1:20 the word *episkope* is used as a synonym for *apostole*, which indicates that visiting and overseeing are part of the role of apostles.[5] This verse also draws attention to the overlap in the ministry and leadership of apostles and elders.

### 4.1.3 Activities of the initial apostles after Acts 8:1

Table 2 lists for each of the original 12 apostles where they served and the manner and location of their death. I have only included service outside of Israel. With the exception of the martyrdom of James

---

2. Matt. 10:5-16 (commands associated with the initial ministry journey of the twelve), Matt. 28:19 ("Go therefore and make disciples of all nations"), Acts 1:8 ("you will be my witnesses in Jerusalem and in all Judea and Samaria, and to the end of the earth").
3. Matt. 10:5, 16, Mark 3:14, 6:7, John 4:35-38, 20:21, Acts 8:14, 26:17-18, 1 Cor. 1:17. *Apostello* is used in 130 verses in the New Testament. Jesus often uses this word to describe His being sent by the Father (Matt. 10:40, John 5:36, 6:57, 17:3). It is also used to describe the sending of prophets (Matt. 11:10, 13:41, 23:34), angels (Matt. 13:41, 24:31, Luke 1:26) and apostles. It can apply to sending an individual on a long journey (Luke 14:32, 19:12-14) or on a short journey (Acts 13:15).
4. In 2 Cor. 8:23 and Phil. 2:25 the word is used of messengers sent by church assemblies on church business.
5. *Cf.* Acts 1:25. Appendix 3.2.3

recorded in Acts 12:2, only Peter and John are mentioned in the Bible by name after Acts 1. I will discuss their ministry after Acts 8:1 below. Most of the information in Table 2 concerning areas of service and the manner of death of each apostle is drawn from church traditions recorded by later authors. In some cases, it is likely that these

| Lists of Apostles | | | |
|---|---|---|---|
| **Matt 10:2-4** | **Mark 3:16-19** | **Luke 6:14-16 Acts 1:13, 26** | **Areas of ministry outside Judea, Galilee and Samaria. Information in this table comes from the New Testament and church traditions. Not all of these church traditions are reliable. Some traditions contradict other traditions.** |
| Simon Peter | Simon Peter | Simon Peter | Preached in Antioch, Pontus, Galatia, Cappadocia, Asia Minor, Bithynia and Rome and possibly in Corinth and Egypt. Martyred in Rome. |
| Andrew Peter's brother | Andrew | Andrew Peter's brother | Preached in Asia Minor, Scythia, along the Black Sea, in Byzantium and Thrace. Martyred in Patrae in Greece. |
| James Son of Zebedee | James Son of Zebedee | James Son of Zebedee | Martyred under Herod (Acts 12:2) in about AD 44 most likely in Jerusalem. May have preached in Spain around AD 40. |
| John Son of Zebedee | John Son of Zebedee | John Son of Zebedee | Ministered in Asia Minor including Ephesus where he died of natural causes. Imprisoned on Patmos. |
| Philip | Philip | Philip | Preached in Greece, Syria, Phrygia (central Turkey) and possibly Carthage. Possibly martyred in Phrygia. |
| Bartholomew | Bartholomew | Bartholomew | May have preached in India, Ethiopia, Mesopotamia, Lycaonia and Armenia. Martyred in Albanopolis in Armenia. Possibly the same person as Nathaniel in John's Gospel. |
| Thomas | Thomas | Thomas | Preached in many areas of India from about AD 52 until about AD 72 when he was martyred there. May also have preached in Parthia (North East Iran) and Syria. |
| Matthew | Matthew | Matthew Also called Levi | Preached the Gospel in Ethiopia, Macedonia, Persia, Parthia and Egypt. Died in Ethiopia or Macedonia, possibly as a martyr. |
| James Son of Alphaeus | James Son of Alphaeus | James Son of Alphaeus | Preached the Gospel and probably martyred in Lower Egypt or Persia. Possibly martyred in Jerusalem. |
| Thaddaeus | Thaddaeus | Jude/Judas "of James" | Preached in some or all of Idumaea, Syria, Mesopotamia, Libya, Armenia and Britain. Martyred in Persia or Beirut, Lebanon. |
| Simon The Cananaean | Simon The Cananaean | Simon The Zealot | Preached in some or all of Egypt, Persia, Armenia, Africa, Georgia and Britain. Probably martyred in Armenia, Persia, Britain or Samaria. Possibly martyred with Thaddeus/Jude. |
| Judas Iscariot | Judas Iscariot | Judas Iscariot Luke 6:16 only | Committed suicide near Jerusalem. Matt 27:5, Acts 1:18 |

Table 2. Biblical and non-Biblical information concerning the original apostles.

traditions are accurate. In other cases, the traditions may be partially accurate. In some cases, traditions contradict each other. So at least one must be incorrect.

In all cases, church tradition asserts that the initial group of apostles, excluding Judas Iscariot, obeyed the Great Commission [6] and following the pattern of Acts 1:8 ended up traveling to distant countries planting churches. One tradition asserts that all of the initial apostles except John (and Judas Iscariot) died as martyrs. This tradition is supported by specific traditions associated with each apostle describing their martyrdom. In almost all of these traditions the apostles died far from home. In spite of the uncertainty associated with some of the specific traditions, they record an understanding within the early church that the essence of apostleship is church planting in unevangelized areas.

Acts 8:25 mentions Peter and John ministering in the villages of Samaria, presumably evangelizing and planting churches. Acts 9:31-32 mentions Peter traveling in Judea, Galilee and Samaria. Galatians 2:11 says Peter visited Antioch and he may have also visited Corinth. [7] The implication of 1 Peter 2:11 and 4:12 is that this epistle is written to individuals Peter loves, which implies that he traveled to Pontus, Galatia, Cappadocia, Asia, and Bithynia. [8] It is possible that he did pioneer church planting in some of these regions. Ancient tradition maintains that Peter was martyred in Rome. John wrote Revelation on Patmos and ancient tradition says that he was based in Ephesus for the latter portion of his life. [9]

In summary of Section 3.1 and Appendix 4.1, it seems that apostleship was primarily about planting and supporting churches in areas where there were no churches. The New Testament and early church historians confirm that the New Testament apostles gave their lives to plant churches all over the known world. The prophecy of Acts 1:8 was fulfilled.

### 4.2 *Profetes* - *Profeteuo* - *Profeteia* - *Profetikos* - *Profetis* – Prophet - To prophesy - A prophecy - Prophetic - Prophetess

The dominant understanding of the meaning of this family of words in modern English focuses on predicting the future. This was a part

6. Matt. 28:18-20
7. 1 Cor. 1:12
8. 1 Pet. 1:1
9. Rev. 1:9

of the meaning of these words during the time of the New Testament church, but as a subset of a broader understanding of the prophet acting as a spokesman or interpreter for another, especially for a deity. This broader role was also expected to include teaching. The fuzzy boundary between the prophetic and teaching roles is implicit in Acts 13:1.

About half of the uses of this family of words, in the New Testament, relate to the Old Testament prophets and about half relate to New Testament prophets. The numerous mentions of the Old Testament prophets show the dependence of the New Testament church on the Old Testament prophets both for evidence that Jesus is the Christ and for developing doctrine. [10] The numerous mentions of prophecy in the context of the New Testament church show that this gift was an important part of the life of the New Testament church.

**4.2.1 *Profetes* (4396)** – spokesman for another especially a spokesman or interpreter for a deity, a prophet or seer, a person gifted for the exposition of divine truth, a foreteller of the future, (in plural) the prophetic scriptures of the Old Testament

This noun is used about 150 times in the New Testament. About 60 percent of these references are to Old Testament prophets. The root meaning of *profetes* (spokesman for another) is very close to the root meaning of *apostolos* (one sent as a messenger or agent). The major difference is that *apostolos* has a connotation of traveling to deliver the message.

**4.2.2 *Profeteuo* (4395)** – to exercise the function of a prophet, to prophesy, to foretell the future, to set forth matter of divine teaching by special faculty

This word is used 28 times in the New Testament. Only five of these references are to Old Testament prophets. The other references are to prophesying in the New Testament church. It seems that prophesying was widespread in the New Testament church.

**4.2.3 *Profeteia* (4394)** – prophecy, a prediction of future events, matter of divine teaching set forth by special gift

This word is used 19 times in the New Testament. Three times it is used to refer to Old Testament prophecy. The other 16 references are to New Testament prophecy. These words vary from personal

---

10. Matt. 1:22, 5:17, 27:35, Acts 3:12-26, 8:27-39, 15:13-21

prophecy, to words given publicly in house church meetings, to words for the church for all time. [11]

**4.2.4 *Profetikos* (4397)** – prophetic, uttered by prophets

This word is used twice in the New Testament. In both cases, it refers to the Old Testament prophetic literature.

**4.2.5 *Profetis* (4398)** – prophetess, a divinely gifted female teacher

This word is used twice in the New Testament: once of Anna and once of Jezebel. [12] Acts 2:17, 21:9 and 1 Cor. 11:5 show that women in the New Testament church prophesied.

**4.3 *Euaggelistes* - *Euaggelizo* - *Euaggelion*** – Evangelist - Evangelize - Good news

**4.3.1 *Euaggelistes* (2099)** – one who announces glad tidings, an evangelist, preacher of the Gospel, teacher of the Christian religion

This word is only used three times in the New Testament: once in the gift list of Ephesians 4:11; once as a title for Philip; and once as part of a command to Timothy. [13]

**4.3.2 *Euaggelizo* (2097)** – to address with glad tidings, to proclaim as glad tidings, to address with gospel teaching, evangelize, preach good news

This word is used 55 times in the New Testament. All but one of these references are associated with the Gospel. English translations very commonly render this word as "preach." For example, in the KJV it is translated "preach" 49 times. This translation is unfortunate as the word "preach" has become strongly associated with the sermons delivered as part of church services. More than three quarters of the times this word is used it is linked to traveling leaders. In only one case is this word explicitly linked to all believers. [14]

**4.3.3 *Euaggelion* (2098)** – glad tidings, good or joyful news, the Gospel, doctrines of the Gospel, the preaching of or instruction in the Gospel

---

11. 1 Tim. 1:18, 4:14; 1 Cor. 14:6, 22; Rev. 1:3, 22:18-19
12. Luke 2:36, Rev. 2:20
13. Acts 21:8, 2 Tim. 4:5
14. Acts 8:4

This word is used 77 times in the New Testament. It is one of Paul's favorite words. He uses it 61 times in his epistles. Every time this word is used in the New Testament it appears to be specific to the Gospel.

**4.4 *Kerusso* - *Kerugma* - *Kerux* - *Kataggello*** — To proclaim - Proclamation - Herald - To announce

**4.4.1 *Kerusso* (2784)** — publish, proclaim (as a herald), announce openly, inculcate, preach

This word is used 61 times in the New Testament. In about half of the passages where this word is used it is explicitly linked to evangelism. [15] In about a third of the passages, where his word is used, there is no specific indication of the content of what is being proclaimed/preached; but a proclamation of the Gospel would fit well with the context. In four other places this word is used of individuals who were so excited by the healing/deliverance that Jesus had done for them that they went around proclaiming it. [16] Many individuals became interested in Jesus because of these testimonies. Similarly, Saul (Paul) started proclaiming Jesus immediately after his conversion. [17]

In five verses proclaiming/preaching and teaching are mentioned together in a way which may indicate that the New Testament authors saw proclaiming/preaching and teaching as different activities. [18] Obviously, there is some overlap as information about Jesus has a place both in evangelistic proclamation and in the teaching of believers.

It seems that the modern Christian use of the word "preaching" to describe a sermon aimed at believers is not consistent with the meaning of this word in the New Testament. The vast majority of what we call sermons would be referred to as teaching by the authors of the New Testament, though it is unlikely that this monologue format was used in New Testament churches. [19] Only evangelistic presentations would be called "preaching" by New Testament authors. It is unlikely that these presentations were extended monologues.

**4.4.2 *Kerugma* (2782)** — proclamation, proclaiming, public annunciation, public inculcation, preaching

---

15. Matt. 4:17, 26:13, Mark 1:14, 6:12, Luke 3:3, 8:1, Acts 8:5, Rom. 10:14-15
16. Mark 1:45, 5:20, 7:36, Luke 8:39
17. Acts 9:20
18. Matt. 4:23, 9:35, 11:1, Acts 28:31, 2 Tim. 4:2
19. Section 6.1

This word is used eight times in the New Testament. In six verses the context is referring to evangelistic preaching. In the other two verses it is likely that Paul is discussing evangelistic preaching.

**4.4.3 *Kerux* (2783)** – herald, public messenger, proclaimer, publisher, preacher

This word is used twice of Paul and once of Noah. [20]

**4.4.4 *Kataggello* (2605)** – announce, proclaim

This word is used in 17 places in the New Testament. It is typically translated to proclaim or preach. In most cases where this word is used the context shows that the proclamation is evangelistic, but in a few cases the proclamation is not evangelistic. [21]

**4.5 *Didaskolos* - *Didasko* - *Didaktos* - *Didaktikos* - *Didaskalia* - *Didache* - *Kathegetes*** – Teacher - To teach - Taught - Qualified to teach - Act of teaching - Instruction

**4.5.1 *Didaskolos* (1320)** – teacher, master

This word is used 58 times in the New Testament. In 42 of these references, all of which are in the Gospels, they apply to Jesus. Eight references, all of which are in Acts and the Epistles, refer to teachers in the church. Three references are specific to Jewish teachers.

**4.5.2 *Didasko* (1321)** – to teach, to direct, to admonish

This word is used 99 times in the New Testament. 58 of these references are in the Gospels and the vast majority of these references are to Jesus. The 17 references in Acts mainly apply to the apostles. The 22 references in the epistles are a mix of references to traveling leaders, local leaders and other believers. The final two references are in Revelation and both refer to false teachers as do some other references.

**4.5.3 *Didaktos* (1318)** – taught, teachable

This word is used in two verses in the New Testament. Both of these verses relate to being taught directly by God. In John 6:45 Jesus emphasizes the criticality of all believers being taught directly by God.

---

20. 1 Tim. 2:7, 2 Tim. 1:11, 2 Pet. 2:5
21. Acts 16:21, Rom. 1:8. In 1 Cor. 11:26 this word is used in the context of the Lord's supper.

**4.5.4 *Didaktikos* (1317)** – apt or qualified to teach

This word is used twice in the New Testament. One reference is specific to elders and the other reference is broader than elders and most likely applies to all believers. [22]

**4.5.5 *Didaskalia* (1319)** – the act or occupation of teaching, information, instruction, matter taught, precept, doctrine

This word is used 21 times in the New Testament mostly in the Pauline epistles. It is often translated doctrine or teaching. This word is used to refer both to godly and to false/demonic teaching. [23] Several verses emphasize the importance of good doctrine. [24]

**4.5.6 *Didache* (1322)** – instruction, the giving of instruction, teaching, what is taught, doctrine, mode of teaching and kind of doctrine taught

This word is used 30 times in the New Testament and is usually translated teaching in the NIV and ESV. KJV typically translates it "doctrine." This word seems to be substantially interchangeable with *didaskalia*. It is the preferred word of the non-Pauline New Testament authors who used it 24 times. When used of Jesus it is often coupled to comments about the amazement of the crowds at his teaching. [25]

**4.5.7 *Kathegetes* (2519)** – guide, leader, teacher, instructor

This word is used twice in modern editions of the Greek New Testament. Both occurrences are in Matthew 23:10. Older editions of the Greek New Testament including the edition used by Strong also have *kathegetes* in Matthew 23:8. The meaning of this word appears to be somewhat broader than just teaching. This is reflected in the range of translations of *kathegetes* offered by English Bibles. For example the NRSV and ESV use "instructor" and the NIV and NEB use "teacher." The NASV and GNB use "leader" and the Amplified Bible gives "master (leader)." The KJV and RSV translate *kathegetes* as "master." The translation "master" may be more appropriate in the sense of a schoolmaster than in the sense of a slave master.

---

22. 1 Tim. 3:2; 2 Tim. 2:24
23. Col. 2:22, 1 Tim. 4:1
24. 1 Tim. 4:6, 13, 16
25. Mark 1:22, Luke 4:32

# Appendix 5
# Submission

This appendix complements Sections 4.1 and 4.2 by providing a more detailed discussion of New Testament teaching on submission. The first section of this appendix discusses the various Greek words, which are translated submission or submit. The second section provides a summary of all the relationships of submission commanded in the New Testament. The final two sections discuss the relationship between submission and obedience.

## 5.1 Greek words translated submission/submit

### 5.1.1 *Hupotasso* (5293) – to place or arrange under, to subordinate, to bring under influence

Thirty two verses in the New Testament contain the Greek verb *hupotasso*, which is typically translated submit, subject, submission or submissive. Strong's (5293) gives the following translations for this word: to arrange under, to subordinate; to subject, put in subjection; to subject one's self, obey; to submit to one's control; to yield to one's admonition or advice; to obey, be subject. The root meaning of this word is a military term meaning "to arrange [troop divisions] in a military fashion under the command of a leader." In non-military use, it was "a voluntary attitude of giving in, cooperating, assuming responsibility, and carrying a burden."[1] Evidence from papyri indicates that this verb also meant to support, append or uphold.[2]

This family of words is used in seven verses in the Septuagint translation of the Old Testament. In three of these verses[3] the ESV

---

1. Thayer's Greek Lexicon
2. Ann Nyland, "Papyri, Women & Word Meaning in the New Testament," *Priscilla Papers*, Volume 17, Number 4, Fall 2003, p. 6, published by Christians for Biblical Equality (www.cbeinternational.org)
3. Ps. 37:7, 62:1, 5

translation is "Be still before the Lord and wait patiently for Him" and "For God alone, O my soul, wait in silence." Being still and waiting in silence are dimensions of submission. In Haggai 2:18 the Septuagint uses *hupotasso* to mean "consider." Reflecting on someone else's perspective on a situation is part of our submission to that individual.

### 5.1.2 *Hupotage* (5292) – subordination, submissiveness

Four verses in the New Testament contain the Greek noun *hupotage*, which is related to *hupotasso*.

### 5.1.3 *Hupeiko* (5226) – yield, give way, be submissive

This verb is only used in Hebrews 13:17.

## 5.2 Who should submit to whom?

The following subsections discuss the primary relationships, mentioned in the New Testament, concerning submission. These relationships are listed in the order of prevalence in the New Testament. In each case, I also discuss whether or not the Bible commands obedience within the relationship.

### 5.2.1 Submission to God and his law

In seven verses the New Testament teaches that "God has put all things in subjection under his [Jesus'] feet." [4] This subjection includes angels, authorities and powers. In many cases this submission will not be voluntary. As noted in Hebrews 2:8, we do not yet see everything in subjection to Jesus. In Hebrews 12:9 and James 4:7 believers are commanded to submit to God and Ephesians 5:24 says that the church submits to Christ. Romans 8:7 and 10:3 imply that we should also submit to God's law and righteousness. Many references say that we should obey God.

### 5.2.2 Wives to Husbands

In six verses, the New Testament teaches that wives should submit to their husbands. [5] There is no direct command in the New Testament that wives should obey their husbands. However, Peter cites Sarah's obedience to Abraham as an example to follow. [6]

In the best Greek manuscripts, Ephesians 5:22 does not include the word "submit." The presence of this verb is implied from Ephesians

---

4. 1 Cor. 15:27, 28, Eph. 1:22, Phil. 3:21, Heb. 2:5, 8, 1 Pet. 3:22
5. Eph. 5:22, 24, Col. 3:18, Titus 2:5, 1 Pet. 3:1, 5.
6. 1 Pet. 3:6

5:21, where mutual submission is commanded among all believers. This emphasizes that mutual submission also applies within Christian marriages: the wife submits to her husband and the husband submits to his wife. This point is also made in 1 Corinthians 7:1-5. Verse 5 says that mutual agreement is required if a couple chooses to abstain from sex for a limited time. It is hard to believe that the principle of mutual decision-making within marriage only applies to sex.

### 5.2.3 Believers to leaders

In Hebrews 13:17 believers are instructed to submit to those who are leading in a particular situation. In 1 Corinthians 16:16 Paul commands the Corinthians to submit to "every fellow worker and laborer." This phrase includes both local and traveling leaders as well as non-leaders who labor in the kingdom.[7]

A potential direct command for believers to obey leaders is found in Hebrews 13:17. As discussed in Section 4.1, it is likely that this is a mistranslation. It is likely that this verse should be translated, "Be persuaded by those who are leading and submit to them." Even if the correct translation of this verse is "Obey those who are leading and submit to them," it is clear from the rest of the New Testament that the scope of this obedience (or this being persuaded) is limited to doctrine and general teaching related to how we should behave, not specific ministry activities. It is plausible that submission to leaders is similarly focused on the same areas.

In 2 Thessalonians 3:14, Paul commands his readers to obey the content of this letter. We now understand this letter as having the authority of Scripture. It is not clear if Paul was thinking that when he wrote this verse. Either way Paul is careful to only ask for obedience to the content of the letter: doctrinal matters and general behavioral teaching. Section 3.6 and Appendix 2.2 provide a detailed discussion of Paul's authority over team members working with him. In these passages I conclude that Paul did not have the authority to direct the ministry activities of other traveling leaders.

### 5.2.4 Civil Authorities

In three passages Paul and Peter command believers to submit to civil authorities.[8] It is likely that the command to obedience in Titus 3:1

---

7. 1 Pet. 5:5 may also command young men to submit to elders, but it can equally well be translated that they should submit to old men.

8. Rom. 13:1-5, Titus 3:1, 1 Pet. 2:13-14

refers to civil authorities. However, this needs to be held in balance with Acts 4:19-20, 5:29 where Peter says that we are only to obey civil authorities when it does not conflict with obeying God. Examples of this include continuing to publicly teach after being commanded to stop teaching and escaping from prison with angelic assistance. [9]

### 5.2.5 Slaves to Masters

In Titus 2:9 Paul commands slaves to submit to their masters and in 1 Peter 2:18 Peter commands servants to submit to their masters, even when they are unjust. The Greek word for servant in this passage (*oiketes*, 3610) is only used five times in the New Testament. It applies to servants or household slaves who live with their master/owner. Slaves are commanded to obey their masters in Ephesians 6:5 and Colossians 3:22.

### 5.2.6 Demons to Believers

In Luke 10:17-20 it is recorded that demons submitted to the 72. This is also implicit in Mark 6:7-13 concerning the 12. In Mark 1:27 it is recorded that demons obeyed Jesus.

### 5.2.7 Children to Parents

Jesus was submissive to his parents. [10] Clearly, this is an example to follow. Also in 1 Timothy 3:4 Paul states that a requirement for being an elder is that your children are submissive to you. Children are commanded to obey their parents in Ephesians 6:1 and Colossians 3:20.

### 5.2.8 All believers to one another

Ephesians 5:21 says that all believers should submit to one another. 1 Corinthians 16:15 -16 says that believers should be subject to individuals like the household of Stephanas who have devoted themselves to the service of the saints. It is likely that this household included many individuals. One or more of them may have been elders, but it is very unlikely that they were all elders. The mutual submission of all believers to one another includes leaders submitting to individuals who are not leading and husbands submitting to their wives. There is no command in the New Testament for believers to obey other believers.

---

9. Acts 5:18-29, 12:6-11
10. Luke 2:51

### 5.2.9 Other relationships of submission

Some other relationships of submission mentioned in the New Testament include:

- Romans 8:20, which states that creation has been subjected to futility or frustration.
- 1 Corinthians 14:32, which states that the spirits of prophets are subject to the prophets. This submission is an important part of the orderly flow of meetings with each member making contributions. [11] Some prophetic individuals receive a steady stream of revelation when they enter into the presence of God. They need to submit each prophecy to themselves to discern which items should be shared aloud. If this is not done, a prophet may inappropriately dominate the meeting.
- 1 Corinthians 14:34, which states that women should be silent in church and be in submission. The meaning of this verse is discussed in Section 6.4.
- Galatians 2:5, which states that Paul did not submit to false brothers.
- 1 Timothy 2:11, which states that women should learn quietly and submissively. This verse is also discussed in Section 6.4.

## 5.3 Is submission the same as obedience?

There are very strong links between submission and obedience. Of the six human-to-human relationships discussed above in two cases the Scripture definitely commands both submission and obedience (children, slaves), and in one case the scripture probably commands both submission and obedience (civil authorities). Wives are commanded to submit to their husbands. They are not directly commanded to obey their husbands, but obedience is presented as an example to follow. However, this needs to be held in balance with consensual decision-making between husbands and wives. This is commanded concerning sexual relations. Believers are commanded to submit to those who are leading and to be persuaded by them especially on matters of doctrine and general ethical behavior. Believers (including leaders) are to submit to other believers. There is no hint in the Bible that the mutual submission of all believers to one another means that all believers should obey all other believers. If we attempted to do this it would result in chaos. So there is at least one human to human relationship where submission is commanded in the Bible but where the submission does not also involve obedience.

---

11. Section 1.1

It seems to me that there are two types of submission and both types of submission are subtly different from obedience. The first type of submission is forced. Examples of this include the submission of demons to believers with appropriate authority and the submission of rebellious creation to Jesus. [12] In this case the demon, which is forced to submit loses its freedom to disobey. Sometimes in deliverance ministry a demon is forced to leave even though the demon is doing its best to disobey the command to leave. (In other deliverances it appears that the demon may choose to obey the command to leave). This dynamic sometimes plays out in interactions with civil authorities. For example, an individual may be moving in disobedience to a police officer and still end up being forced into submission and arrest. In summary, in the case of forced submission the individual being subjected may or may not be choosing to obey.

The second type of submission is freely chosen. Examples of relationships of freely chosen submission include the relationship between leaders and non-leaders in a local Christian assembly, relationships between believers and the relationship between a husband and his wife (assuming that they freely chose to marry each other). The essence of this type of submission is a flexible and cooperative heart attitude within the context of a relationship of mutual respect. This heart attitude will usually result in the individual, who is submitting, choosing to obey. But this obedience will often come after dialog, which influences and possibly changes, what the individual who is submitting is asked to do. Occasionally it is appropriate to obey God and not the individual to whom one is submitting. When it is right to do this, it is very important to maintain an appropriate heart attitude.

The essence of walking in mutual submission with other believers is submitting ideas, suggestions and recommendations to other believers. We are to open ourselves up to be influenced by all believers, especially leaders. This means that we will often, but not always, end up doing what they suggest. Discernment is important to ensure that we are not being influenced in a bad direction.

We should not tell other believers that they must do X or Y, instead we submit to them the suggestion that they do X or Y and maybe give some good reasons supporting the recommendation. The point is that we leave it up to them to decide what to do. When we do this

---

12. 1 Cor. 15:27

we are demonstrating respect and humility. Ordering another person around is disrespectful and proud. We do not know everything about their lives and circumstances so it is presumptuous to think we know what they should do. The exception to this is unambiguous ethical matters. It is, of course, acceptable to say things like, "Do not commit adultery." In Philippians 2:2-4 Paul provides a good summary of walking in mutual submission:

> Complete my joy by being of the same mind, having the same love, being in full accord and of one mind. Do nothing from rivalry or conceit, but in humility count others more significant than yourselves. Let each of you look not only to his own interests, but also to the interests of others.

Another piece of the meaning of the word *hupotasso* is to support. This part of the meaning of this word directly applies to several, but not all the *hupotasso* relationships mentioned in the New Testament. Wives should support their husbands and all believers should support one another. This includes husbands supporting their wives and leaders supporting other believers as well as believers supporting leaders. However, when demons *hupotasso* to believers they are not supporting them!

A key piece of walking in mutual submission to other believers is the need to submit prophetic words and pictures to the relevant individual or group. If we assume that we have heard God correctly and that the relevant individual or group should receive our word without question, we may be inadvertently attempting to take ungodly control. This behavior may also come across as proud and disrespectful. No one hears God correctly all of the time. We all make mistakes and sometimes we do not know when we are making them. The worst mistakes are sometimes made when we are most sure we are right. Subsection 1.1.5 discusses New Testament teachings related to the testing of revelatory words.

There is a great deal of overlap between the command in Hebrews 13:17 to "Be persuaded by those who are leading" and the command in the same verse to submit to (or "to be under influence" of) those who are leading. The dynamics of "being persuaded by those who are leading" are discussed in Section 4.1. These dynamics also apply to other relationships of freely chosen submission. These dynamics are different to the dynamics that apply to a relationship of obedience.

## 5.4 Discussion of submission and obedience

In Scripture there is a clearly stated caveat associated with obedience to human authority figures. We need to be sure that the commands we are receiving from any human are consistent with God's commands. Acts 4:19 and 5:29 teach that the delegation of authority to leaders is partial and there are circumstances where we need to obey God rather than any human leader. In Luke 2:41-50 Jesus obeyed His heavenly Father and caused his human parents "great distress." It is not stated if he directly disobeyed them. He certainly felt justified behaving in a manner contrary to their wishes.

Jesus is the one who has ultimate authority and He delegates certain limited authority to specific people in specific situations to do specific things. [13] We only need to obey human authority figures when they are moving within their range of delegated authority and when they are giving commands that are not in conflict with God's commands. For example, we need to obey a police officer when he is directing traffic. But we do not need to obey a police officer if he tells us to support his favorite sports team!

This caveat against unthinking obedience to human authority figures is implicit in commands against idolatry. [14] Idolatry is giving a piece of the created order (in this case the human authority figure) honor due only to God (in this case unquestioning obedience). To give the honor of total obedience to any person (except God) is idolatry. All human leaders make mistakes and if they attempt to provide detailed direction to the lives and ministry of other believers they will sooner or later get it wrong and end up directing someone to do something counter to God's will.

Walking in a relationship of freely chosen submission often requires more thought and wisdom than walking in obedience. A relationship of freely chosen submission also typically involves more dialog than a relationship of obedience. It is healthy for a wife (to her husband) or for a believer (to a leader) to submit suggestions and questions. If the husband or leader is in a healthy place he (or she) will welcome such dialog and will often end up agreeing with his wife/the believer. The husband or leader must never forget that he also has a duty to walk in submission within this relationship. The goal is to reach

---

13. Matt. 23:10, 28:18
14. Deut. 6:13, Luke 4:8

consensus in an amicable manner. However, the essence of freely chosen submission generally includes the wife/believer choosing to submit to her husband/the leader even if consensus is not reached. 1 Corinthians 7:1-5 teaches that in at least one area, sexual relations, marital decision-making should be entirely by consensus with the husband and wife both having an equal say in the decision. Wise husbands and leaders will seek to make as many decisions as possible by full consensus.

Given the New Testament teaching that each believer is expected to follow Jesus' personal lead in specific ministry matters, it is unlikely that the command for believers to submit to leaders is giving leaders the right to direct their ministry. [15] To be consistent with the rest of the New Testament, it seems likely that submission to leaders primarily applies to doctrine and general teaching related to how we should behave, not to specific ministry activities. Obviously, if a discussion of a specific ministry matter comes up, the believer should have a gracious and submissive attitude towards the leader. However, believers have more freedom to respectfully differ with leaders in matters of ministry than in matters of doctrine and appropriate behavior.

If the husband or leader is not in a healthy place, a great deal of wisdom is required. In this situation it is sometimes appropriate to challenge the husband or leader about their sin. Submission can sometimes include humbly submitting an invitation to return to Biblical doctrine or Biblical standards of behavior. Careful consideration and prayer is appropriate before doing this. In 1 Timothy 5:19-20, Paul discusses challenging elders about their sin, so this can definitely happen within a relationship where submission is commanded. [16] This is also consistent with the example of John the Baptist challenging Herod about his sin. [17] John's submission to King Herod included a very blunt challenge concerning Herod's sin, which eventually resulted in John's execution. Very clear guidance from God is required before such blunt challenges are delivered.

In Acts 13:50-51 and 14:5-6 Paul and Barnabas leave the city where they are ministering to avoid persecution. These incidents demonstrate that godly submission to civil authorities sometimes involves getting a safe distance away from them. On the other hand,

---

15. Subsection 1.1.3
16. Section 2.8
17. Matt. 14:3-4

Jesus went to Jerusalem knowing He would be crucified, and Paul chose to go to Jerusalem even though he expected to be arrested there.[18] So godly submission to civil authorities may sometimes involve allowing oneself to be arrested and martyred. On a case-by-case basis we need God's wisdom and guidance to know when to get away from persecution and when to walk right into it.

This principle is directly applicable to other relationships of submission, including husband/wife and leader/believer relationships. If the husband or leader is behaving abusively, godly submission may involve leaving. The decision to leave a husband (even temporarily) or a church to avoid abuse should not be taken lightly. Case-by-case wisdom and guidance is needed.

Paul says in Galatians 2:4-5 that he chose not to submit to false brothers. It is reasonable to assume that some believers considered these false brothers to be leaders.[19] So, just as Peter teaches in Acts 4:19, 5:29 that we must obey God rather than men, Paul is providing an example of not submitting to Christian leaders when they are in error. This is not a light thing to do and we should only go down this path after considerable thought and prayer. This example may in some cases be applicable to other relationships of submission. Examples of this may include when a husband tells his wife to do something sinful, or when he asks her to believe something, which is contrary to Scripture. However prayerful consideration also needs to be given to 1 Peter 3:6 where Peter commends the example of Sarah who obeyed her husband Abraham even though he told her to sin.[20]

1 Peter 2:18 teaches that the appropriate heart attitude of the person commanded to submit does not depend on the leader behaving appropriately. A partial exception to this principle is righteous anger. In some cases righteous anger may be an appropriate response to an abusive leader or husband. However, as commanded in Ephesians 4:26 it is important not to dwell on this anger.

Sometimes it is hard to identify when a relationship of freely chosen submission has become abusive. It may also be very hard

---

18. Matt. 16:21, Acts 21:10-15
19. *E.g.*, based on Gal. 1:6-9
20. Gen. 12:10-20

for the individual being abused to admit the reality of the abuse even if it is obvious to others. A Christian leader or husband who delights in his "right" to expect unquestioning submission/obedience, and does not take seriously all the balancing scriptures that constrain his behavior is at or has crossed the line into abuse. It is also highly likely that this husband or leader is failing to move in appropriate mutual submission to his believing wife or to the believers he is seeking to lead.

After an individual realizes that a relationship of freely chosen submission has become abusive the really hard question is how to respond. God will provide appropriate wisdom and guidance for each situation. Once that wisdom is received, which may take longer than we would like, it becomes more important to obey God than the husband or leader. God may lead the wife/believer to forgive the husband/leader and to do things his way with a gracious heart attitude. In other situations God may lead the wife/believer to challenge the husband/leader concerning his sin or He may lead the wife/believer to withdraw from the relationship. None of these options are to be undertaken lightly. There is no simple answer that applies in all situations. God's wisdom is needed on a case-by-case basis. If a wife/believer thinks that she has received wisdom from God that allows her to treat a husband/leader disrespectfully or proudly, she has got it wrong.

# Appendix 6
# Rebuking

This appendix complements Section 4.3 by providing a more detailed study of New Testament teaching concerning rebuking. Most occurrences of the word rebuke in the KJV, ESV and NIV are translations of the Greek verbs *elegcho* and *epitimao*. In all three of these Bible translations, several different English words are used to translate these two Greek words. The meaning of these words and the New Testament teaching associated with these words are discussed in the first two sections of this appendix.

Six other Greek words are occasionally translated rebuke/rebuked/rebuking in at least one of these three translations. These words are briefly discussed in the third section of this appendix.

**6.1 *Elegcho* (1651)** – put to proof, test, convict, refute, detect, lay bare, expose, reprove, rebuke, discipline, chastise

Table 3 shows how this word is translated in the KJV, ESV, and NIV translations.[1] Consistent with the definition given above, it can

| Translation | KJV | ESV | NIV |
|---|---|---|---|
| Reprove | 6 | 4 | |
| Rebuke | 5 | 4 | 6 |
| Convince | 4 | | 1 |
| Tell one's fault | 1 | 1 | 1 |
| Convict | 1 | 4 | 2 |
| Refute | | | 1 |
| Expose | | 3 | 3 |
| Prove guilty | | | 1 |
| Correct | | | 1 |

Table 3. Words used to translate *elegcho*

1. The edition of the Greek New Testament used by ESV and NIV contains *elegcho* 16 times, whereas the edition used by the KJV contains *elegcho* 17 times. The extra occurrence in the KJV is John 8:9.

be seen that all three Bible translations use a wide range of English words to translate *elegcho*.

In 10 of the ESV/NIV passages, which contain *elegcho*, the context is associated with sin.[2] John 16:8 states that the Holy Spirit "will convict the world concerning sin and righteousness and judgment." It is highly plausible that Paul has this multi-faceted work of conviction in mind in 1 Corinthians 14:24. When Paul uses this word in Titus 1:9 the context is the teaching of false doctrine and in Titus 1:13 the context may be sin or false doctrine or both.

So in summary, *elegcho* is almost always associated with sin and is occasionally associated with false doctrine or convincing individuals of the truth about Jesus. Based on this, I conclude that an *elegcho* rebuke to an individual is only appropriate concerning sin or concerning the teaching of false doctrine. As commanded in Galatians 6:1, we should seek to correct others gently first and only move to a rebuke, if gentle correction is rejected. There is absolutely no hint in scripture that it is ever appropriate to give an *elegcho* rebuke to an individual, who senses a leading to approach ministry in a different way to our preference, or who misunderstands or who is slow to learn. Unfortunately, some current day Christian leaders assume they have the right to rebuke other believers in these types of circumstances.

### *Who may elegcho?*

On five occasions *elegcho* is associated with God.[3] On four occasions *elegcho* is associated with Timothy and Titus who were traveling leaders.[4] Both 1 Timothy 5:20 ("As for those who persist in sin, rebuke them in the presence of all, so that the rest may stand in fear") and Titus 1:13 ("rebuke them sharply") are describing strong rebukes, which are focused on the person as well as their sin. So there are some circumstances where it is appropriate for traveling leaders to issue strong rebukes. Titus 2:15 teaches that authority is available to traveling leaders for exhortation and rebuking. The circumstances

---

2. Matt. 18:15, Luke 3:19, John 3:20, 8:46, Eph. 5:11, 13, 1 Tim. 5:20, Heb. 12:5, James 2:9, Rev. 3:19. This is also the context of *elegcho* in John 8:9 in KJV.
3. John 3:20, 16:8, Eph. 5:13-14, Heb. 12:5, Rev. 3:19
4. 1 Tim. 5:20, 2 Tim. 4:2, Titus 1:13, 2:15. In all four of these verses the verb form is second person singular, which show that these commands are a specific word to Timothy and Titus both of whom were traveling leaders (Appendix 7).

in which it is appropriate for traveling leaders to rebuke an individual and their associated authority is discussed in Sections 3.7, 4.3 and 5.2. In particular, Section 5.2 discusses how this fits into the overall balance of power associated with New Testament church leadership.

In two places *elegcho* is associated with all believers. Matthew 18:15 says "If your brother sins against you, go and tell him his fault," and Ephesians 5:11 commands us to "Take no part in the unfruitful works of darkness, but instead expose them." So, there is a Scriptural basis for any believer (including elders) to *elegcho* in response to sin. Of course Galatians 6:1 applies in these circumstances.

In Luke 3:19 *elegcho* is associated with a prophet, John the Baptist, who reproved/rebuked Herod. In 1 Corinthians 14:24, this Greek verb is associated both with prophets and the full congregation in describing the convicting/convincing that may occur when an unbeliever attends a meeting.

Only in Titus 1:9 is *elegcho* explicitly associated with elders. The focus here is on responding to false teaching. As discussed in Section 4.3, it appears from the context of this passage and the New Testament as a whole that a relatively soft translation is appropriate in this verse.

**6.2 *Epitimao* (2008)** — to set a value upon, to assess a penalty, to allege as a crimination, to reprove, chide, censure, rebuke, reprimand, admonish strongly, enjoin strictly

This verb is used 29 times in the New Testament. 27 of these references occur in the synoptic Gospels and two in the epistles. Many of the times *epitimao* is used in the Gospels are parallel passages so there are many less than 29 independent uses of this verb. Table 4 shows how this word is translated in the KJV, ESV and NIV translations. It can be seen that for all three translations in the majority of verses *epitimao* is translated "rebuke." These translations use a

| Translation | KJV | ESV | NIV |
|---|---|---|---|
| Rebuke | 24 | 25 | 23 |
| Charge | 5 | 2 | |
| Warn | | | 3 |
| Speak sternly | | | 2 |
| Order | | 2 | 1 |

Table 4. Words used to translate *epitimao*

narrower range of words to translate *epitimao* than is provided by the lexicon. In general it appears that *epitimao* describes a stronger rebuke than *elegcho*.

### *To whom or what is an epitimao rebuke addressed?*

Table 5 lists the recipients of *epitimao* rebukes. In 12 cases rebukes are directed towards non-human entities including demons, winds and a fever. [5] The strong linkage between *epitimao* and deliverance ministry is an indicator that *epitimao* describes a stronger rebuke than *elegcho*.

| Demons | 8 |
|---|---|
| Individuals/crowds coming to Jesus | 7 |
| Individual apostles or all apostles | 5 |
| Winds | 3 |
| Jesus | 2 |
| Believer(s) | 2 |
| Fever | 1 |
| Criminals executed with Jesus | 1 |

Table 5. Recipients of *epitimao* rebukes

### *Who may epitimao?*

In 17 verses Jesus is the one doing the rebuking/commanding. This includes eight verses where he rebuked demons, four verses where He rebuked/commanded one or more apostles, three verses where He rebuked winds, one verse where He rebuked a fever and one verse where he commanded individuals who had been healed to not tell others who He was. [6] Clearly, all of these rebukes/commands were appropriate. Most of the other rebukes/commands recorded in the Gospels are inappropriate. This includes three verses where the disciples rebuke individuals bringing children to Jesus and three verses where the crowds rebuke individuals, who were loudly calling out to Jesus. [7] It also includes two verses where Peter rebukes Jesus and one verse where the Pharisees told Jesus to rebuke the disciples. [8] There is only one appropriate *epitimao* rebuke given by an individual

---

5. Matt. 17:18, Mark 1:25, 3:12, 9:25, Luke 4:35, 41, 9:42, Jude 1:9; Matt. 8:26, Mark 4:39, Luke 8:24; Luke 4:39
6. Mark 8:30, 33, Luke 9:21, 55; Matt. 12:16
7. Matt. 19:13, Mark 10:13, Luke 18:15; Matt. 20:31, Mark 10:48, Luke 18:39
8. Matt. 16:22, Mark 8:32; Luke 19:39

other than Jesus recorded in the New Testament. [9] I think that this is a warning to us to not be too hasty about rebuking others.

The incident where the disciples rebuked individuals for bringing children to Jesus is a good example of the inappropriateness of rebuking someone for approaching ministry differently to the way we think is reasonable. Similarly, the three references to the crowds rebuking individuals who were shouting out to Jesus is an example of the inappropriateness of rebuking someone for seeking to approach Jesus in a manner of which we disapprove.

In Luke 17:3, Jesus commands believers to *epitimao* rebuke the brother who sins repeatedly. In 2 Timothy 4:2 Paul uses *epitimao* in the second person singular. So this verse is a command to Timothy as an individual not a broad command to the church as a whole to *epitimao*. The context of this verse does not make clear which of the possible translations of *epitimao* is most appropriate. Given other scriptural teaching on the role of Christian leaders it is likely that this verse applies to situations of repeated sin or teaching of false doctrine. In other words it is highly plausible that 2 Timothy 4:2 is consistent with Luke 17:3. A potential difference between these two verses is that Luke 17:3 only mentions the individual who is sinned against *epitimao* rebuking the person committing the offense. This verse does not tell individuals to take up the offense of others. 2 Timothy 4:2 Paul commands Timothy, a traveling leader, to *epitimao* rebuke, with patience and teaching, as part of his broader ministry to the church he is visiting. This may include situations where the sin was not directed towards Timothy.

## 6.3 Other Greek words translated rebuke

Six other Greek words are occasionally translated rebuke/rebuked/rebuking in at least one of the KJV, NIV and ESV translations. The teaching associated with these words is consistent with the teaching associated with *elegcho* and *epitimao*. For example Mark 14:5 records some people "rebuk[ing] harshly" (NIV, Greek *embrimaomai*) the woman anointing Jesus with perfume. This is a good example of the inappropriateness of rebuking an individual for ministering to Jesus in a manner which is outside of our comfort zone.

9. Luke 23:40

# Appendix 7
# Were Timothy and Titus Traveling Leaders or Elders?

This appendix documents the travels of Timothy and Titus as recorded in the New Testament. Their pattern of travel shows that they were both traveling leaders. This means that Paul's commands to them, which are recorded in his letters to them, describe Paul's expectations of traveling leaders. These commands do not necessarily apply to local leaders of Christian assemblies.

## *Timothy's Travels*

Timothy lived in Lystra prior to joining Paul and Silas on Paul's second missionary journey. [1] He remained in Berea with Silas when Paul went on to Athens and he rejoined Paul in Corinth. [2] Acts 18:18 implies Timothy did not leave Corinth at the same time as Paul. Timothy was sent by Paul to Macedonia with Erastus. [3] In Acts 20:4 Timothy is included in a list of people traveling with Paul. He is also noted as being with Paul in the following Scriptures: Romans 16:21 (AD 57 Corinth?), 2 Corinthians 1:1 (AD 55-57 Macedonia?), Philippians 1:1 (AD 61 Rome?), Colossians 1:1 (AD 60 Rome?), 1 Thessalonians 1:1 (AD 51 Corinth?), 2 Thessalonians 1:1 (AD 51-52 Corinth?), Philemon 1 (AD 60 Rome?).

1 Corinthians 4:17 says Paul sent Timothy to Corinth. 1 Corinthians 16:10 talks about a potential future visit of Timothy to Corinth. Philippians 2:19 notes that Paul hopes to send Timothy to Philippi. 1 Thessalonians 3:2, 6 mention that Timothy was sent from Athens to the Thessalonians by Paul and then returned. Paul writes his first letter to Timothy while Timothy is in Ephesus. [4] It is unclear how long

---

1. Acts 16:1-4
2. Acts 17:14,15, 18:5
3. Acts 19:22
4. 1 Tim. 1:3. This epistle may have been written in AD 64.

Timothy was in Ephesus at this time. At most he may have been there a handful of years. It is possible that Timothy was only in Ephesus a few months. By the time Paul writes 2 Timothy he wants Timothy to come to him. [5] 2 Timothy 4:12 may imply that Timothy had moved on from Ephesus prior to the writing of 2 Timothy in about AD 66 or 67. It seems that wherever he was located at the time of 2 Timothy he was facing similar issues to those mentioned in 1 Timothy. [6] An individual called Hymenaeus is mentioned in both epistles. Even if this is the same individual, it does not prove that Timothy was in the same city. My take on the two references is that Hymenaeus is a relevant example of the kind of problem Timothy is addressing not necessarily an individual in the same city as Timothy.

Hebrews 13:23 raises the possibility of Timothy traveling with the author of Hebrews to meet the recipients of Hebrews. This implies that Timothy also worked with other key New Testament leaders. [7] Based on this extensive pattern of ministry travel it is clear that Timothy was a traveling leader. This may also be implied by Paul calling him a "fellow worker" in Romans 16:21. Timothy was serving as a traveling leader at the time that Paul wrote his two letters to him. So it is appropriate to interpret commands and directions given by Paul to Timothy as an individual [8] in these letters as direction to a traveling leader. We should not assume that these commands apply to individuals who are not traveling leaders unless other passages support this broader application. [9]

### *Titus' Travels*

The earliest reference to Titus in the New Testament is Galatians 2:1, 3 which record that Titus traveled with Paul and Barnabas to Jerusalem in about AD 49 for the Acts 15 Council. There are several references to Titus in 2 Corinthians, which was written around AD 55 to 57. In 2 Corinthians 2:13 Paul mentions that he had expected to find Titus in Troas. In 2 Corinthians 7:6,13,14, 12:18 Paul says that he connected with Titus in Macedonia after Titus had completed a ministry trip to Corinth. In 2 Corinthians 8:6 Paul says that he

---

5. 2 Tim. 4:9
6. 1 Tim. 1:3-4, 20, 2 Tim. 2:14-18
7. Unless Paul wrote Hebrews.
8. In the Greek, it can be seen that the verb is in the second person singular, which means the command is directed to one person.
9. See Section 2.9 for a discussion of the appropriate leadership style to be followed by individuals who serve both as elders and as traveling leaders.

was urging Titus to visiting Corinth again. Titus' commitment to the Corinthian church assembly is mentioned in 2 Corinthians 8:16, 23.

Titus 1:4, 5 says that Paul left Titus in Crete to appoint elders in every town. So this was a traveling assignment. The length of this assignment is unclear. In Titus 3:12 Paul says that he wants Titus to come to Nicopolis for the winter. This letter may have been written in about AD 64. 2 Timothy 4:10 mentions that Titus is in Dalmatia. This may have been about AD 66 or 67. In summary, Titus was a traveling leader for several years including the time when he received his letter from Paul. So we should interpret commands to Titus as an individual as commands to a traveling leader.

# Appendix 8
# Detailed Outline

**Appendices**

**Figures and Tables**

Made in United States
Orlando, FL
21 November 2024